Lecture Notes in Economics and Mathematical Systems

627

For further volumes:
http://www.springer.com/0075-8442

Christian Korth

Fairness in Bargaining and Markets

 Springer

Dr. Christian Korth
School of Law, Business and Economics
University of Bayreuth
Universitätsstraße 30
95447 Bayreuth
christian.korth@uni-bayreuth.de

ISSN 0075-8442
ISBN 978-3-642-02252-4   e-ISBN 978-3-642-02253-1
DOI 10.1007/978-3-642-02253-1
Springer Dordrecht Heidelberg London New York

Library of Congress Control Number: 2009931060

Cover design: SPi Publisher Services

Printed on acid-free paper

Springer is part of Springer Science+Business Media (www.springer.com)

I dedicate this book to my beautiful wife, Karolina. Thank you for your infinite patience, understanding, support, and, most importantly, unending love.

Acknowledgements

Stefan Napel did an exemplary job as my Ph.D. supervisor. Without his valuable contributions, inspiring discussions, reliable support, high standards, and willingness to give me the freedom to explore new ideas, writing this book would not have been possible. I owe him many thanks. The design of the laboratory experiment and the implementation of the trial session were made possible by the support of David Huffman. The classroom study was a joint project with Philipp Reiss, who, in addition to collaborating on the classroom study, contributed to some sections of this book. Sigfried Berninghaus contributed his thoughts to the evolutionary study. Many helpful discussions I had with Werner Güth, Nicholas Shunda, and Sven Fischer proved to be valuable assets in writing certain sections of this book. The gift of inspiration was given to me by many conference, summer school, and seminar participants who asked the right questions. Gunnar Oldehaver, Jürgen Zerth, and Martin Leroch helped keep me motivated over the years. Heidi Rossner-Schöpf and Herta Wolf provided important organizational assistance whenever needed. To all of them, I give many thanks. Finally, I would like to thank my wonderful family for always believing in me.

Erlangen, April 2009   *Christian Korth*

Contents

Symbols

$\mathbb{N}$	set of natural numbers
$\mathbb{R}$	set of real numbers
$\mathbb{R}_+$	set of non-negative real numbers
$x \geqq y$	$(\forall i \in I): x_i \geq y_i$
$x \geq y$	$x \geqq y$ and $(\exists i \in I): x_i > y_i$
$x > y$	$(\forall i \in I): x_i > y_i$
$(x)^+$	$\max\{0, x\}$
a, b	constants
a_i	strategy chosen by player i
b	share of buyers given by $B/(B+S)$
b_i	belief of player j about the strategy a_i chosen by player i
$\tilde{b}$	share of buyers for which $p^* = p_{\mathrm{ref}}$
c	offer in the ultimatum or dictator game / a constant
$c(\cdot)$	offer in the ultimatum or dictator game
$c^*(\cdot)$	equilibrium offer in the ultimatum or dictator game
c_i	(second-order) belief of player i about b_i
$c(e)$	cost function of effort
e	effort decision
$f(\cdot)$	some (unspecified) function
$\tilde{f}_j(\cdot)$	kindness term: kindness player i experiences
$f_i(\cdot)$	reciprocation term: player i's reaction to player j's expected behavior
i, j	a player
k	role of player: proposer ($k = X$) or responder ($k = Y$)
k_i	exogenous sensitivity of player i to a relevant norm
n	number of players / a node in the game tree / a natural number
o	a deterministic bargaining outcome
p	price / units of a divisible good
p^*	equilibrium price / acceptance probability in equilibrium
p^{**}	equilibrium price in the limit of $\delta \to 1$
$p^\dagger$	equilibrium price for standard preferences without fairness concern

p°	equilibrium price for preferences without fairness concern for $\delta \to 1$
$p_B(t), p_S(t)$	price offered by a buyer/seller that is selected to make an offer
p_{ref}	exogenous reference price
$\underline{p}, \bar{p}$	lower/upper bound of intermediate case for p^* (see equation 5.6)
$p(c, \rho_R)$	acceptance probability for offer c in a ultimatum game by responder R
s_i	strategy of player i
$\hat{s}$	a strategy in the preference game $\hat{\Gamma}$ (a preference)
$\mathbf{s}$	a strategy profile
$\mathbf{s}_{-i}$	a strategy profile of players other than player i
$\hat{\mathbf{s}}$	a preference profile
t	time or period index / terminal node / test statistic of an OLS regression
$u(\cdot)$	(social) utility function
$u_i(x^i)$	immediate utility of player i of goods x^i
$u_i(x, t)$	immediate utility of player i of share x in period t
$u_i(\omega)$	utility of player i at end node ω of a game tree
$u_i^k(\cdot)$	utility of player i in the role k
x	price offer in an ultimatum game
x^i	player i's amount of goods
$\bar{x}^i$	endowment of player i
x_i	amount of good i / market length of market number i
x_j^i	player i's amount of good j
$\bar{x}_j^i$	endowment of player i of perfectly divisible good j
z	test statistic of a Probit regression
B	amount of buyers
F	bargaining solution
F^N	Nash bargaining solution
$F_X(t)$	distribution function of the exponential distribution
I	set of players
$\mathbf{L}_{-i}$	subset of strategy profiles $\mathbf{S}_{-i}$ for which a social norm exists
M	pie size or maximum price
N_i	fair price the proposer ought to offer according to the norm of player i
P	a population
$\bar{P}$	a upper bound
R	a behavioral rule
R_i	a behavioral rule or norm for player i
$R_{i,j}$	player j's belief about R_i
S	amount of sellers / set of strategy profiles
S_i	strategy set of player i
$\hat{S}$	set of feasible preference outcomes in Γ
$\mathbf{S}_{-i}$	set of strategy profiles of players other than player i
$\hat{T}$	a set of stable preference strategies $\hat{s}$ in $\hat{\Gamma}$
$V_B(t), V_S(t)$	utility of an unmatched buyer/seller at the beginning of period t
$\mathscr{B}$	set of bargaining problems
$\mathscr{N}$	set of nodes of the game tree
$\mathscr{N}_i$	set of nodes at which player i has to move

$\mathscr{O}$	set of bargaining outcomes
$\mathscr{S}$	set of situation types
$\mathscr{T}$	set of terminal nodes
$\mathscr{U}$	set of all feasible payoff combinations
α_i, β_i	exogenous (fairness) parameters of player i
β	a regression variable
$\hat{\beta}$	regression coefficient for regression variable β
δ_i	discount factor of player i
ε	tolerable gap between between p_{ref} and p^*
ε_i	pure outcome concern parameter of player i
ε_i^k	pure outcome concern parameter of player i in role k
ε_l	exogenous lower bound for parameter ε
λ	exogenous probability or share
μ	a mapping from preference profiles $\hat{\mathbf{s}}$ to equilibrium strategy profiles $\mathbf{s}$
$\nu(n,t)$	successor of node $n \in \mathscr{N}$ on the path to a terminal node $t \in \mathscr{T}$
ω	end node of a game tree
$\pi_i(\cdot)$	expected material payoff to player i
$\hat{\pi}(\cdot)$	payoff function in higher-level preference game $\hat{\Gamma}$
ρ_i	reciprocity parameter of player i
ρ_i^k	reciprocity parameter of player i in role k
σ_β	standard errors of individual regression coefficients for β
$\tau(\upsilon)$	strictly increasing affine transformation of payoffs
ϑ	probability that a potential match is formed
$\vartheta_j(n)$	intention factor for player j in a node $n \in \mathscr{N}_i$
υ	payoff combination selected from $\mathscr{U}$ by outcome o
υ^D	disagreement point or status quo point
$\Delta_j(n)$	outcome term for player j in a node $n \in \mathscr{N}_i$
Γ	a game / the "game of life"
$\hat{\Gamma}$	a higher-level preference game
$\Omega(\cdot)$	degree of attributed intention
$\Pi_i(n)$	set of payoff combinations at node $n \in \mathscr{N}_i$

Introduction

This book focuses on economic bargaining theory. Economic bargaining theory seeks to predict the outcomes of *bargaining situations*. In such situations, governments, firms, or individuals share a mutual interest in cooperation; however, they also have conflicting interests regarding the terms of an agreement. A classic example of such a situation is wage bargaining between unions and employers. More commonplace examples also exist. For instance, a discussion between partners on how to spend an evening can be understood as a bargaining situation.

Economic bargaining theory explores the relationship between bargaining situations and the outcomes of the bargaining. Economists have two primary reasons to show interest in this relationship. The first reason is that many important human interactions, including economic interactions, are bargaining situations. The second reason is that the understanding of these situations may inform the economic theory of markets.

The tool utilized in this study is the mathematical theory of games. Predictions for bargaining outcomes are developed by modeling the bargaining situation as a strategic game and using game-theoretic equilibrium concepts in order to solve the game. In this approach, the specific identified bargaining outcome depends on the *assumptions* underlying the model. The neoclassical and fundamental assumption is that of rational agents—called *economic men*—who strive to maximize their utility based on stable preferences.

Over the last few decades, a new branch of economics has emerged: experimental economics. Experimental economics investigates human economic behavior in laboratory studies. In these studies, subjects are incentivized with real monetary payoffs. For many decision situations, including bargaining situations, human behavior observed in the laboratory contradicted predictions of neoclassical economic models which were based on purely self-concerned and materialistic preferences. This led some behavioral economists to develop behavioral models which seek to integrate insights from psychology, sociology, and anthropology into neoclassical economics.

This book is a contribution to this kind of behavioral economic research. It develops new insights into the implications of *social fairness norms*. It is based on game-theoretic analysis and supports the view that a *preference for reciprocity* is evolutionarily stable in a "game of life" that consists of bilateral bargaining situations. Such a preference depends on a fairness benchmark or reference. This dependence is addressed by a classroom experiment in which the following hypothesis is investigated: that the fairness reference depends in a predictable way on the framing of the specific bargaining situation, and therefore, the framing affects behavior. Afterwards, this book explores the implications of fairness concern for price formation in *matching markets*, which involve temporary bilateral bargaining. This is examined by the theoretical analysis of a market model, and by an experimental laboratory study of such a market. The more detailed structure of this book is as follows.

Chapter 1 provides a brief introduction to the classic bargaining theories which are used as foundations in the subsequent chapters. Chapter 1 begins with Edgeworth's (1881) early formalization of the bargaining problem; it explains the necessity of further assumptions to narrow down the set of potential solutions to a unique equilibrium prediction. The chapter then introduces the cooperative game-theoretical approach of Nash (1950) as well as the non-cooperative approach. The chapter uses some exemplary applications to ultimatum and alternating offers bargaining for clarification. Finally, the matching market model of Rubinstein and Wolinsky (1985) is explained, and relevant ties to the literature are pointed out.

Chapter 2 begins with some of the empirical evidence that initiated the economic research on social utility. The chapter presents a comparison of recent approaches to the definition of *preferences* that result in *fair* behavior. These approaches can be grouped into two categories: equity-based and intention-based (psychological) approaches. Intention-based approaches explain more stylized facts from experiments but, in terms of tractability, come at a cost. Nevertheless, their explanatory power justifies their complexity. Specifically, the model of Falk and Fischbacher (2006) is identified as a very versatile approach because it unifies equity-based and pure intention-based models into one framework.

Chapter 3 combines the methods of evolutionary and behavioral game theory. The chapter addresses the questions of under what circumstances is behavior closer to the standard *homo economicus*-type, i.e., maximizing monetary payoffs, and which environments induce human beings to act more like *homo reciprocans*, with a preference for reciprocity. The chapter is based on the *indirect evolutionary approach* which was derived from the classic evolutionary approach in connection with social preferences. To account for human abilities, classical game theory is used to predict strategic behavior. However, the *preferences* of the players are based on evolutionary stability. Therefore individual preferences are seen in a new way: not as exogenously given, but as evolving over time. The chapter investigates agents who face a stylized, pecuniary "game of life" which comprises the ultimatum game and the dictator game. Utility may, but need not, be attached to equity and reciprocity as formalized by Falk and Fischbacher (2006). However, critically, this social component of preferences cannot be conditioned on whether an ultimatum or a dictator game is played. The evolutionary fitness of agents is determined solely by material success. While a strong preference for reciprocity evolves under these conditions, little interest in equity evolves. It is shown, in line with experimental observations, that a preference for reciprocity plays a significant role in games with punishment opportunities. Possible exogenous constraints that link reciprocity and equity concerns imply long-run levels of both that depend on the relative frequency of ultimatum vs. dictator interaction in agents' multi-game environment. Chapter 3 was a joint project with Siegfried K. Berninghaus and Stefan Napel. It was published 2007 in the *Journal of Evolutionary Economics*.

A preference for reciprocity is a social fairness norm. Chapter 4 addresses the reference dependence of such fairness norms. What is perceived as fair, may depend on the context. Therefore, context may affect behavior. This hypothesis was tested in a classroom experiment that involved more than 1000 students. All subjects made a decision in the same strategic environment, but the framing that described the bargaining situation varied across treatments. The observation made was that behavior varies significantly depending on the framing and that behavior varies in a predictable manner. One possible explanation is the potential reference dependence of social norms. Subjects may derive utility, not only from the material payoff, but also from a norm-related payoff. The norm-related payoff may depend on the relation of the pecuniary payoff and a reference point. This reference point may be a belief about what one "ought to share" or a similar reference dependent social norm. The chapter was a joint project with Philipp Reiss who not only subjected his students to the experiment, but also contributed to parts of the chapter at hand.

Fair behavior in bilateral bargaining is one of the most discussed topics in microeconomics today. However, its implications for markets are not yet completely clear. Double-auction markets appear to have a strong built-in tendency toward the competitive equilibrium. This tendency, however, does not necessarily translate to all other market forms. To address this shortfall, chapter 5 extends the scope to a market setting that involves temporary one-on-one interactions: it investigates price formation in a decentralized market with random matching à la Rubinstein and Wolinsky (1985). In contrast to the original model, agents are assumed to have subdued social preferences. Buyers, for example, prefer a lower price to a higher one, but experience smaller utility increases below a reference price that serves as a common fairness benchmark. The strategic equilibrium reflects market fundamentals. However, it is markedly affected by the fairness concern of agents, and less sensitive to the buyer–seller ratio near the fair-price benchmark. If the fairness benchmark is influenced by the market experience of traders, for example, in a manner consistent with the theory of cognitive dissonance, prices may be sticky around very different reference levels in markets with otherwise identical fundamentals. The implied history dependence turns out to be mitigated rather than exacerbated by friction. These results have important practical implications. For example, they can explain a potential mechanism behind soft policy measures like the publication of the rent indices common in several German municipalities: Such measures may affect the fairness benchmark of market participants. This may, in turn, affect behavior. Chapter 5 is based on collaboration with Stefan Napel. It is forthcoming as a joint paper in the *Journal of Economic Behavior & Organization*.

The model described in chapter 5 is built on several limitative assumptions. One of these limitative assumptions is perfect homogeneity of agents on each side of the market. All agents are assumed to hold a common reference price and discount factor. Chapter 6 relaxes these and other assumptions of the model. Heterogeneity with respect to reference prices, discount factors, and the degree of fairness concern does not render the results of the original model invalid. For example, it is *not* necessary that all agents have a preference for fairness, or that they agree on the same reference price. As long as *some* participating agents hold a sharp notion of the reference price, the effects of fairness on equilibrium market prices are sustained. Corresponding to intuition, the larger the share of agents in the market with fairness concern, the more pronounced the effect. Interestingly, the share of gains from trade that an agent can capture is increasing in fairness concern. This fact is analogous to the findings regarding reciprocity in the "game of life" (see chapter 3). In contrast to the finding for heterogeneity under the premise of perfect information, assuming imperfect information may eliminate the uniqueness of the equilibrium. Overall, the model proves to be very robust, and the major findings translate into more generalized settings.

The final chapter provides a robustness check of a different kind. Chapter 7 investigates price formation in an *experimental* market that involves random matching. Specifically, it investigates whether market prices are in line with the predictions of standard theory based on material payoff maximization, or if, instead, market prices exhibit inflexibility with respect to market conditions in a way that is consistent with the fairness preferences discussed in chapters 5 and 6. In the chapter, a proposed laboratory study is described in detail, and the study's feasibility is demonstrated by a trial session which was conducted with 20 paid subjects at the BonnEcon-Lab. Preliminary results of this trial session indicate that market prices are indeed sticky and that the behavioral model is a better predictor of outcomes than standard theory based on material payoff maximization. This result is contrary to the result typically obtained through experimental studies of markets. Most such studies find that fairness has either limited or no effects on market prices. However, typically double-auction or similar setups are investigated. These are distinct from the setup investigated here because they have an inherent tendency to converge to the competitive equilibrium. By contrast, markets involving a matching and bargaining process allow the fairness concerns of the subjects to affect market prices. Given that such markets are typically utilized in the analysis of labor and monetary markets, these findings may have far-reaching consequences.

Because they are designed to be self-contained, the first five chapters and chapter 7 can be read in any sequence. However, chapter 6 is closely tied to chapter 5.

References

Berninghaus SK, Korth C, Napel S (2007) Reciprocity—An indirect evolutionary analysis. J Evol Econ 17(5):579–603

Edgeworth FY (1881) Mathematical Psychics: An Essay on the Application of Mathematics to the Moral Sciences. C. Kegan Paul & Co., London, UK, reprinted by New York, NY: A.M. Kelley, 1961

Falk A, Fischbacher U (2006) A theory of reciprocity. Games Econom Behav 54(2):293–315

Korth C, Napel S (2009) Fairness, price stickiness, and history dependence in decentralized trade. J Econ Behav Organ (in press)

Nash JF (1950) The bargaining problem. Econometrica 18(2):155–162

Rubinstein A, Wolinsky A (1985) Equilibrium in a market with sequential bargaining. Econometrica 53(5):1133–1150

Chapter 1
Bargaining Theory

This chapter provides a short introduction to bargaining problems and the basic approaches to solve them. It draws mainly on the thorough and at the same time concise introductions to bargaining theory that are given by Napel (2002, chap. 1) and Osborne and Rubinstein (1990). Here, only a very basic summary is given, which cannot replace the study of more elaborate works as the aforementioned books. See also Binmore et al. (1986) for another good introduction on this topic.

A classic example of a bargaining problem is bilateral exchange. Assume that two agents, denoted by 1 and 2, have initial endowments of two perfectly divisible goods. These endowments are formally described as $\bar{x}^i = (\bar{x}_1^i, \bar{x}_2^i) \in \mathbb{R}_+^2$ for $i \in \{1,2\}$. Assume further that the utility of each agent is given by a differentiable, strictly increasing, and quasi-concave utility function denoted by $u_i(\bar{x}^i)$ for $i \in \{1,2\}$. The two agents may then be able to improve the status quo that is given by the endowments and described by $(u_1(\bar{x}^1), u_2(\bar{x}^2))$ by a *bilateral exchange* of goods: by trading with each other, they might be able to mutually increase their utility. Economists are then concerned with the question: which allocation is reached through voluntary exchange by rational agents without the support of an exogenous arbitrator? The first formal investigation of this problem was given by Francis Edgeworth (1881). He proposes that both agents would exchange goods as long as this exchange is increasing the utility for both of them. The resulting potential allocations are called the *contract curve*. For all points on the contract curve

$$\frac{\partial u_1 / \partial x_2}{\partial u_1 / \partial x_1} = \frac{\partial u_2 / \partial x_2}{\partial u_2 / \partial x_1}$$

holds, which describes tangential indifference curves. An agent's indifference curve is a set of allocations for which the utility level is the same; that is, the set of allocations an agent is indifferent between. Because exchange is assumed to be voluntary, individual rationality prescribes that agents only agree on allocations that yield them at least as much utility as their respective initial endowments. This narrows down the set of allocations agents would agree on from the contract curve to the bargaining set or *core*, which is the individually rational subset of the contract curve. Which

C. Korth, *Fairness in Bargaining and Markets,*
Lecture Notes in Economics and Mathematical Systems, 627
DOI: 10.1007/978-3-642-02252-4_1, © Springer-Verlag Berlin Heidelberg 2009

allocation from this bargaining set the agents will finally agree on remains unspecified. Without further assumptions, no single allocation can be determined as the only possible solution.

The following sections give a very brief overview on some classic attempts to further specify a unique solution. Section 1.1 describes the seminal axiomatic approach that was taken by John Nash (1950). It determines the solution without detailing any bargaining process; instead, some axioms are defined and the solution is derived from these axioms. Section 1.2 describes the strategic approach, which defines the bargaining process as a strategic game. Then, the solution can be derived as an equilibrium of this game. Section 1.3 extends the scope from bilateral bargaining to a market setting, and introduces the market model of Rubinstein and Wolinsky (1985). Section 1.4 concludes.

1.1 The Axiomatic Approach

Nash (1950) introduced a new approach to the bargaining problem. His approach belongs to cooperative bargaining theory, which assumes that agents can make voluntary but binding agreements of any kind. Bargaining *outcomes* $o \in \mathscr{O}$ are cooperation agreements that can either specify a certain surplus distribution or final disagreement. The set of all feasible payoff combinations is denoted by $\mathscr{U} \subset \mathbb{R}^2$, and the outcome o selects a unique payoff combination of this set, denoted by $\upsilon \in \mathscr{U}$. The disagreement point is described by $\upsilon^D \in \mathscr{U}$ and corresponds to the status quo. As already found by Edgeworth (1881) and described above, agents would agree on an allocation from the bargaining set. The theory of Nash (1950) provides an answer to the question: which specific agreement results between rational and perfectly informed agents, if some further assumptions are made? He achieves this without assuming any specific bargaining process. Instead, he takes an *axiomatic approach* (Nash, 1953, p. 129):

> One states as axioms several properties that it would seem natural for the solution to have and then one discovers that the axioms actually determine the solution uniquely.

A bargaining problem is a pair $\langle \mathscr{U}, \upsilon^D \rangle$, which is considered common knowledge by the agents. Note that this primitive of the model describes payoffs, not the agreements. There may be multiple agreements resulting in the same payoffs. $\mathscr{U}$ is assumed to be compact, convex, and to contain at least one element $\upsilon > \upsilon^D$ that is preferred over υ^D by both agents.[1] The set of all bargaining problems satisfying these assumptions is denoted by $\mathscr{B}$. A bargaining solution $F(\mathscr{U}, \upsilon^D) \in \mathscr{U}$ can then be defined as a function $F \colon \mathscr{B} \to \mathbb{R}^2$ which maps each bargaining problem to a uniquely feasible payoff vector. For a given bargaining problem $\langle \mathscr{U}, \upsilon^D \rangle$, $F(\mathscr{U}, \upsilon^D)$ denotes the *solution to the bargaining problem* $\langle \mathscr{U}, \upsilon^D \rangle$. The solution F^N identified

---

[1] For $x, y \in \mathbb{R}^2$, let $x > y$ denote $x_1 > y_1 \wedge x_2 > y_2$, let $x \geq y$ denote $x_i > y_i \wedge x_{-i} \geq y_{-i}$, and let $x \geqq y$ denote $x_1 \geq y_1 \wedge x_2 \geq y_2$.

by Nash is called the Nash bargaining solution. It is characterized by the following four axioms:

The first axiom states that the agent's preferences are basic. The physical outcome of the bargaining problem should not change for strictly increasing affine transformations of payoffs. Let the mapping $\tau_i : \mathbb{R} \to \mathbb{R}$ be a such a transformation with $\tau_i(v_i) = av_i + b$ for $a, b \in \mathbb{R}$ and $a > 0$.

Invariance to Equivalent Utility Representations (INV):
Given $\tau(v) \equiv (\tau_1(v_1), \tau_2(v_2))$ *and any bargaining problem* $\langle \mathscr{U}, v^D \rangle$

$$F(\tau(\mathscr{U}), \tau(v^D)) = \tau(F(\mathscr{U}, v^D)) .$$

The second axiom formalizes that the solution abstracts from any "bargaining ability" of the agents. Any asymmetry must be captured in $\langle \mathscr{U}, v^D \rangle$. If the agents are interchangeable, the solution must also assign them the same utility.

Symmetry (SYM):
Given $\rho(v_1, v_2) \equiv (v_2, v_1)$ *and any bargaining problem* $\langle \mathscr{U}, v^D \rangle$

$$F(\rho(\mathscr{U}), \rho(v^D)) = \rho(F(\mathscr{U}, v^D)) .$$

The third axiom describes that deleting irrelevant alternative potential solutions from the set of feasible solutions would not change the outcome.

Independence of irrelevant alternatives (IIA):
For any $\langle \mathscr{U}, v^D \rangle$ *and all* $\mathscr{U}' \subseteq \mathscr{U}$ *with* $v^D \in \mathscr{U}'$

$$F(\mathscr{U}, v^D) \in \mathscr{U}' \Longrightarrow F(\mathscr{U}', v^D) = F(\mathscr{U}, v^D) .$$

The fourth axiom states that the solution must be Pareto efficient: no alternative feasible solution exists that makes both agents better off than the solution.

Pareto efficiency (PAR):
For any $\langle \mathscr{U}, v^D \rangle$

$$v \geq F(\mathscr{U}, v^D) \in \mathscr{U} \Longrightarrow v \notin \mathscr{U} .$$

Nash proves that from these axioms, a unique solution of the bargaining problem can be derived. This solution maximizes the product of agents' gain over the disagreement outcome:

$$F^N(\mathscr{U}, v^D) \equiv \underset{v \in \mathscr{U}, v \geq v^D}{\arg\max} \ (v_1 - v_1^D)(v_2 - v_2^D) . \tag{1.1}$$

The following simple example clarifies the application of Nash's approach and the role of risk aversion:

Two agents may decide how to split a dollar. If they agree on a division, the dollar is split according to their agreement, and each agent receives his or her share. If they disagree, both agents receive nothing. They may also destroy a share of the dollar if they wish. Formally, $\mathcal{O} = \{(x^1, x^2) \in \mathbb{R}^2 : x^1 + x^2 \leq 1 \text{ and } x^1, x^2 \geq 0\}$ describes all possible divisions of the dollar. Both agents are assumed to have preferences only about their own share of the dollar, to be risk-averse, and to have preferences that can be described by a differentiable concave utility function denoted by $u_i(x^i)$ for $i \in \{1, 2\}$ with domain $[0, 1]$. For these utility functions we assume $u_1(0) = u_2(0) = 0$. Given these assumptions the set $\mathcal{U}$ denoting all feasible payoff combinations is compact and convex:

$$\mathcal{U} = \{(\upsilon_1, \upsilon_2) \in \mathbb{R}^2 : (\upsilon_1, \upsilon_2) = (u_1(x^1), u_2(x^2)) \text{ for some } (x^1, x^2) \in \mathcal{O}\} \ .$$

And the disagreement payoff υ^D, that is given by $\upsilon^D = (u_1(0), u_2(0)) = (0, 0)$, is also contained in $\mathcal{U}$. In addition, there is at least one point $\upsilon \in \mathcal{U}$ that is preferred over υ^D by both agents (for which $\upsilon > \upsilon^D$ holds). Taken together, $\langle \mathcal{U}, \upsilon^D \rangle$ is a bargaining problem.

For the case of symmetric preferences of both agents, the solution of this symmetric bargaining problem is given by axioms PAR and SYM. It is simply the equal split given by $F^N(\mathcal{U}, \upsilon^D) = (u_1(1/2), u_2(1/2))$.

For the case that the preferences of the two agents differ, the solution may be different. Take a simple scenario, in which one agent's utility function is a concave function of the utility function of the other agent. By applying the Nash solution given by equation 1.1 one finds that for this scenario the more risk-averse agent (the one with the more concave utility function) receives a smaller share of the dollar than the other agent.[2]

This simple game described in the example also resembles a basic model of trade: Imagine one agent (the seller) holds one unit of an indivisible good that is worthless to him. The other agents (the buyer) holds one unit of some divisible good (e.g., money). The seller's utility for receiving p units (p denoting the price) of the divisible good is given by $u_1(p)$, with $u_1(0) = 0$. The buyer's utility for trading the good against p is given by $u_2(1 - p)$, with $u_2(0) = 0$. In case of disagreement (no trade) both agents' utility is assumed to be 0. This trading problem is then formally equivalent to the split-a-dollar game that was described above.

1.2 The Strategic Approach

The axioms given in section 1.1 uniquely define the Nash bargaining solution F^N without assuming or explicitly modeling any bargaining process. They try to predict which solution can be expected to result when rational agents negotiate an agreement. Non-cooperative bargaining theory takes a different approach: The bargaining process is explicitly modeled as a fully specified strategic game. Agreements

---

[2] See Osborne and Rubinstein (1990) for more details on this example.

made before playing the game are assumed to be non-binding, and thus cannot influence the outcome of the game. With this approach, the structure of the game may influence the predicted solution, which is an equilibrium of the game. The non-cooperative approach, and the relation between the cooperative and the non-cooperative approach to bargaining were well described by Nash (1953, p. 129):

> ... one makes the players' steps of negotiation ... moves in the non-cooperative model. Of course, one cannot represent all possible bargaining devices as moves in the non-cooperative game. The negotiation process must be formalized and restricted, but in such a way that each participant is still able to utilize all the essential strengths of his position. ... The two approaches to the problem, via the negotiation model or via the axioms, are complementary; each helps to justify and clarify the other.

A popular simple bargaining game in the domain of non-cooperative games is the *ultimatum game*: A proposer offers a division of a given sum of money to a responder. The responder can either accept the proposed split and receive his share, or reject the offer. If he rejects, both players receive nothing. Under the assumption that both agents maximize their material payoff,[3] the simple solution of this game in extensive form is the following:[4] The responder should accept any offer. Therefore the proposer should offer the smallest possible amount to him. This solution indicates the strong bargaining power the proposer has; the proposer can appropriate nearly the full sum of money, because he can make the take-it-or-leave-it offer, and the responder can only accept or reject this offer.

A more complex bargaining game is the infinite horizon *alternating offers* bargaining game, which extends the bargaining game to infinitely many stages. In this game, counteroffers are possible: The first two stages of the game resemble the ultimatum game. One of the agents is selected to propose a division—let this be agent 1. Then the other agent (agent 2) can accept or reject this proposal. If agent 2 rejects, he may subsequently propose a division to agent 1, and agent 1 can accept or reject the proposal. In case of rejection, the game continues with a proposal by agent 1, and so on. The game ends with agreement when one of the agents accepts a proposal.[5]

The following simple example clarifies the subgame perfect equilibrium outcome of this game. Denote a proposal for the division by which agent 1 would receive the amount x and agent 2 would receive the amount $1 - x$ by $(x, 1 - x)$. Assume that the two agents have preferences over the divisions and time (denoted by t), that can be represented by the following utility functions:

---

[3] Güth and Peleg (2001, p. 480) comment that "payoff maximization, e.g., in the sense of profit maximization on markets, represents the orthodox rationality assumption in economics. This has either been stated as behavioral assumption, or justified by an as if-hypothesis in the sense that, in markets, only profit-maximizing behavior can survive." However, neoclassic economic theory only assumes that agents are rational, that is, their preferences are complete and transitive, but it does not limit preferences to material payoffs. Therefore, it would be in line with neoclassic economic theory if utility was derived from other, non-material sources like, for example, fairness considerations.

[4] This solution is based on the solution concept of a *subgame perfect equilibrium*, which is typically applied to this game. See Selten (1975) for details on this equilibrium concept.

[5] This version of the game was first considered by Rubinstein (1982), and a similar game with finite horizon by Ståhl (1972).

$$u_1(x,t) = \delta_1^t x \quad \text{and} \quad u_2(x,t) = \delta_2^t (1-x) .$$

The discount factors δ_1 and $\delta_2 \in (0,1)$ describe the agent's patience. The subgame perfect equilibrium outcome of this game is then for agent 1 to propose the division $(x^*, 1-x^*)$ with

$$x^* = \frac{1-\delta_2}{1-\delta_1 \delta_2}$$

in the first period, and for agent 2 to accept this proposed division.[6]

This equilibrium outcome has some interesting features. In case both agents are equally impatient ($\delta_1 = \delta_2 = \delta$), the equilibrium division is simply

$$\left(\frac{1}{1+\delta}, \frac{\delta}{1+\delta} \right) . \tag{1.2}$$

Because $\delta < 1$ holds, a first mover advantage also exists in this game, only in the limit for $\delta \to 1$ the division approaches the equal split $(1/2, 1/2)$. In case the discount factors for one of the two agents approaches unity while it does not for the other agent, the infinitely patient agent appropriates the whole pie. Formally, for some fixed $\delta' \in (0,1)$ and $\delta_1 \to 1, \delta_2 = \delta'$ the equilibrium split is $(1,0)$ and for $\delta_1 = \delta', \delta_2 \to 1$ the equilibrium split is $(0,1)$.

1.3 A Strategic Perspective on Market Exchange

In sections 1.1 and 1.2, bargaining models involving two agents were discussed. However, in market situations, typically more than two agents are involved. Classic market models that involve bilateral bargaining are the *search* and *matching* markets that were described by Diamond and Maskin (1979), Mortensen (1982), or Rubinstein and Wolinsky (1985). All these models have a common general setup: The markets run over time, and there is some mass of buyers and sellers in the market. Buyers and sellers are matched, and subsequently bargain about a potential agreement. Matches may be resolved (e.g., disagreement after a certain time), after which the agents return to the pool of agents for a potential new match. The first two papers focus on an explicit model of the search function, which formally describes a mapping from the *search efforts* to the likelihood of a *successful match*. They take a straightforward approach to the bargaining by assuming the Nash bargaining solution (see above). The third paper has a different focus: The search and matching is not explicitly modeled, but a random matching process without search is assumed. Instead, Rubinstein and Wolinsky explicitly model the bargaining process as a strategic bargaining game, and discuss the bargaining outcomes in detail.

A simplified setup of the matching market by Rubinstein and Wolinsky (1985) is given in Rubinstein (1989, Model A): All relevant information is assumed to be

---

[6] See, for example, Osborne and Rubinstein (1990, chap. 3) for a detailed discussion of this game and the proof of this equilibrium.

common knowledge. Time is discrete and indexed by $t = 0, 1, 2, \ldots$. There are two sets of agents, buyers and sellers, with the cardinalities B and S, respectively. All sellers are endowed with one unit of a single indivisible good, and all buyers are endowed with at least one unit of disposable income. The buyers and sellers wish to trade the indivisible good for the disposable income. All sellers have a reservation price of zero, and the reservation price of all buyers is normalized to one. Every period, buyers and sellers are matched into pairs. The matching technology is assumed to be frictionless, so that in every period, as many pairs as possible $(\min(B, S))$ are formed. Only some agents on the long side of the market remain unmatched in each period. The matching is completely random, so that each potential match is equally likely and independent of the history of play. Once a match is formed, agents engage in a simple bargaining process. Either the buyer or the seller is determined with equal probability to propose a price $p \in [0, 1]$ the buyer is supposed to pay the seller in exchange for the good, and the other agent may accept or reject this offer. If the offer is rejected, the match is resolved and both agents return to the set of active buyers and sellers. If the offer is accepted, the price essentially determines how the total surplus generated by the trade (normalized to one unit) is split between the two agents. The seller receives the share p, and the buyer receives the share $1 - p$. After carrying out the trade, both agents leave the market. They are replaced by two new agents, so that the number of buyers and sellers in the market remains constant over time. This loosely resembles, for example, real-life markets like the market for housing, in which tenants approximately vacate apartments at the same rate as new rental agreements are made.

The symmetric subgame perfect equilibrium in (semi-)stationary strategies[7] can be determined the following way: Denote by $V_S(t)$ the expected utility of an unmatched seller at the beginning of period t, and by $V_B(t)$ the expected utility of an unmatched buyer. The utility functions of sellers and buyers for an agreement in period t on the price p are given by $u_S(t, p) = \delta^t p$ and $u_B(t, p) = \delta^t(1 - p)$, respectively, with $\delta \in (0, 1)$ as common discount factor. These utility functions satisfy $u_S(t, 0) = 0$ and $u_B(t, 1) = 0$, and $u_S(t, p) + u_B(t, p) \leq 1$ for any t. The utility for perpetual disagreement is set to zero for buyers and sellers.

Matched sellers and buyers can both be selected to propose a price. The price proposals of sellers in period t will be denoted by $p_S(t)$ and those of buyers by $p_B(t)$. As both are selected with equal probability, the resulting average market price in period t is given by $p(t) \equiv 1/2(p_S(t) + p_B(t))$. In any equilibrium, $\delta V_S(t) + \delta V_B(t) < 1$ must hold because $u_S(p, 0) + u_B(p, 0) \leq 1$ for all $p \in [0, 1]$ and $\delta < 1$. This implies that in equilibrium, every match ends in immediate agreement. Otherwise,

---

[7] Semi-stationary strategies (as defined by Rubinstein and Wolinsky 1985) are strategies that prescribe the same bargaining tactics against all bargaining partners an agent might meet, independently of the period and the bargaining outcomes an agent experienced. Rubinstein and Wolinsky (1985) allow a bargaining process between matched agents over multiple periods, and agents may have "non-stationary" strategies for this bargaining process, but they may not condition this strategy on the history of play up to the point that they met their bargaining partner. The simplified model described here contains a simplified bargaining protocol (one-period ultimatum bargaining) without multiple rounds of bargaining. Therefore, the original "semi-stationary strategies" may simply be described as "stationary strategies" in this context.

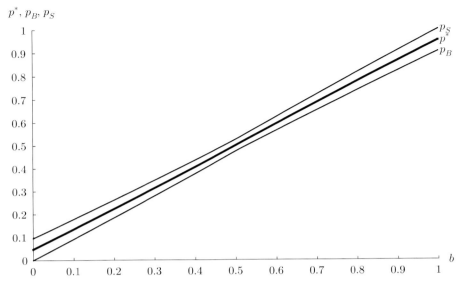

Fig. 1.1 Prices in a matching market for $\delta = 0.95$

there would be a period t in which some proposed price is rejected. In this case, the proposer could increase his payoff by making a deviating offer p that satisfies $u_S(p,t) > \delta V_S(t+1)$ and $u_B(p,t) > \delta V_B(t+1)$, and any rational responder strategy would prescribe acceptance of this offer.

In equilibrium, the buyer will always offer exactly $p_B = u_S^{-1}(\delta V_S(t+1))$, and the seller will always offer $p_S = u_B^{-1}(\delta V_B(t+1))$. This renders the responder indifferent between accepting and rejecting the offer, and will lead him to accept it. If we assume that sellers are on the short side of the market, or that the market is balanced $(S \leq B)$,[8] then the following equations hold for all t:

$$u_S(p_B,t) = \delta V_S(t+1)$$
$$u_B(p_S,t) = \delta V_B(t+1)$$
$$V_S(t) = \frac{1}{2}(u_S(p_B,t) + u_S(p_S,t))$$
$$= \frac{1}{2}(\delta V_S(t+1) + u_S(u_B^{-1}(\delta V_B(t+1))))$$
$$V_B(t) = \frac{S}{B}\left[\frac{1}{2}(u_B(p_S,t) + u_B(p_B,t))\right] + \left(1 - \frac{S}{B}\right)[\delta V_B(t+1)]$$
$$= \frac{S}{2B}\left[\delta V_B(t+1) + u_B(u_S^{-1}(\delta V_S(t+1)))\right] + \left(1 - \frac{S}{B}\right)[\delta V_B(t+1)]$$

---

[8] For the symmetric problem with $(S > B)$, analogous equations hold. See Rubinstein (1989) for details.

$$p(t) = \frac{1}{2}\left[p_B + p_S\right] = \frac{1}{2}\left[u_B^{-1}(\delta V_B(t+1)) + u_S^{-1}(\delta V_S(t+1))\right] \ .$$

For simplicity, denote the share of buyers in the market by $b \equiv B/(B+S)$. The above set of equations can be solved for $p(t)$ and the resulting equilibrium price $p^* \equiv p(t) \in (0,1)$ turns out to be time-independent, and unique:

$$p^* = \frac{b}{2b(1-\delta)+\delta} \ .$$

See figure 1.1 for a graphical representation of this result. This equilibrium price has some features that conform to general intuition: the higher the share of buyers in the market, the higher the price, and with it $V_S(t)$:

$$\frac{\partial p^*}{\partial b} = \frac{\delta}{(2b(1-\delta)+\delta)^2} > 0 \ .$$

The same holds for the discount factor: the equilibrium price is increasing in δ, i.e.,

$$\frac{\partial p^*}{\partial \delta} = \frac{b(2b-1)}{(2b(1-\delta)+\delta)^2} > 0 \ .$$

And in the limit for $\delta \to 1$, one obtains the attractive equation

$$p^* = b \ .$$

As Rubinstein and Wolinsky (1985) point out, this limit result ($p^* = b$) is equivalent, if the Nash bargaining solution is assumed instead of the strategic approach as in the models by Diamond and Mortensen (see above); nevertheless, the outcomes diverge, if agents are not completely patient. Furthermore, the results of this model depend on the specific representation of agent's preferences over payoffs, as described in chapter 5.

The model sparked a discussion mainly between Rubinstein, Wolinsky, and Gale about the relation of these findings to the competitive (Walrasian) equilibrium. Most assumptions made by Rubinstein and Wolinsky (1985) are comparable to standard descriptions of competitive markets; therefore, their result seems to contradict the competitive equilibrium. At first sight, the competitive equilibrium would prescribe that the short side of the market appropriates all gains from trade. Therefore, Rubinstein and Wolinsky originally concluded that the competitive equilibrium does not well predict the outcome for markets, because a different result is obtained when the mechanism for price formation and frictions are taken into account. However, this was not the last insight on this topic. Gale (1987) demonstrates the opposite result with a similar model. He points out that the competitive equilibrium needs to be defined in terms of the flows of agents into the market, and not based on the stock of agents in the market at any period. The flows of buyers and sellers in the model of Rubinstein and Wolinsky (1985) are equal, and thus any price could be the competitive equilibrium, including the one identified by them; this resolved the initial discrepancy. For a thorough discussion of this topic, see Gale (1986a; 1986b), Rubinstein (1989), Rubinstein and Wolinsky (1990), and Kunimoto and Serrano (2004).

1.4 Discussion

This chapter gave a brief introduction to bargaining theory. First, the classic bargaining problem of bilateral exchange was introduced to explain why assumptions are necessary to determine a unique solution. Without assumptions, every agreement that renders at least the disagreement payoff to every agent is a feasible solution. Edgeworth (1881) made an early proposal to model exchange between agents based on initial endowments and indifference curves. He could determine a *bargaining set* of potential allocations on which agents are likely to agree on, but did not further narrow down the outcome prediction of successful bilateral exchange.

John Nash (1950) employed game-theoretic concepts to solve this problem. He based his model on agent's preferences over feasible outcomes that were represented by expected utility functions and axioms describing characteristics of the solution with regard to outcomes. His approach was successful in narrowing down the solution from a set of potential solutions to one unique equilibrium of a cooperative game, as described in section 1.1.

Following Nash's (1950) cooperative solution, strategic, non-cooperative models were proposed to address the same problem. These models explicitly describe the bargaining procedure as a strategic game. The solution is then derived as an equilibrium of the game. The exemplary models described in section 1.2 demonstrate that this approach may confirm the cooperative bargaining solution (compare the limit result for the alternating offers bargaining game), but can also result in a completely different equilibrium prediction (as for the ultimatum game). Contrasting these models demonstrates that the bargaining process—if incorporated into the model—may affect the bargaining outcome. The ultimatum game, which generates a very unequal equilibrium prediction, is further analyzed in chapters 2 to 4.

A brief introduction to the strategic model of market exchange by Rubinstein and Wolinsky (1985) was given in section 1.3. It extends the interaction from a purely bilateral exchange to a market setting. On this market, buyers and sellers are matched into pairs and the price is determined by a bargaining process. This model forms the basis of analysis in chapters 5 to 7.

References

Binmore KG, Rubinstein A, Wolinsky A (1986) The nash bargaining solution in economic modelling. Rand J Econ 17(2):176–188

Diamond PA, Maskin E (1979) An equilibrium analysis of search and breach of contract, I: Steady states. Bell J Econ 10(1):282–316

Edgeworth FY (1881) Mathematical Psychics: An Essay on the Application of Mathematics to the Moral Sciences. C. Kegan Paul & Co., London, UK, reprinted by New York, NY: A.M. Kelley, 1961

Gale D (1986a) Bargaining and competition Part I: Characterization. Econometrica 54(4):785–806

Gale D (1986b) Bargaining and competition Part II: Existence. Econometrica 54(4):807–818

Gale D (1987) Limit theorems for markets with sequential bargaining. J Econ Theory 43(1):20–54

Güth W, Peleg B (2001) When will payoff maximization survive? An indirect evolutionary analysis. J Evol Econ 11(5):479–499

Kunimoto T, Serrano R (2004) Bargaining and competition revisited. J Econ Theory 115(1):78–88

Mortensen DT (1982) The matching process as a noncooperative bargaining game. In: McCall JJ (ed) The Economics of Information and Uncertainty, The University of Chicago Press, Chicago, IL, pp 233–254

Napel S (2002) Bilateral Bargaining: Theory and Applications, Lecture Notes in Economics and Mathematical Systems, vol 518. Springer, Berlin, Germany

Nash JF (1950) The bargaining problem. Econometrica 18(2):155–162

Nash JF (1953) Two-person cooperative bargaining games. Econometrica 21(1):128–140

Osborne MJ, Rubinstein A (1990) Bargaining and Markets. Academic Press, San Diego, CA

Rubinstein A (1982) Perfect equilibrium in a bargaining model. Econometrica 50(1):97–109

Rubinstein A (1989) Competitive equilibrium in a market with decentralized trade and strategic behavior: An introduction. In: Feiwel GR (ed) The Economics of Imperfect Competition and Employment: Joan Robinson and Beyond, Macmillan, London, UK, chap 7, pp 243–259

Rubinstein A, Wolinsky A (1985) Equilibrium in a market with sequential bargaining. Econometrica 53(5):1133–1150

Rubinstein A, Wolinsky A (1990) Decentralized trading, strategic behaviour and the Walrasian outcome. Rev Econ Stud 57(1):63–78

Selten R (1975) Reexamination of the perfectness concept for equilibrium points in extensive games. Int J Game Theor 4(1):25–55

Ståhl I (1972) Bargaining theory. PhD thesis, Stockholm School of Economics

Chapter 2
Game Theory and Fairness Preferences

During the last three decades a lot of attention was given to experimental investigations of the ultimatum game.[1] Contrary to the theoretical "standard" prediction based on maximization of the monetary payoff (responders accepting the smallest possible offer and proposers offering the minimum possible offer), experiments with ultimatum games show that players are typically not simply maximizing their monetary payoff. Instead, responders frequently *reject* offers they perceive as *unfair* and proposers anticipate this by offering a substantial share, usually with modal and median offers between 40 and 50 percent. A good overview of the various experiments done with ultimatum games is given by Camerer (2003, chap. 3, tables 2–5). The following section 2.1 very briefly summarizes further experimental evidence that subjects are not always maximizing material payoffs.

How can this behavior be in line with classical game theory? The theory of games as defined by von Neumann and Morgenstern is based on *preferences*, and these preferences are described by a utility function. The *payoffs* that classical game theory is based on are *utility levels*. However, as Weibull (2004, p. 6) states:[2]

> The formal machinery of non-cooperative game theory does not require that a player's payoff value $u_i(\omega)$ at an end node ω be a function of the material consequences at that node. Indeed, two plays resulting in identical material payoffs to all players may well differ in terms of information sets reached, choices made or not made during play and so on—aspects that may be relevant for players' preferences and hence influence their Bernoulli functions. Standard game theory only requires the *existence* of a Bernoulli function u_i for each (personal) player i. Indeed, several laboratory experiments have convincingly—though perhaps not surprisingly for the non-economist—shown that human subjects' preferences are not driven only by their own monetary payoffs.

Therefore it is *not contradictory* to classical game theory to define a player's utility function not only on his own monetary payoff, but, for example, on his own payoff *and* the monetary payoff of others. This way, it is possible to explain and predict behavior by using classical game theory in conjunction with a new class of

---

[1] See section 1.2 for a short description of the ultimatum game.

[2] In the original text a player's payoff value was denoted by $\pi_i(\omega)$. To keep consistency with the rest of this book this was replaced by $u_i(\omega)$.

C. Korth, *Fairness in Bargaining and Markets,*
Lecture Notes in Economics and Mathematical Systems, 627
DOI: 10.1007/978-3-642-02252-4_1, © Springer-Verlag Berlin Heidelberg 2009

social preferences and *social utility functions*. The area of research concerned with social preferences is called *social utility* and is part of behavioral game theory.

Some economists argue that altering the utility function makes it possible to explain anything. For example, Güth (1995, p. 342) remarked:

> Very often this type of research resembles, however, a neoclassical repair shop in the sense that one first observes behaviour for a certain environment and then defines a suitable optimisation or game model which can account for what has been observed.

Comments like this show how behavioral game theory can be misunderstood. The goal is not to explain all kinds of experimental results but to find *adjusted utility functions* on the basis of *psychological analysis*, which help to *explain* and *predict* human behavior.

Based on the idea that a preference for fairness can explain rejections in experimental ultimatum games, two classes of fairness-models evolved: *outcome-based* and *intention-based* models. Outcome-based models treat the intentions that players attribute to one another as unnecessary for predicting behavior and focus solely on the *monetary payoffs*. Section 2.2 summarizes two prominent contributions in this domain: the equity-based approaches by Fehr and Schmidt (1999) and Bolton and Ockenfels (2000). In contrast, intention-based approaches, in particular the reciprocity and trust hypothesis, rely on the attribution of *intentions* (i.e., players not only observing their actions but forming beliefs on each other's *motives*) in an essential way. Depending on the available alternatives, identical outcomes may be interpreted in different ways. For outcome-based approaches, this is not the case: since it is only the intrinsic properties of outcomes that drive behavior, the alternatives the players face are irrelevant. Section 2.3 gives a detailed exposition of the reciprocity model that was developed by Falk and Fischbacher (2006) and points out some differences to the models of reciprocity by Rabin (1993) and by Dufwenberg and Kirchsteiger (2004).

This chapter lays some foundations for later chapters: chapter 3 is based on the model of reciprocity by Falk and Fischbacher (2006), while chapters 5 to 7 employ a utility representation that is closely related to the model of Fehr and Schmidt (1999).

2.1 Evidence from Experiments

In most applications of economic models, it is assumed that people maximize their own material well-being without caring for "social" goals. In contrast to this, a large body of experimental evidence suggests that there are other determinants of human behavior.

In experimental *ultimatum games*, most proposers offer between forty and fifty percent of the total pie to the receiver while offers below twenty percent are rarely observed. Small offers are usually rejected, with the rejection rate decreasing in the amount offered to the responder. Another observation is that responders accept lower offers when they are made by a random device instead of a human.[3]

A similar game is the *best-shot game*, in which the proposer can only choose between two payoff distributions. He can either propose a split that is very advantageous or disadvantageous to himself. Participants in experiments usually accept a higher degree of inequity than in the ultimatum game.[4]

The *dictator game* is similar to the ultimatum game, but the second player has no choice and must accept the first player's offer. Experiments show that proposers in dictator games usually offer less than in the ultimatum games. About 80 percent offer a positive amount while practically nobody offers more than 50 percent.[5]

In the *gift-exchange game*, the first mover (firm) offers a wage w to the second mover (worker). The worker can reject the offer so that both earn nothing, or he can accept. If he accepts, he makes a costly effort decision with a convex cost function $c(e)$. Higher wages yield lower monetary payoffs for the firms and higher ones for workers, while higher effort levels have the reverse effect on payoffs. The standard game-theoretic prediction based on monetary payoff maximization is that workers will invariably choose the lowest possible effort level, since this choice is dominant in a pecuniary sense. In anticipation of this, firms will only make the lowest possible wage offer. In contrast to this, some firms offer wages above the market rate, and a positive relationship between wages and effort levels is usually observed.[6]

In *public-goods games*, agents simultaneously decide whether to pay for the provision of a public good or not. The good is said to be public because every agent, regardless of whether he paid for it or not, enjoys the same benefit from this good. Experiments show that the amount subjects contribute is increasing in their expectation about the contributions of others.[7]

These experimental results suggest that subjects do not only care about their own material payoff but also about something like fairness. Fehr and Schmidt (2006) give a good overview of recent papers written based on these results.

---

[3] Analysis of the ultimatum game was pioneered by Güth et al. (1982). For surveys on ultimatum games, see Thaler (1988), Güth and Tietz (1990), Camerer and Thaler (1995) and Roth (1995).

[4] The best-shot game was introduced by Harrison and Hirshleifer (1989) and Prasnikar and Roth (1992). See also Falk et al. (2003) for experimental results.

[5] See, for example, Forsythe et al. (1994) and Andreoni and Miller (2002).

[6] See, for example, Berg et al. (1995), Gächter and Falk (2002), or Fehr et al. (1996). Falk (2007) reports findings from a field study that demonstrates—in a setting outside the labor market—how gift-giving to donors induces them to reciprocate the gift by donating more.

[7] For surveys on public-goods games, see Ledyard (1995) and Dawes and Thaler (1988). Another interesting study was published by Falk et al. (2005), who find that besides fairness considerations, spitefulness is an important driver of sanctioning behavior in multi-person games.

2.2 Equity-based Approaches

This section introduces two papers that try to reconcile the above-mentioned stylized facts from experiments with traditional Bayesian equilibrium behavior of optimizing agents: Fehr and Schmidt (1999) and Bolton and Ockenfels (2000). They describe models in which agents have preferences that exhibit *inequity aversion*. Agents can increase their utility by sacrificing their own material payoff if by doing so their payoff is closer to the payoff the other players receive. Preferences depend only on the *payoff distribution* but not on a measure for the *intentions* attributed to the opponents' behavior.

In Fehr and Schmidt (1999), subjects are introduced that dislike inequitable outcomes, but dislike them less when they are to their own advantage. The utility function for player $i \in \{1, \ldots, n\}$ is given by

$$u_i(\pi) = \pi_i - \frac{\alpha_i}{n-1} \sum_{j \neq i} \max(\pi_j - \pi_i, 0) - \frac{\beta_i}{n-1} \sum_{j \neq i} \max(\pi_i - \pi_j, 0),$$

or simplified for the two-player case $i \in \{1, 2\}$:

$$u_i(\pi) = \pi_i - \alpha_i \max(\pi_j - \pi_i, 0) - \beta_i \max(\pi_i - \pi_j, 0), \quad i \neq j,$$

with $\alpha_i \geq \beta_i$ and $0 \leq \beta_i < 1$. π_i denotes the material payoff to player i; α_i and β_i are capturing how much the subject suffers from inequitable outcomes, where $\alpha_i \geq \beta_i$ captures the idea that the subject suffers more from inequality that is to his disadvantage. The share of individuals with a concern for equity (in the model, part of the total population consists of purely selfish players), where α_i and β_i are positive is exogenously given and common knowledge. The assumption that individuals are heterogenous is an important ingredient of the model.

Despite its simplicity, many stylized facts can be explained. The model is consistent with giving in dictator, trust, and gift-exchange games and with the rejection of low offers in ultimatum games. However, since the model does not account for intentions, the model fails to explain why people behave differently when playing against a random device instead of a real player, or why low offers in a best-shot game are more readily accepted than in an ultimatum game.

The approach by Bolton and Ockenfels (2000) is similar to this model although there are some differences in detail. For example, in their model, the subjects compare their material payoff to the material *average* payoff of the group, so there is a difference regarding the *reference point* for fairness considerations. Another difference is that the marginal disutility of small deviations from equality is zero. Therefore, if subjects are non-satiated in their own material payoff, they will never propose an equal split in the dictator game. The utility function is given by

$$u_i(\pi) = \begin{cases} (\pi_i, \frac{\pi_i}{\sum_{j=1}^n \pi_j}) & \text{if } \sum_{j=1}^n \pi_j > 0 \\ f(\pi_i, \frac{1}{n}) & \text{if } \sum_{j=1}^n \pi_j = 0. \end{cases}$$

This utility function is assumed to be weakly increasing and concave in player i's own material payoff π_i for any given u_i. For any given π_i, the utility function is strictly concave in player i's share of total income. The specific functional form is not fixed, so this utility function is more flexible than the one in the model of Fehr and Schmidt.

The model of Bolton and Ockenfels (2000) can also explain giving in dictator and gift-exchange games as well as rejections in ultimatum games. However, the model fails to explain punishment patterns in the public-goods games,[8] and because the reference point is the average payoff, it cannot explain behavior dependent on inequities among other players.[9]

2.3 Reciprocity

The concept of *reciprocity* captures a motivational force behind human behavior. Reciprocity can be distinguished from simple altruism, which corresponds to unconditional generosity. Positive (negative) reciprocity is the impulse or the desire to be kind (unkind) to those who have been kind (unkind) to us.[10]

A crucial feature of the psychology of reciprocity is obviously that people decide about their actions towards others not only according to the *material consequences* resulting from the actions taken by the latter, but also dependent on the *intentions* attributed to them. One example are people who are motivated by *positive reciprocity*. They differentiate between people who take a generous action by choice and those who are forced to do so.[11]

This section reviews some of the literature which tries to integrate the phenomenon of reciprocal behavior into standard game theory.[12] The focus is on the approach of Falk and Fischbacher (2006). Some important differences to the approaches by Rabin (1993), and Dufwenberg and Kirchsteiger (2004) are pointed out

---

[8] For example, Fehr and Gächter (2000) provide evidence that free riders in public-goods games are punished if there is an opportunity for the other players to do so. The more the free riders negatively deviate from the group standard, the more they are punished—even if punishing is costly to the punisher.

[9] For an example of behavior dependent on inequities among other players, see Charness and Rabin (2002). They let a player C choose between the material payoff allocations (575,575,575) and (900,300,600). In both allocations, player C receives the fair share of $1/3$, so the Bolton and Ockenfels model predicts the second choice as the payoff for player C is higher. However, in experiments, 54% of subjects choose the first allocation.

[10] See, for example, Fehr and Gächter (1998) for more detailed observations regarding reciprocity.

[11] Experimental evidence is given in Falk et al (2003) where the authors performed four different mini-ultimatum games. In each game, the proposer had two choices, one of which was always to offer 20%. The alternatives have been 0%, 20%, 50%, or 80%. The rejection rate of the 20% offer was highest when the alternative was equal division; it was lowest when the only alternative was to offer nothing to the second player. The fact that the rejection rate was not zero in this case suggests that pure equity considerations indeed play a role.

[12] See Klein (2000) for a detailed comparison of literature on reciprocity.

to clarify why the model of Falk and Fischbacher was chosen to be further analyzed in chapter 3.

Rabin was the first who adapted the framework of psychological games of Geanakoplos et al (1989) to suit the phenomenon of reciprocity. He introduced so-called *fairness games* in which a reciprocity payoff is added to the material payoff of the players. This reciprocity payoff can be described as the product of a *kindness* and a *reciprocation term*. The kindness term is positive if a player feels he is treated well. The player then wants to make the reciprocation term positive in order to increase his overall payoff. He can achieve this by behaving nicely in return, as the reciprocation term is defined to be positive when the player chooses a kind action. The motivation for negative reciprocity is modeled analogously. Because the kindness and the reciprocation term depend explicitly on *belief*s, a psychological game is formed.

However, Rabin's model is restricted to simultaneous, two-player normal-form games. This implies a drawback when a sequential game is rewritten in normal form and solved accordingly: Rabin's model cannot not take the sequential structure of the game into account. Therefore, an equilibrium in Rabin's model may allow for non-optimizing behavior at information sets that are not reached. The paper by Dufwenberg and Kirchsteiger (2004) is closely related to Rabin (1993). They generalize Rabin's model to *n*-person extensive-form games of imperfect information. In contrast to Rabin, they impose not only subgame perfection but also *sequential rationality* in non-proper subgames. The main idea behind their extension is to keep track of players' beliefs about the strategy profile being played as the game evolves. Falk and Fischbacher (2006) also extend Rabin's approach, but to extensive-form games of perfect information. They use a more complex utility function that allows for equity concerns *and* for intentions.

Each of these papers has four basic "ingredients": the *kindness term* $\tilde{f}$, the *reciprocation term* f, a *social utility function* u,[13] and an *equilibrium concept*. In the following subsections, each "ingredient" of the approach by Falk and Fischbacher (2006) is discussed, and some relevant differences to the other approaches are briefly pointed out. All discussed models boil down to games with only two players, so the *n*-player case, which is important for market environments, for example, is not discussed.

2.3.1 Kindness Term

Consider a two-player game with strategy sets S_i and S_j for the two players i and j with $\pi_i \colon S_i \times S_j \longrightarrow \mathbb{R}$ describing the expected payoff for player i. The *kindness term* $\tilde{f}_j(\cdot)$ measures the kindness player i experiences from player j's expected actions. It is positive if player j is considered as acting kindly and negative if he is considered as acting unkindly. Player i's kindness term depends on the strategy $a_j \in S_j$

---

[13] The social utility function is usually a sum of the material payoff π and the reciprocity payoff, which is the product of kindness term $\tilde{f}$ and reciprocation term f. For example, $u = \pi + \tilde{f} \times f$.

chosen by player j, player i's belief $b_j \in S_j$ about the strategy a_j, and player i's second-order belief $c_i \in S_i$ about what he believes player j believes he is choosing; or in other words: c_i is player i's belief about b_i. In the following $i \in \{1,2\}$ and $j = 3 - i$.

Falk and Fischbacher (2006) base their model on extensive-form games with a finite number of stages and with complete and perfect information. They define $\mathcal{N}_i$ as the set of nodes at which player i has to move. Furthermore they define $\pi_i(n, s_i, s_j) \equiv \pi_i(s_i | n, s_j | n)$ as the expected payoff of player i conditional on node $n \in \mathcal{N}_i$, that is, the expected payoff of player i in the subgame starting from node n, given that the strategies s_i and s_j are played.

The kindness term combines the psychological approach with equity considerations. The kindness term $\tilde{f}_j(n)$ in a node $n \in \mathcal{N}_i$ is given by[14]

$$\tilde{f}_j(n) = \vartheta_j(n)\Delta_j(n) .$$

The second expression $\Delta_j(n)$ is called the *outcome term*. It is positive if player i experiences a higher payoff than his opponent:

$$\Delta_j(n) = \pi_i(n, b_j, c_i) - \pi_j(n, b_j, c_i)$$

with $\pi_i(n, b_j, c_i)$ being player i's *belief* about the material payoff player j is offering to player i if player j chooses to play a_j and expects player i to choose b_i. In the following, let $(\pi_i^0, \pi_j^0) = (\pi_i(n, b_j, c_i), \pi_j(n, b_j, c_i))$ to simplify notation.

The first component $\vartheta_j(n)$, which is called the *intention factor*, is given by

$$\vartheta_j(n) = \max\{\Omega(\tilde{\pi}_i, \tilde{\pi}_j, \pi_i^0, \pi_j^0) | (\tilde{\pi}_i, \tilde{\pi}_j) \in \Pi_i(n)\} .$$

This factor measures how much intention player i attaches to the actions he expects player j to choose and which would result in the payoffs (π_i^0, π_j^0). $\vartheta_j(n)$ is calculated in two steps.

First, (π_i^0, π_j^0) is compared with all the alternatives player j has. These alternatives are denoted by $(\tilde{\pi}_i, \tilde{\pi}_j)$ and are collected in the set of payoff combinations $\Pi_i(n)$. Every comparison is summarized by $\Omega(\tilde{\pi}_i, \tilde{\pi}_j, \pi_i^0, \pi_j^0)$ and results in a value of $\Omega(\cdot)$ between 0 and 1. A value of 1 resembles *full intentionality* while a smaller value of $\Omega(\cdot)$ expresses a lower degree of intention.

In a second step, the *maximum value* of all these comparisons is taken to be the *overall intention* player i attaches to (π_i^0, π_j^0). The main intuition behind this approach is the following: if player j has at least one alternative, where he could give more to player i without suffering any loss himself, then (π_i^0, π_j^0) is considered as fully intentional.

The value of Ω is calculated as follows:

---

[14] $\tilde{f}_j(n)$ corresponds to $\varphi_j(n)$ in their paper.

$$\Omega(\tilde{\pi}_i, \tilde{\pi}_j, \pi_i^0, \pi_j^0) = \begin{cases} 1 & \text{if } \pi_i^0 \geq \pi_j^0 \text{ and } \tilde{\pi}_i < \pi_i^0 \quad \text{(a)} \\ \varepsilon_i & \text{if } \pi_i^0 \geq \pi_j^0 \text{ and } \tilde{\pi}_i \geq \pi_i^0 \quad \text{(b)} \\ 1 & \text{if } \pi_i^0 < \pi_j^0, \tilde{\pi}_i > \pi_i^0 \text{ and } \tilde{\pi}_i \leq \tilde{\pi}_j \text{ (c)} \\ \max(1 - \frac{\tilde{\pi}_i - \tilde{\pi}_j}{\pi_j^0 - \pi_i^0}, \varepsilon_i) & \text{if } \pi_i^0 < \pi_j^0, \tilde{\pi}_i > \pi_i^0 \text{ and } \tilde{\pi}_i > \tilde{\pi}_j \text{ (d)} \\ \varepsilon_i & \text{if } \pi_i^0 < \pi_j^0 \text{ and } \tilde{\pi}_i < \pi_i^0. \quad \text{(e)} \end{cases}$$

In cases (a) and (b), player i receives a higher payoff than player j. While in case (a), this is interpreted as being fully intentional ($\Omega = 1$), it is not in case (b). This is because in case (a), the alternative which player j could choose would leave him a smaller payoff ($\tilde{\pi}_i < \pi_i^0$), while in case (b), the alternatives would make him even better off ($\tilde{\pi}_i \geq \pi_i^0$). In this latter case, player j's action is not seen by player i as being really generous and therefore the intention factor is set to be $\Omega = \varepsilon_i$. This means that the choice of (π_i^0, π_j^0) in case (b) is not seen as intentional, but evaluated with the individual *pure outcome-concern parameter* $0 \leq \varepsilon_i \leq 1$.[15] Case (b) is also relevant when player j has no alternative to choose from. Then the intuition behind setting $\Omega = \varepsilon_i$ is that kindness or unkindness is perceived to be weak but not zero, regardless of the actual material distribution.

In cases (c), (d), and (e), player i's payoff is smaller than the payoff of player j ($\pi_i^0 < \pi_j^0$). In case (c), player j could have put player i in a better position ($\tilde{\pi}_i > \pi_i^0$) without giving up his relatively better position ($\tilde{\pi}_i \leq \tilde{\pi}_j$). This is evaluated by player i as fully intentional *meanness* of player j by setting $\Omega = 1$. In case (d), player j could also have improved player i's situation ($\tilde{\pi}_i > \pi_i^0$), but at the expense of making himself worse off ($\tilde{\pi}_i > \tilde{\pi}_j$). How player i evaluates this depends on how much player j could have decreased the payoff difference between the player relative to the chosen outcome (π_i^0, π_j^0). The smaller the resulting difference in the alternative, the higher the intention factor player i attributes to this choice. If player j would have to sacrifice a lot to decrease the inequity, then $\Omega = \varepsilon_i$ as above. In this case, ε_i could be interpreted as an *"envy term."* Finally, case (e) captures the situation where player j has no possibility at all to offer a higher payoff to player i, so no intention is visible which results in $\Omega = \varepsilon_i$.

This measure of kindness is robust against additions of supposedly irrelevant alternatives to the game, which does not hold for Rabin's model. Furthermore, Rabin (1993), and Dufwenberg and Kirchsteiger (2004) limit the kindness term to behavior which is driven only by intentions; pure equity consideration cannot play a role in their models. In this regard, the model of Falk and Fischbacher (2006) is more general, as it can encompass not only intention-based behavior, but also pure concern for equity ($\varepsilon_i = 1$).

---

[15] As the parameter ε_i measures player i's *pure* concern for an equitable *outcome*, it can be used to model behavior which is purely intention driven ($\varepsilon_i = 0$), as in Rabin (1993) and Dufwenberg and Kirchsteiger (2004), or a behavior which is purely outcome oriented ($\varepsilon_i = 1$), as in the equity-based approaches by Fehr and Schmidt (1999) and Bolton and Ockenfels (2000).

2.3.2 Reciprocation Term

The *reciprocity payoff* consists of two terms—the *fairness term* as given above, and a *reciprocation term*. The reciprocation term captures player i's reaction to player j's expected behavior and gives an interpretation of player i's *reaction* as either nice or mean. The product of kindness and reciprocation terms are part of the utility function. Therefore, both terms will have the same sign in equilibrium.

The reciprocation term of Falk and Fischbacher (2006) captures the influence player i's reaction has on player j's payoff:[16]

$$f_i(n,t,b_j,c_i) = \pi_j(v(n,t),c_i,b_j) - \pi_j(n,c_i,b_j)$$

with $v(n,t)$ denoting the unique node that directly follows node $n \in \mathcal{N}$ on the path to a terminal node $t \in \mathcal{T}$. The reciprocation term $f_i(\cdot)$ describes the *change* in player j's *expected payoff* implied by player i's move when he selects a path on the game tree towards the terminal node t. The second term is player j's expected payoff before this move and the first term is player j's expected payoff after player i's move. Falk and Fischbacher call $f_i(\cdot)$ the *"alteration"* of player j's payoff from $\pi_j(n,c_i,b_j)$ to $\pi_j(v(n,t),c_i,b_j)$. The intuition that a positive change in player j's payoff means a "reward" for him is misleading. In fact, it does measure how much player j is pleased or upset, after each realization of player i's mixed strategy. The reciprocation utility player i receives does depend on how much he is able to surprise player j with his action, given player j's beliefs. However, in equilibrium, beliefs are consistent, and therefore it is not possible for player i to surprise player j by his moves. Because of this, the reciprocity payoff $f_i(\cdot)$ in equilibrium is always zero by definition. Still, this concept helps to understand how an equilibrium is reached. In principle, $f_i(\cdot)$ is defined so that player i tries to reward player j for kind moves and tries to punish him for unkind actions.[17]

This shows the role beliefs play in psychological games. They do not have any deeper meaning, but are a helpful device to construct equilibria.[18]

2.3.3 Utility Function

The total utility that the players maximize is a sum of the material payoff and a reciprocity payoff. In the model of Falk and Fischbacher (2006), the utility for player i at each end node $t \in \mathcal{T}$ is given by

---

[16] $f_i(n,t,b_j,c_i)$ corresponds to $\sigma_i(n,f)$ in their paper.

[17] See Klein (2000) for this explanation.

[18] In the literature, it is not clear if or how beliefs are given or formed before the equilibrium choices are made, or if they are formed according to equilibrium choices after equilibrium is reached. We leave this question open for discussion.

$$u_i(t) = \pi_i(t) + \rho_i \sum_{\substack{n \in \mathcal{N}_i \\ n \to t}} \tilde{f}_j(n) \times f_i(n, t, b_j, c_i) \,. \qquad (2.1)$$

As above, the *pure material payoff* $\pi_i(t)$ at the end node t is combined with an expression representing the *reciprocity payoff*. In Falk and Fischbacher's model, this reciprocity payoff is calculated as the sum over all nodes in the game tree on the path from the root node to the terminal node t (that is denoted by $\substack{n \in \mathcal{N}_i \\ n \to t}$). For each node, the fairness expression $\tilde{f}_j(\cdot)$ is multiplied with the reciprocation term $f_i(\cdot)$, and finally, the sum is weighted with the reciprocity parameter ρ_i against the material payoff. If the reciprocity parameter for both players is zero ($\rho_i = \rho_j = 0$), then the game is reduced to a standard game.

To clarify how the calculations actually work, the following demonstrates how the concept is applied to the ultimatum game.

In a first step, the decision of the responder is analyzed. The responder can either accept or reject the offer. His payoff is the sum of the actual material payoff he receives and his reciprocity payoff. For offers of exactly or more than half of the pie, the responder is in a (weakly) advantageous position. Because the proposer could have offered less, this move is considered as fully intentional and therefore $\Omega = 1$. The outcome term is also positive, because the responder's payoff is weakly higher than the proposer's. Taken together, the kindness term is positive, too. Therefore, the responder tries to reciprocate and always accepts the offer. If the offer is strictly below half of the pie, it is regarded as being fully intentional with $\Omega = 1$, because the proposer could have offered half. This would have improved the responder's situation without putting the proposer at a relative disadvantage. The outcome term is negative because the responder's payoff is smaller than the proposer's. So in this case, the kindness term is negative. Now the receiver's reciprocity payoff is positive when he rejects, as this would result in a negative reciprocation term. Whether he indeed rejects depends on a trade-off between the reciprocity payoff he gains and the material payoff he forgoes by rejecting.

In a second step, the behavior of the proposer can be analyzed. Whenever he offers a positive amount, the responder has the choice to accept or to reject. The responder's behavior is considered fully intentional ($\Omega = 1$) because rejecting would leave the proposer with a smaller payoff than accepting. For offers of more than half, the outcome term from the proposer's point of view is negative. So in these cases, the utility is decreasing in the amount offered, which in turn leads the proposer to offer half of the pie, at the most. For offers of less than half, the outcome term is positive, so the proposer gains reciprocity utility by offering more to the receiver. Again, the result is a trade-off between reciprocity payoff and material payoff. Note that this definition of the utility function can allow for pure altruism. This is, for example, ruled out in the model by Rabin (1993).

2.3.4 Equilibrium Concepts

The utility function used by Falk and Fischbacher (2006) has the properties as in the definition by Geanakoplos et al. (1989) of a psychological game—all information sets are singletons and beliefs do not depend on the history of play.[19] So the result of Geanakoplos et al. (1989) applies: the concept of subgame perfection is also a suitable equilibrium refinement in psychological games. Falk and Fischbacher (2006) call a subgame perfect psychological Nash equilibrium a *reciprocity equilibrium*. For $\rho_i = \rho_j = 0$, the definition is equivalent to the definition of a subgame perfect Nash equilibrium.

In contrast to the models of Rabin (1993) and Dufwenberg and Kirchsteiger (2004), the model of Falk and Fischbacher (2006) makes *unique* equilibrium predictions for most relevant games. Application to several games shows that it is possible to derive plausible predictions for different games with the same utility function and even the same parameter constellation.

The example of the ultimatum game given in section 2.3.3 can be extended to equilibrium considerations. Because the model allows for backward induction, the responder's behavior is derived first. Recall that the strategy of the responder R depends on a trade-off between material and reciprocity payoff. Calculations show that offers c above a certain threshold $c_0(\rho_R) \leq 1/2$ are always accepted, with $c_0(\rho_R)$ increasing in ρ_R. For offers below this threshold, the responder plays a mixed strategy of randomly choosing between accepting and rejecting with an acceptance-probability $p(c, \rho_R)$, which is increasing in c and decreasing in ρ_R. A higher offer is more likely to be accepted, while a more reciprocal responder rejects the same offer more often.

There are two cases for the proposer P. If he has a relatively low concern for reciprocity, he simply maximizes his expected material payoff, which results in an offer of exactly $c_0(\rho_R)$. This is the smallest offer which assures acceptance by the responder. However, when his concern for reciprocity is relatively high, he can gain additional utility by offering more, so in this case, the equilibrium offer is $c(\rho_P) > c_0(\rho_R)$. Nevertheless, he will always offer at most half of the pie.[20]

Falk and Fischbacher (2006) call a subgame perfect psychological Nash equilibrium a *reciprocity equilibrium*. For a proof of existence in the considered class of games and more details on the following equilibrium derivations, see their paper. The following paragraphs give a formal proof of the equilibrium for the ultimatum game:

Assume that the following equations (2.2) and (2.3) describe the unique reciprocity equilibrium of the ultimatum game: Equilibrium play results in *acceptance probability*

---

[19] The utility function in Falk and Fischbacher (2006) as given here is not continuous. However, Falk and Fischbacher show that a minor technical modification in the definition of Ω guarantees the existence of a reciprocity equilibrium.

[20] This is a result of the considerations at the end of section 2.3.3.

$$p^*(c) = \begin{cases} \min\left\{1, \frac{c}{\rho_R \times (1-2c)(1-c)}\right\} & \text{if } c < \frac{1}{2} \\ 1 & \text{if } c \geq \frac{1}{2} \end{cases} \qquad (2.2)$$

for offer c if $\rho_R \neq 0$, and $p^* \equiv 1$ if $\rho_R = 0$. The share c^* offered by the proposer P to responder R in equilibrium is given by

$$c^* = \max\left\{\frac{3\rho_R + 1 - \sqrt{1 + 6\rho_R + \rho_R^2}}{4\rho_R}, \frac{1}{2} \times (1 - \frac{1}{\rho_P})\right\} \qquad (2.3)$$

for $\rho_P, \rho_R \neq 0$.

First, let p' denote the proposer's belief about acceptance probability p and let p'' denote the responder's belief about p'. Let $\vartheta_P(c)$ be the intentionality factor at the decision node after the proposer P's choice of c. The responder's utility is

$$u_{R_A} = c + \rho_R \times \vartheta_P(c)\, p'' \left[c - (1-c)\right] \times \left[(1-c) - p''(1-c)\right]$$

in case she accepts the offer and

$$u_{R_R} = \rho_R \times \vartheta_P(c)\, p'' \left[c - (1-c))\right] \times \left[0 - p''(1-c)\right]$$

if she rejects. The former is greater for $c \geq 1/2$, implying acceptance. For $c < 1/2$ define (by setting $u_{R_A} = u_{R_R}$)

$$p''_{\text{crit}} = \frac{c}{\rho_R \vartheta_P(c)(1-2c)(1-c)}. \qquad (2.4)$$

Note that $p'' > p''_{\text{crit}}$ would ask for $p = p'' = 0$ in contradiction to $p''_{\text{crit}} \geq 0$ (for $c < 1/2$). Hence, either $p'' < p''_{\text{crit}}$ so that optimal responder behavior in equilibrium (involving consistent beliefs) requires $p = p'' = 1$, or we have $p'' = p''_{\text{crit}}$ so that $p = p'' = p''_{\text{crit}}$ is optimal for consistent beliefs. Optimal responder behavior can thus be summarized by $p^*(c) = \min\{1, p''_{\text{crit}}\}$. If $c < 1/2$, then responder R is disadvantaged and the proposer P's move is considered as fully intentional because $c = 1/2$ would lead to a higher payoff for responder R without making P worse off. Therefore, $\vartheta_P(c) = 1$ in equation (2.4).

The expected utility of a proposer with a correct belief p' determined by $p^*(\cdot)$ is

$$u_P = p^*(c) \times (1-c) + \rho_P \times \vartheta_R(c)\, p^*(c'')\,(1 - 2c'') \times \left[p^*(c)c - p^*(c'')c''\right] \quad (2.5)$$

where c'' denotes the proposer P's second-order beliefs.[21] In equilibrium, we must have $c \leq 1/2$ because u_P is decreasing in c for $c'' \geq 1/2$. For $c > 0$, the responder's move $p^*(\cdot)$ is fully intentional, as she has the option of rejecting the offer, which leads to a smaller payoff for the proposer; so $\vartheta_R = 1$.

---

[21] One can think of c'' as an offer that proposer P conjectures R's response to be based on in order to evaluate her kindness. This kindness renders a particular reciprocation and corresponding actual offer c optimal, which must coincide with c'' in equilibrium.

Now define

$$c_0 = \frac{1 + 3\rho_R - \sqrt{1 + 6\rho_R + \rho_R^2}}{4\rho_R}$$

as the smallest c such that $p^*(c) = 1$. u_P is increasing in c for $c < c_0$; so a rational proposer must choose $c^* \geq c_0$, implying acceptance with probability 1. Setting $p^* = 1$ and $c \geq c_0$ in equation (2.5), one obtains

$$u_P = (1 - c) + \rho_P \times (1 - 2c'') \times (c - c'')$$

and

$$\frac{\partial u_P}{\partial c} = -1 + \rho_P \times (1 - 2c'') .$$

So u_P is decreasing in c for

$$c'' > c''_{\text{crit}} = \frac{1}{2}\left(1 - \frac{1}{\rho_P}\right)$$

and increasing for $c'' < c''_{\text{crit}}$. First, consider $c''_{\text{crit}} < c_0$: Since, in equilibrium, $c = c''$, we get $c''_{\text{crit}} < c_0 \leq c = c''$ and u_P is decreasing in c. Then, the optimal proposal is $c^* = c_0 (= \max(c_0, c''_{\text{crit}}))$. Second, consider $c''_{\text{crit}} \geq c_0$: If $c'' > c''_{\text{crit}}$, u_P is decreasing in c and therefore c would have to be chosen equal to c_0 which is, however, incompatible with $c = c''$ because $c'' > c''_{\text{crit}} \geq c_0 = c$. If $c'' < c''_{\text{crit}}$, u_P is increasing in c and therefore c is chosen equal to 1, which is also incompatible with $c = c''$ because $c'' < c''_{\text{crit}} < 1/2 < 1 = c$. Therefore, $c^* = c'' = c''_{\text{crit}}(= \max(c_0, c''_{\text{crit}}))$.

The equilibrium in the dictator game for agents with preferences based on Falk and Fischbacher (2006) is easily derived. The key difference from the ultimatum game is that acceptance is not intentional in the dictator game. So the intentionality factor at the proposer's decision node equals ε_P. Then

$$u_P = (1 - c) + \rho_P \varepsilon_P (1 - c'' - c'') c$$

and the first order condition yields

$$c''_{\text{crit}} = 1/2\left(1 - \frac{1}{\rho_P \varepsilon_P}\right) .$$

2.3.5 Explanatory Power

In the reciprocity equilibrium as defined by Falk and Fischbacher (2006), the responder's strategy in the ultimatum game is mixed. The acceptance probability is monotonically increasing in the amount offered up to a point, called *cutoff point*,[22] from which on the offer is always accepted. The cutoff point is decreasing in the responder's reciprocity parameter and always lower than one half.

The offer of a selfish proposer matches this cutoff point and is therefore also increasing in the responder's reciprocity parameter. If the proposer himself is reciprocal, his offer can be more generous. This depends on how reciprocal he is relative to the responder.

The equilibrium in random-offer ultimatum games, in which the offer is not determined by a human but by a random device, demonstrates the role of intentions: because no intentions are attributed to a random offer, the acceptance probability of a given offer is weakly higher than in the regular ultimatum game. The acceptance probability is not always one, because equity considerations also play a role.

The model of Falk and Fischbacher (2006) correctly predicts the main stylized facts for the gift-exchange game, in which positive reciprocity plays a major role. The worker's effort choice is increasing in the wage paid and in his reciprocity parameter. This is because the higher the wage paid by the company, the higher the kindness term from the worker's point of view. A reciprocal worker tries to react kindly by increasing his effort choice. The results are strictly positive wages.

In analyzing the best-shot game, the dictator game, and the public-goods game the results of Falk and Fischbacher (2006) are also consistent with the experimental evidence discussed above.

2.4 Summary of Fairness Approaches

The models discussed in sections 2.2 and 2.3 fall in two categories: equity-based and intention-based psychological approaches to fairness. One important difference between them is that the former assume that players are either intrinsically fair or intrinsically egoistic or that each player randomizes whether he acts fairly or not. The ex-ante probability of a player being fair is common knowledge. In psychological games, beliefs are built independently of information. A shortcoming of this approach is that beliefs do not have any inherent meaning, and therefore might be formed strategically.

The approaches further differ in what matters to the players: only the outcomes, only the intentions, or both. This is achieved by different definitions of the utility function. The more degrees of freedom the utility function of a fairness game does allow for, the more a model can explain. Unfortunately, equilibrium calculations in psychological games are very complex and sometimes result in ambiguous predictions. Therefore, equity-based models are much easier to handle. However, according to most experimental evidence, human behavior depends on *both* intentions and considerations regarding the distribution of material payoffs.[23]

---

[22] The cutoff point is formally given by $c_0(\rho_R)$, see above.

[23] For example, the mini-ultimatum game experiment conducted by Falk et al (2003) shows this explicitly.

Of all discussed models, only the one developed by Falk and Fischbacher (2006) is able to account for this. Not surprisingly, it is most successful in predicting behavior observed in experiments with computable unique equilibria for many games. With two free parameters ρ and ε for each player's utility function, it is furthermore possible to model pure selfish behavior, pure inequity aversion, or pure intentional reciprocity by simply using limit cases. This makes it a very powerful tool for predicting behavior resulting from a variety of preferences in many different games.

References

Andreoni J, Miller JH (2002) Giving according to GARP: An experimental test of the consistency of preferences for altruism. Econometrica 70:737–753

Berg J, Dickhaut J, McCabe K (1995) Trust, reciprocity and social history. Games Econom Behav 10(1):122–142

Bolton GE, Ockenfels A (2000) ERC: A theory of equity, reciprocity, and competition. Am Econ Rev 90(1):166–193

Camerer CF (2003) Behavioral Game Theory: Experiments in Strategic Interaction. Princeton University Press, Princeton, NJ

Camerer CF, Thaler RH (1995) Ultimatums, dictators, and manners. J Econ Perspect 9(2):209–219

Charness G, Rabin M (2002) Understanding social preferences with simple tests. Q J Econ 117(3):817–869

Dawes RM, Thaler RH (1988) Cooperation. J Econ Perspect 2:187–197

Dufwenberg M, Kirchsteiger G (2004) A theory of sequential reciprocity. Games Econom Behav 47(2):268–298

Falk A (2007) Gift exchange in the field. Econometrica 75(5):1501–1511

Falk A, Fischbacher U (2006) A theory of reciprocity. Games Econom Behav 54(2):293–315

Falk A, Fehr E, Fischbacher U (2003) On the nature of fair behavior. Econ Inq 41(1):20–26

Falk A, Fehr E, Fischbacher U (2005) Driving forces behind informal sanctions. Econometrica 7(6):2017–2030

Fehr E, Gächter S (1998) Reciprocity and economics. The economic implications of homo reciprocans. Eur Econ Rev 42(3–5):845–859

Fehr E, Gächter S (2000) Cooperation and punishment in public goods experiments. Am Econ Rev 90(4):980–994

Fehr E, Schmidt KM (1999) A theory of fairness, competition and cooperation. Q J Econ 114(3):817–868

Fehr E, Schmidt KM (2006) The economics of fairness, reciprocity and altruism—Experimental evidence and new theories. In: Kolm SC, Mercier Ythier J (eds) Handbook on the Economics of Giving, Reciprocity and Altruism, vol 1, Elsevier, Amsterdam, Netherlands, chap 8, pp 615–691

Fehr E, Gächter S, Kirchsteiger G (1996) Reciprocal fairness and noncompensating wage differentials. Journal of Institutional and Theoretical Economics 152(4):608–640

Forsythe R, Horowitz J, Savin N, Sefton M (1994) Fairness in simple bargaining games. Games Econom Behav 6:347–369

Gächter S, Falk A (2002) Reputation and reciprocity: Consequences for the labour relation. Scand J Econ 104(1):1–26

Geanakoplos J, Pearce D, Stacchetti E (1989) Psychological games and sequential rationality. Games Econom Behav 1(1):60–79

Güth W (1995) On ultimatum bargaining experiments—A personal review. J Econ Behav Organ 27(3):329–344

Güth W, Tietz R (1990) Ultimatum bargaining behavior—A survey and comparison of experimental results. J Econ Psychol 11(3):417–449

Güth W, Schmittberger R, Schwarze B (1982) An experimental analysis of ultimatum bargaining. J Econ Behav Organ 3(4):367–388

Harrison GW, Hirshleifer J (1989) An experimental evaluation of weakest link/Best shot models of public goods. J Polit Econ 97(1):201–225

Klein A (2000) Reciprocity, endogenous incomplete contracts, and the role of options in law. PhD thesis, Berlin, Germany: dissertation.de

Ledyard J (1995) Public goods: A survey of experimental research. In: Kagel JH, Roth AE (eds) The Handbook of Experimental Economics, Princeton University Press, Princeton, NJ

Prasnikar V, Roth AE (1992) Considerations of fairness and strategy: Experimental data from sequential games. Q J Econ 107(3):865–888

Rabin M (1993) Incorporating fairness into game theory and economics. Am Econ Rev 83(5):1281–1302

Roth AE (1995) Introduction to experimental economics. In: Kagel JH, Roth AE (eds) The Handbook of Experimental Economics, Princeton University Press, Princeton, NJ, chap 1, pp 3–110

Thaler RH (1988) The ultimatum game. J Econ Perspect 2(4):195–206

Weibull JW (2004) Testing game theory. In: Huck S (ed) Advances in Understanding Strategic Behaviour: Game Theory, Experiments and Bounded Rationality. Essay in Honour of Werner Güth, Palgrave, Basingstoke, UK, pp 85–104

Chapter 3
Reciprocity—An Indirect Evolutionary Analysis

In experimental investigations of the *ultimatum game*, participants quite consistently offer 30–50% of an available monetary surplus as first-moving proposers. They reject offers of less than 20% as second-moving responders, which results in zero payoff for both players. Particularly the latter observation is hard to reconcile with the assumption that economic actors are rational maximizers of their monetary payoffs.[1] However, observations can be explained very well by including a consideration for fairness and reciprocity in players' preferences. This is also true regarding many other games for which experimental findings are puzzling from a monetary-payoff maximization point of view.

Neoclassical theory does not restrict preferences to those based solely on monetary payoffs or to strict monotonicity. However, economic agents who are spiteful, enjoy a warm glow donating money to anonymous strangers, or feel it worthwhile to incur private costs to punish free-riders of public goods have not been the conventional assumption in economics. The award of 2002's Nobel Prize to Daniel Kahneman and Vernon Smith is only one indicator that this is changing fast.

In adopting a more realistic view of homo economicus, however, one needs to be careful not to jump to the other extreme, that is, to count any observation of supposedly odd behavior as evidence that "standard assumptions" are wrong and to suppose that human beings universally have the nicer-than-expected character exhibited in some laboratory experiments. The latter would be invalidated by many other experiments, for example, on most market games, in which participants' behavior is typically explained well by egoistic maximization of monetary rewards. Also, the tale—told in different versions before the advent of behavioral economics—that (an unspecified kind of) evolution would make economic agents behave *as if* they maximized payoffs in a world of scarce material resources in our view contains some grain of truth. The question is: under which circumstances is behavior more of the

---

[1] It is unlikely that stakes are just too small for people to bother: experiments in which the available surplus amounted to several monthly wages of participants (e.g., in Indonesia by Cameron 1999 or in the Slovak Republic by Slonim and Roth 1998) produce roughly the same results. Findings are also very robust concerning the subject pool. See, for example, the large cross-cultural study in non-student populations by Henrich et al. (2001).

C. Korth, *Fairness in Bargaining and Markets,*
Lecture Notes in Economics and Mathematical Systems, 627
DOI: 10.1007/978-3-642-02252-4_1, © Springer-Verlag Berlin Heidelberg 2009

standard *homo economicus*-type, and which environments defined by which conditions induce human beings to act, for example, like *homo reciprocans* (cp. Fehr and Gächter 1998) or benevolent dictators?

This chapter combines methods of evolutionary and behavioral game theory to address the above question in a simple but still powerful model. The analysis concentrates on a possible preference for reciprocity as formalized by Falk and Fischbacher (2006). The key departure from the literature is that we consider an environment consisting of not just one, but two distinct distribution tasks (or games) and impose restrictions on the degree to which social preferences can be conditioned on the particular task at hand. This serves as a first approximation of the complexities of the real "game of life" and the observation that it has to be tackled with a limited set of social norms, moral rules and emotions pertaining to general classes of interaction rather than to specific situations. To be concrete we study evolution of particular reciprocity-based preferences in a world where agents randomly face either the ultimatum or the dictator game.[2]

Positive (negative) *reciprocity* refers to the impulse or desire to be kind (unkind) to those who have been kind (unkind) to us.[3] Reciprocity is to be distinguished from simple altruism, i.e., unconditional generosity. While the narrow self-interest hypothesis in "standard theory" fails to explain stylized facts of many experiments, the notion of reciprocity preference sheds a fairly consistent light on possible motivational forces behind a number of observations.

A related motive which seems to guide behavior of economic agents in situations of social exchange is *inequity aversion*.[4] Fehr and Schmidt (1999) and Bolton and Ockenfels (2000) have provided prominent models of agents with preferences that exhibit inequity aversion. In these models, agents may increase their utility by sacrificing their own material payoff if by doing so their payoff is closer to their counterparts' payoffs. Preferences can depend on the entire payoff distribution, but crucially not on any intentions ascribed to other players.

Still, it is a key feature of the psychology of reciprocity that decisions to be kind or unkind to others are based not only on material consequences implied by other players' actions but also on the *intentions* attributed to these players. Agents who are motivated by reciprocity discriminate between players who take an (un)generous action by choice and those who are forced to do so.[5]

---

[2] What we in the following refer to as a multi-game environment may also be viewed as a recurrent version of a comprehensive single game, in which Nature has the first move and selects either an ultimatum or a dictator subgame.

[3] See Fehr and Gächter (1998) for a more detailed account.

[4] Inequity aversion even seems to be an important determinant of social networks: subjects in recent experiments form equilibrium networks involving nearly equal payoffs; they abstain from forming a network with a player designed to earn significantly less than others (see, e.g., Falk and Kosfeld 2003 or Berninghaus et al. 2006).

[5] Experimental evidence is given, for example, by Falk et al. (2003) for four different mini ultimatum games. In each game the proposer had two choices, one of which always was to offer 20%. The alternatives were 0%, 20%, 50% or 80%. When the alternative was equal division, the rejection rate of the 20% offer was highest. When the only alternative was to offer nothing to the

Prominent formalizations of reciprocity based on intentions have been given by Rabin (1993), Charness and Rabin (2002), Dufwenberg and Kirchsteiger (2004) and Falk and Fischbacher (2006). Rabin was the first to adopt the framework of psychological games of Geanakoplos et al. (1989) to model reciprocity. He introduced so-called fairness games in which a reciprocity payoff is added to the material payoff of the players. The reciprocity payoff is calculated as the product of a kindness term and a reciprocation term. The kindness term is positive whenever a player feels treated well. Then he or she tries to make the reciprocation term positive, too, in order to increase his or her total utility payoff. This is achieved by being nice in return. Negative reciprocity is modeled analogously.

While Rabin's original model only applies to two-player normal-form games, Charness and Rabin (2002, app. 1) consider reciprocity and the parallel concern for social welfare in multiperson settings. They define a reciprocal-fairness equilibrium, which imposes homogeneity in preferences and does not entail sequential rationality. It is, therefore, unsuitable to analyze the stylized "game of life" focused on in this chapter. The model of Dufwenberg and Kirchsteiger (2004) incorporates sequential rationality in general n-person extensive-form games. Its main restriction is that it captures intention-based reciprocity, but not any direct equity or social welfare orientation.[6]

Falk and Fischbacher (2006), first, extend Rabin's approach to extensive-form games of perfect information with finitely many stages and, second, propose a utility function that allows for both intention-based reciprocity *and* pure equity concern. Equilibrium calculations and parameter calibrations are quite complex but predictions of Falk and Fischbacher's hybrid model are very consistent with a broad range of experimental evidence. This, and its comprehensiveness—nesting "traditional" preferences, pure inequity aversion and pure intentional reciprocity—make it a very powerful tool for the joint analysis of different games and therefore the focus of this chapter.

Our choice of Falk-Fischbacher preferences obviously entails a loss of generality. However, permitting *all* possible preferences would, in fact, lead back to allowing unimpeded context-dependent specialization of social preferences. So any model that considers the evolution of a limited set of behavioral norms pertaining to distinct interaction types would have to impose similar restrictions.

We have selected combinations of ultimatum and dictator games as the environment because these rather simple games already capture two very fundamental forms of conflictual social and economic interaction, admittedly in a highly stylized fashion: In the first, individual success depends on mutual cooperation and is influenced by both agents' behaviors. In the second, an agent either has no power at all, or full control over own and someone else's success. Bolton and Ockenfels (2000,

---

second player, that is, when the 20% offer revealed good intentions, the rejection rate was lowest but remained positive. The latter suggests that pure equity concern also plays a role.

[6] Another restriction of psychological games more generally (hence also the Falk-Fischbacher model) is that players are assumed to have consistent second-order beliefs, that is, to anticipate correctly not only others' strategy choices but even their respective beliefs about one's own choice. This contrasts with evidence, for example, on human overconfidence or wishful thinking.

p. 188) explicitly show how "many facets of behavior, over a wide class of games, can be deduced from [these] two … most elementary games." In particular, knowledge about respective dictator offers and lowest accepted ultimatum offers allows fairly accurate predictions of their behavior in other bargaining, market, and social dilemma games. Insights about the evolutionary (in)stability of social preferences in our quite specific set-up may, therefore, also have more general economic relevance.

We study the evolution of preferences among rational decision makers. Agents have preferences satisfying the usual axioms and select strategies with the goal to maximize *expected utility*. Preferences can, but need not, depend on an agent's individual material payoff alone; they may, for example, exhibit reciprocity in the way indicated above. However, it is assumed that (average) material payoffs ultimately determine the *fitness* of the agents having particular preferences and hence preferences themselves in an evolutionary process: agents with preferences that earn material payoffs above (below) the average reproduce more (less) successfully, and their preferences' population share increases (decreases).

The considered agents make choices based on anticipated consequences, evaluating their options by preferences which evolve dependent on past success. Thus, as argued in more detail, for example, in Berninghaus et al. (2003) and Güth et al. (2003), an *indirect evolutionary* model such as this combines the main elements of the traditional neoclassical approach (rational purposeful actions selected according to their anticipated consequences or the "shadow of the future") and the direct evolutionary approach (agents carry out fixed behavioral programs that evolve based only on past success or the "shadow of the past").[7]

Throughout this chapter, agents are assumed to know their opponents' preferences before they interact. This allows them to anticipate their opponents' action and optimally respond to it, as formalized by the (subgame perfect) Nash equilibrium concept. These are somewhat restrictive but not overly critical assumptions of the indirect evolutionary approach: immediate play of an equilibrium could be replaced by an adaptive learning process that operates sufficiently faster than evolution; general perfect observability of preferences—a standard assumption in game theory—could be relaxed to only occasional bilateral encounters with complete information, or the possibility that players collect and process information about their opponents at non-prohibitive costs, which they compare to population-dependent benefits.

The following analysis is closely related to that of Güth and Napel (2006). There, equity-based preferences similar to those of Fehr and Schmidt (1999) are considered in the same stylized "game of life." Here, the multi-game indirect evolutionary analysis of Güth and Napel is extended to the domain of psychological games.[8]

The remainder of the chapter is organized as follows: The following section presents our model, which is analyzed in section 3.2 with focus on the question:

---

[7] The indirect evolutionary approach was pioneered by Güth and Yaari (1992) and Güth (1995). Good overviews over research in the domain of indirect evolution are given by Samuelson (2001), and Sethi and Somanathan (2001).

[8] Cf. Stahl and Haruvy (2008) for an experimental study of multi-game environments. Also see Poulsen and Poulsen (2006) for simultaneous preference evolution in several games.

under which circumstances is a reciprocity-based notion of fairness evolutionarily stable? Section 3.3 compares results to those obtained in the related model of Güth and Napel (2006). Section 3.4 concludes.

3.1 The Model

Repeatedly, two agents who are randomly drawn from a single population are given the chance to create a surplus (the "pie"), and subsequently to decide about its distribution. Taking the population to be large enough to rule out repeated-game effects, agents are assumed to act fully rationally according to commonly known preferences for the possible outcomes of the game presented to them. Utility is not restricted to own material payoff, but (average) material payoff alone defines an agent's fitness or reproductive success in a—not explicitly modeled—payoff-monotonic evolutionary process imposed on the population.[9] As expressed in a pointed way by Samuelson (2001, p. 226f): "Nature can thus mislead her agents, in that preferences and fitness can diverge, but cannot mislead herself, in that high fitness wins the day."

3.1.1 The Material World

A matched pair of agents randomly faces either of two different games: the ultimatum game or the dictator game. In the ultimatum game, one of the two players is randomly (with probability 0.5) selected to be the proposer (role X), who proposes how to split the pie of one unit. The amount he or she offers is denoted by $c \in [0,1]$. The other player (the responder, role Y) decides whether to accept the proposed split or to reject it. The resulting material payoffs are $(\pi_X, \pi_Y) = (1 - c, c)$ and $(\pi_X, \pi_Y) = (0,0)$, respectively.

In the dictator game, one agent is similarly assigned to the proposer role and decides how to split the pie by offering $c \in [0,1]$ to the responder. In contrast to the ultimatum game the responder must accept, so resulting material payoffs are $(\pi_X, \pi_Y) = (1 - c, c)$.

Which game the agents play is determined randomly, with exogenous probability $\lambda \in [0,1]$ for the ultimatum game and $1 - \lambda$ for the dictator game. The game realization becomes common knowledge to the agents. In both events, material payoffs (π_X, π_Y) determine reproductive success.

Differences between the dictator game and the ultimatum game very loosely resemble those between private interaction and anonymous market interaction: success in the ultimatum game depends on mutual cooperation and is influenced by both agents' behavior; in the dictator game, one player is a mere price taker without

---

[9] See Benaïm and Weibull (2003) for a concise overview of models with agents who learn or imitate rather than biologically reproduce, which can be very closely approximated by evolutionary models coming from a purely biological background.

influence on terms of trade. It will be interesting to see if and how evolutionarily stable preferences depend on the frequency or "importance" of each type of interaction in agents' lives.

3.1.2 Agents' Preferences

Agents can have fairness preferences, as defined by Falk and Fischbacher (2006). Details about the utility representation are discussed in section 2.3.[10] Basing reciprocity on intentions has a price in terms of model complexity, even in simple ultimatum or dictator games. Paying it, however, cannot be avoided if one does not want to rule out a priori that intentions matter in the considered context. Most important is that the utility functions $u_i^X(\cdot)$ and $u_i^Y(\cdot)$ which represent preferences of a given agent i in the roles of proposer X or responder Y have the free parameters $\rho_i^X, \varepsilon_i^X$ and $\rho_i^Y, \varepsilon_i^Y$, respectively. Reciprocity parameter $\rho_i^k \in \mathbb{R}_+$ describes how much weight agent i places on reciprocal behavior in role $k \in \{X, Y\}$. For $\rho_i^k = 0$, the considered agent is purely interested in his or her own material payoff, behaving as in most orthodox economic models. The equilibrium rejection probability of ultimatum game offers below 50% increases in ρ_i^Y (see section 3.2.1). The second parameter, $\varepsilon_i^k \in [0,1]$, measures agent i's pure concern for an equitable outcome in role k. Agents without any pure equity concern have an entirely intention-driven notion of fairness: whenever no good or bad intentions can be attributed to the other player, the agent simply maximizes material payoff. In contrast, for agents with positive equity concern more equitable splits of the pie are more valuable even in the absence of intentions. This is best seen in the dictator game, where there is no scope for reciprocation: an agent with $\varepsilon_i^X = 0$ offers $c = 0$, whereas an agent with $\varepsilon_i^X = 1$ may offer up to half of the pie.[11]

In principle, the intensities of reciprocity and equity concern could be different in ultimatum and dictator games and also in the proposer or responder roles of each game. This would correspond to a setting in which agents can have moral sentiments that are tailor-made to very specific economic situations.[12] Here, we prefer to focus on social preferences that reflect the general character of a given agent, i.e., which are the same in randomly assigned roles and randomly selected distribution tasks.

---

[10] In short, player i's utility at any terminal node t of the game tree is the sum of his or her material payoff associated with t and a reciprocity payoff which is calculated decision node by decision node and weighted by parameter ρ_i. For each of i's decision nodes n along the path to t, the products of a term measuring the (un)kindness of others to i which has lead to n (here, parameter ε_i may matter) and a term measuring i's reciprocated (un)kindness from choosing to move further towards t are added up.

[11] The actual offer depends on the pure equity concern *and* the reciprocity parameters.

[12] The possibility that agents can condition equity concern on the game and/or their role in it is explored in Güth and Napel (2006). If real economic agents' fair behavior is adequately described by a utility function with one or a few fairness-related parameters at all, the same parameters should, in our view, be valid for more than a very special class of games. Admittedly, to expect them to be valid in *all* games would be too much.

Therefore, we will apply $\rho_i^X \equiv \rho_i^Y \equiv \rho_i$ and $\varepsilon_i^X \equiv \varepsilon_i^Y \equiv \varepsilon_i$ for agent i in his or her entire stylized "game of life."

Allowing preferences of the Falk-Fischbacher type (which nest material pay-off maximization, purely intention-based reciprocity, and inequity aversion) but excluding other types clearly is a restriction. It entails some arbitrariness, but can be motivated by the former type's descriptive success and generality. Giving up *any* restriction in the spirit of Dekel et al. (2007) would go too far in our view: it would implicitly allow for moral discrimination between the components of any mixed habitat. One would thus force about a simple superimposition of preference types that are each tailor-made for a specific single-game environment.

3.1.3 Stability Concepts

The approach pursued here can formally be subsumed under classical (direct) evolutionary game theory.[13] In particular, preference evolution for a two-player game Γ in which fitness is determined by strategy profiles $\mathbf{s} \in S^2$ can be regarded as evolution in a higher-level game $\hat{\Gamma}$ in which payoffs and fitness are (indirectly) determined by *preference profiles* $\hat{\mathbf{s}} \in \hat{S}^2$. Namely, $\hat{\Gamma}$'s "strategy space" $\hat{S}$ is the set of feasible preferences over outcomes in Γ and its payoff function $\hat{\pi}$ is the composition $\pi \circ \mu$ of original payoff function π and a mapping μ from preference profiles in $\hat{S}^2$ to equilibrium strategy profiles of Γ.

In the following, we will not explicitly model a dynamic evolutionary process. Our goal is to identify preferences $(\rho, \varepsilon) \equiv \hat{s}$ that are stable at least in the sense of being a *neutrally stable strategy* (NSS) in game $\hat{\Gamma}$. So considering payoffs $\hat{\pi}$ defined by the outcome of the respective (unique) subgame perfect equilibrium (SPE) of the underlying material game, we call preferences $\hat{s}$ *stable* if and only if for all $\hat{s}' \in \hat{S}$

$$\hat{\pi}(\hat{s}, \hat{s}) \geq \hat{\pi}(\hat{s}', \hat{s}) \tag{3.1}$$

and, moreover, whenever $\hat{\pi}(\hat{s}, \hat{s}) = \hat{\pi}(\hat{s}', \hat{s})$ then

$$\hat{\pi}(\hat{s}', \hat{s}') \leq \hat{\pi}(\hat{s}, \hat{s}') . \tag{3.2}$$

This is equivalent to preferences (ρ, ε) satisfying equation (3.2) for all (ρ', ε') in a neighborhood of (ρ, ε) (see, e.g., Weibull 1995, prop. 2.7).

For finite strategy spaces, close links between static stability concepts such as NSS and stationary points of various dynamic evolutionary processes exist. In particular, a NSS corresponds to a population state which satisfies *(Lyapunov) dynamic stability* under the well-known replicator dynamics, that is, a small group of invading mutants cannot spread (e.g., Weibull 1995, chap. 3). Unfortunately, even

---

[13] The opposite is also true: models that study the direct evolution of behavior can be regarded as the special case of preference evolution where feasible preferences are restricted to those making distinct strategies strictly dominant.

stronger concepts such as *evolutionarily stable strategy* (ESS), which replaces equation (3.2) by a strict inequality and implies actual repelling of a small invasion, do not guarantee that an arbitrary initial preference distribution converges. Static concepts such as ESS and NSS are nevertheless a focal prediction for long-run evolution and have been the benchmark of most related investigations.[14]

As links between static stability concepts and actual evolutionary dynamics are much harder to pin down in the continuous case[15] (and one can argue that the world is fundamentally discrete anyhow, at least at the quantum level), we analyze evolution of preferences on a finite grid. In particular, we consider preference parameters

$$(\rho,\varepsilon) \in \hat{S} \equiv \{0,\frac{1}{n},\frac{2}{n},\ldots,\bar{P}\} \times \{0,\frac{1}{n},\frac{2}{n},\ldots,1\}$$

given an arbitrarily small grid size $1/n$ ($n \in \mathbb{N}$), and a large upper bound $0 < \bar{P} \in \mathbb{N}$.

3.2 Evolutionary Analysis

First, ultimatum and dictator games will be studied in isolation, corresponding to the boundary cases $\lambda = 1$ and $\lambda = 0$. Then, the mixed environment consisting of both games will be analyzed. When agents A and B interact, we will in the following write ρ_X and ε_X (ρ_Y and ε_Y) for the preference parameters of the agent who is assigned to role X (role Y). Recall that we assume agents to have complete and perfect information when they interact.

3.2.1 The Ultimatum Game

Equilibrium play[16] results in *acceptance probability*

$$p^*(c) = \begin{cases} \min\left\{1,\frac{c}{\rho_Y \times (1-2c)(1-c)}\right\} & \text{if } c < \frac{1}{2}, \\ 1 & \text{if } c \geq \frac{1}{2} \end{cases}$$

for offer c if $\rho_Y \neq 0$, and $p^* \equiv 1$ if $\rho_Y = 0$. So an offer of half of the pie or more is always accepted. This is not the case for lower offers, for which the acceptance probability is decreasing in ρ_Y as shown in figure 3.1.

---

[14] A recent exception is Possajennikov (2005), who explicitly studies a dynamic process.

[15] We are aware of no general sufficient condition for dynamic stability if a straightforward definition of "closeness" of two population states is applied. Oechssler and Riedel (2002) obtain a sufficient condition regarding the natural weak topology in the special case of *doubly symmetric games*. General sufficient conditions exist for the much less appealing variational norm, also see Oechssler and Riedel (2001).

[16] The derivations of the equilibrium for the ultimatum and dictator games are sketched in section 2.3.4.

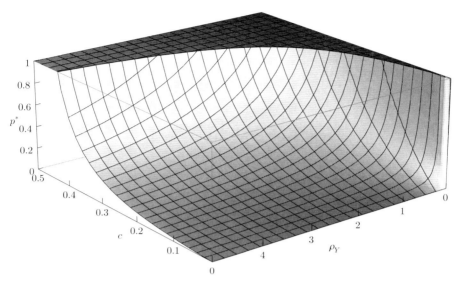

Fig. 3.1 Acceptance probability p^* of agent with reciprocity parameter ρ_Y for offer c in the ultimatum game

The share c^* offered by the proposer X to responder Y in equilibrium is given by

$$c^* = \max\left\{ \frac{3\rho_Y + 1 - \sqrt{1 + 6\rho_Y + \rho_Y^2}}{4\rho_Y}, \frac{1}{2} \times (1 - \frac{1}{\rho_X}) \right\} \tag{3.3}$$

for $\rho_X, \rho_Y \neq 0$. For $\rho_X > \rho_Y = 0$ and $\rho_Y > \rho_X = 0$, c^* is equation (3.3)'s limit for $\rho_Y \downarrow 0$ and $\rho_X \downarrow 0$, respectively, while for $\rho_X = \rho_Y = 0$ one obtains $c^* = 0$ (corresponding to "traditional" preferences). Note that preference parameter ε has no effect in the ultimatum game.

Offer c^* can result from two distinct motives, reflected by the two terms in equation (3.3). The first term depends only on the responder's reciprocal inclination ρ_Y and is the maximizer of the proposer's expected utility in case that the responder's concern for reciprocity is "binding"—dominating a relatively weak reciprocity concern of the proposer. The associated share of the pie is just high enough to ensure acceptance ($p = 1$). The second expression depends only on the proposer's ρ_X and reflects how much the proposer would *voluntarily* offer in order to maximize utility in the light of his or her intrinsic concern for a fair outcome. As either ρ_X or ρ_Y grow large, c^* approaches $1/2$ (see figure 3.2).

The equilibrium offer is the maximum of both expressions. This means that, if a selfish proposer plays against a reciprocal responder, the offer is increasing in ρ_Y. If the responder's concern for reciprocity is low, the offer depends on the fairness concern of the proposer, hence it is increasing in ρ_X. If both players are selfish, the offer is close to zero.

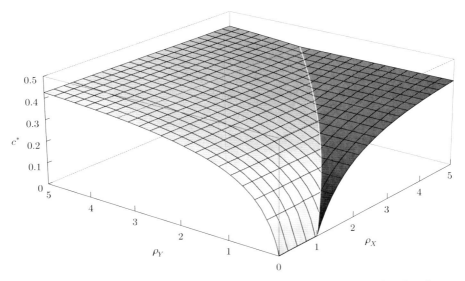

Fig. 3.2 Split c^* proposed by an agent with reciprocity parameter ρ_X to one with reciprocity parameter ρ_Y in the ultimatum game

Agent A's role in interaction with agent B is random, with probability 0.5 for each. The fitness and expected material payoff $\pi^*_{A_U}$ of agent A with preference parameters (ρ_A, ε_A) who is matched with agent B to play the ultimatum game is the average of the payoffs he or she receives in both roles. This turns out to be:

$$\pi^*_{A_U}(\rho_A, \rho_B) = \begin{cases} \frac{5\rho_A + 3 - \sqrt{1 + 6\rho_A + \rho_A^2}}{8\rho_A} & \text{if } \rho_A \geq \frac{-2\rho_B}{\rho_B + 1 - \sqrt{1 + 6\rho_B + \rho_B^2}}, & \text{(a)} \\[2ex] \frac{3\rho_B - 3 + \sqrt{1 + 6\rho_B + \rho_B^2}}{8\rho_B} & \text{if } \rho_A \leq \frac{\rho_B(\rho_B - 1)}{1 + \rho_B}, & \text{(b)} \\[2ex] \frac{3\rho_A + 1 - \sqrt{1 + 6\rho_A + \rho_A^2}}{8\rho_A} \\ + \frac{\rho_B - 1 + \sqrt{1 + 6\rho_B + \rho_B^2}}{8\rho_B} & \text{if } \frac{-2\rho_B}{\rho_B + 1 - \sqrt{1 + 6\rho_B + \rho_B^2}} > \rho_A > \frac{\rho_B(\rho_B - 1)}{1 + \rho_B}. & \text{(c)} \end{cases}$$

$$(3.4)$$

Figure 3.3 illustrates this. Expected payoff depends on both agents' concerns for reciprocity, captured by ρ_A and ρ_B.

There are three cases. In case (a), ρ_A is large compared to ρ_B and thus behavior in *both* possible role realizations is determined by agent A's strong concern for fairness. Agent A's payoff is strictly decreasing in ρ_A, i.e., whenever (a) applies, agents with minimal reciprocity concern (ρ_A at the boundary to case (c)) are fittest.

Case (b) applies if ρ_A is small compared to ρ_B. Then, behavior in both roles is determined by ρ_B. Agent A's payoff is constant in ρ_A, i.e., evolutionary pressures

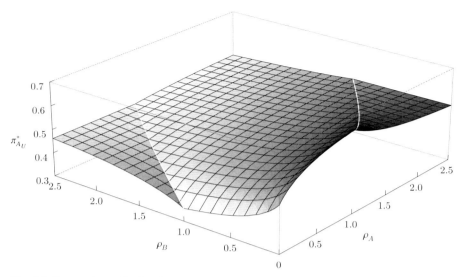

Fig. 3.3 Expected payoff $\pi^*_{A_U}$ of agent A with reciprocity parameter ρ_A in the ultimatum game when matched with an agent B with reciprocity parameter ρ_B

only apply to the agent with greater concern for reciprocity (the smaller ρ_B, the fitter).

In the intermediate case (c), ρ_A and ρ_B do not differ too much. This is the only relevant case for NSS-based stability analysis, since it concerns *symmetric* Nash equilibrium profiles. The proposer offers a split that maximizes his or her own material payoff subject to the binding constraint imposed by the rejection behavior of the responder, i.e., c^* depends only on the responder's reciprocity parameter. It follows from equation (3.4) that agent A's (B's) payoff is strictly increasing in ρ_A (ρ_B). Restricting attention to parameter ρ, the unique symmetric Nash equilibrium of preference game $\hat{\Gamma}$ is thus (ρ^*, ρ^*) with $\rho^* = \bar{P}$, i.e., the highest possible level (see section 3.1.3).[17] Replicator dynamics—and, in fact, all weakly payoff positive selection dynamics—begun from a fully mixed population state must therefore bring about ρ^* if they converge (Weibull 1995, prop. 4.11(c)).

Since agents' pure concern for an equitable outcome, ε, has no effect on payoffs, we can conclude that all preferences

$$\hat{s} \in \hat{T}_U \equiv \{(\bar{P}, \varepsilon) \in \hat{S} \colon \varepsilon \in [0, 1]\}$$

are stable in the ultimatum game played in isolation. This corresponds to an approximately *equal split* (exactly equal for $\bar{P} \to \infty$), which is offered for *strategic reasons*, i.e., to prevent the responder from rejecting and not because of the proposer's intrin-

---

[17] It is even strict and thus corresponds to an ESS.—Preferences with $\rho = \infty$ would correspond to maximization of the so-called reciprocity payoff regardless of own material payoff (compare equation (2.1) in section 2.3.3).

sic motivation. This finding is broadly consistent with various other evolutionary and behavioral investigations of ultimatum bargaining: Huck and Oechssler (1999) consider indirect evolution in a 2×2-version of the ultimatum game and find that a preference for punishing unfair proposers survives and induces equitable offers (even under anonymous interaction). Direct evolutionary studies of the ultimatum game include Gale et al. (1995), Nowak et al. (2000), and Nowak and Page (2002). They each demonstrate the persistence of fair offers given relatively more noise in the responder than the proposer population (or none at all), when proposers have access to observations of past responder behavior, and when at least some fraction of agents are empathetic in the sense of always offering at least what they themselves would accept. The aspiration-based satisficing model investigated by Napel (2003) entails fair ultimatum offers linked to parameters that reflect player characteristics such as stubbornness and capriciousness. Reinforcement learning models, proposed, for example, by Roth and Erev (1995), also predict rather equal offers coupled with rejection of unequal ones, at least in the intermediate run.

3.2.2 The Dictator Game

The split c^* offered by the proposer X in the dictator game in equilibrium depends only on his or her *own* reciprocity parameter ρ_X and pure outcome-concern parameter ε_X:

$$c^* = \max\left\{0, \frac{1}{2} \times (1 - \frac{1}{\varepsilon_X \rho_X})\right\}. \tag{3.5}$$

A proposer offers a positive amount if $\varepsilon_X \rho_X > 1$, which means that he or she is reasonably concerned about reciprocity in the unintentional case. No matter how large $\varepsilon_X \rho_X$, the offer is never greater than half. Equation (3.5) corresponds to the second term in equation (3.3), i.e., the possible "voluntary offer" in the ultimatum game, where $\varepsilon_X \rho_X$ replaces ρ_X. Here, the receiver has no choice but to accept and therefore the outcome is "unintentional" in the sense of Falk and Fischbacher (2006); this is reflected by a "discounting" of reciprocity parameter ρ_X by pure equity concern parameter ε_X in the dictator game. A given agent always offers weakly *less* in the dictator game than in the ultimatum game, because $0 \leq \varepsilon_X \leq 1$.

Agent A is assigned the proposer role in a dictator game with agent B with probability 0.5. His or her expected material payoff $\pi^*_{A_D}$ in equilibrium is then given by:

$$\pi^*_{A_D}(\rho_A, \varepsilon_A, \rho_B, \varepsilon_B) = \begin{cases} \frac{1}{2} & \text{if } \varepsilon_A \rho_A \leq 1 \text{ and } \varepsilon_B \rho_B \leq 1, \text{ (I)} \\ \frac{1}{4} + \frac{1}{4\varepsilon_A \rho_A} & \text{if } \varepsilon_A \rho_A > 1 \text{ and } \varepsilon_B \rho_B \leq 1, \text{ (II)} \\ \frac{3}{4} - \frac{1}{4\varepsilon_B \rho_B} & \text{if } \varepsilon_A \rho_A \leq 1 \text{ and } \varepsilon_B \rho_B > 1, \text{ (III)} \\ \frac{1}{2} + \frac{1}{4\varepsilon_A \rho_A} - \frac{1}{4\varepsilon_B \rho_B} & \text{if } \varepsilon_A \rho_A > 1 \text{ and } \varepsilon_B \rho_B > 1. \text{ (IV)} \end{cases} \tag{3.6}$$

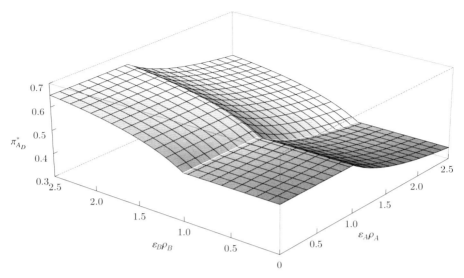

Fig. 3.4 Expected payoff $\pi^*_{A_D}$ of agent A with parameters ε_A and ρ_A in the dictator game when matched against an agent B with parameters ε_B and ρ_B

We have four cases, illustrated by figure 3.4. In cases (II) and (III), either of the two agents offers a positive amount to the other agent when he or she is in the role of proposer. The expected payoff for such "generous" behavior is smaller than in case (I), and strictly decreasing in the agent's parameters ρ and ε. Cases (II) and (III) are hence unstable.

In case (IV), *both* agents as proposers share the pie with the receiver; their payoff need not be smaller than in case (I). Still, material payoff is decreasing in each agent's individual parameters ρ and ε. The smaller they are, the fitter is the agent carrying these preferences. In particular, no preference profile corresponding to case (IV) forms a Nash equilibrium (let alone NSS) of the preference game.

For parameter constellations pertaining to case (I), both agents are only weakly interested in fairness; both offer $c^* = 0$ as proposers. The case applies as long as the product of the parameters for reciprocity ρ and the pure equity concern ε is smaller than or equal to unity for both agents. All such parameter constellations are behaviorally equivalent. It follows from equation (3.6) that any

$$\hat{s} \in \hat{T}_D \equiv \{(\rho, \varepsilon) \in \hat{S} \colon \varepsilon\rho \leq 1\}$$

is a NSS of preference game $\hat{\Gamma}$, and there exist no other stable preferences.[18] Moreover, $\hat{T}_D$ comprises all Nash equilibria of $\hat{\Gamma}$. So, if any given payoff monotone selection dynamic converges from an interior point to some $\hat{s}^* \in \hat{S}$, then $\hat{s}^* \in \hat{T}_D$.

We can thus expect agents to offer zero (i.e., to be indistinguishable from selfish payoff maximizers) in the dictator game in the long run. They may have a preference for fairness to a degree that does not affect behavior.

3.2.3 The Mixed Environment

Now consider the stylized "game of life" in which agents randomly get to interact in either an ultimatum or a dictator game setting. The payoff π_A^* of agent A facing agent B given the probability $\lambda \in [0,1]$ to play the ultimatum game and probability $1 - \lambda$ to play the dictator game is

$$\pi_A^*(\rho_A, \varepsilon_A, \rho_B, \varepsilon_B, \lambda) = \lambda \times \pi_{A_U}^*(\rho_A, \rho_B) + (1 - \lambda) \times \pi_{A_D}^*(\rho_A, \varepsilon_A, \rho_B, \varepsilon_B) .$$

This expected material payoff function is illustrated for $\lambda = 1/2$ and several values of ε_A and ε_B in figure 3.5.[19] Total expected payoff is increasing in payoff $\pi_{A_U}^*(\cdot)$ from the ultimatum game and the payoff $\pi_{A_D}^*(\cdot)$ from the dictator game. Hence evolution would favor preferences that maximize $\pi_{A_U}^*(\cdot)$ and $\pi_{A_D}^*(\cdot)$ at the same time if this were possible.

Indeed, this is possible for the Falk-Fischbacher preferences considered here: The maximum payoff in the dictator game is reached for *any* parameter constellation with $\rho \times \varepsilon \leq 1$. The pure equity concern parameter ε can always totally compensate a high reciprocity concern ρ by being less or equal to $1/\rho$. So, the "optimal," material payoff-maximizing preferences in the dictator game can be reached for any level of ρ. The stable preferences are hence all $\hat{s} \in T_U \cap T_D = \{(\bar{P}, \varepsilon) \in \hat{S}: \varepsilon \leq 1/\bar{P}\}$, which also correspond to the Nash equilibria of preference game $\hat{\Gamma}$ if $\lambda \in (0,1)$.

This implies that agents behave very fairly whenever their counterpart can reciprocate, but show no pure concern for equity. The evolutionary prediction is thus: approximately equal splits in the ultimatum game and full appropriation of the pie in the dictator game, i.e., a superimposition of the stable outcomes in the two components of our stylized "game of life." With large ρ and small ε, agents reciprocate strongly in situations that imply intentionality, but do not care about fairness when it comes to situations where intentions play no role. So from our evolutionary model's point of view, fair behavior should really be a matter of intention-based reciprocity rather than a general concern for equitable payoff distributions.

---

[18] In fact, $\hat{T}_D$ forms an *evolutionarily stable set* (ES set): every $\hat{s} \in \hat{T}_D$ is locally superior to preference strategies outside $\hat{T}_D$ and not inferior to others inside $\hat{T}_D$; this implies asymptotic stability. The same holds for $\hat{T}_U$ in the ultimatum game. See, for example, Weibull (1995, sec. 3.5.4) for details.

[19] Note the saddle points (1,1) and (2,2) in the cases of $\varepsilon_A = \varepsilon_B = 1$ and $\varepsilon_A = \varepsilon_B = 0.5$, respectively. A saddle point—corresponding to an ESS *if* ε were exogenously fixed (or is restricted as in section 3.2.4)—does not exist for $\varepsilon_A = \varepsilon_B \approx 0$.

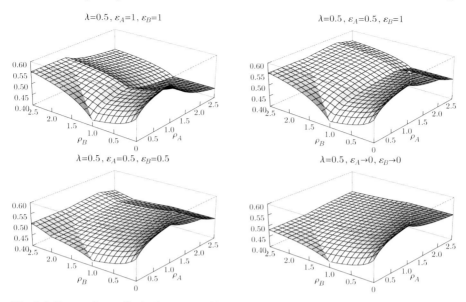

Fig. 3.5 Expected payoff π_A^* of agent A with parameters ε_A and ρ_A in the "game of life" when matched against an agent B with parameters ε_B and ρ_B for $\lambda = 0.5$

3.2.4 Restricted Parameters in the Mixed Environment

With two free parameters and two games, it may not be surprising (though it is not trivial either) that evolution brings about "optimal" behavior for isolated dictator and ultimatum game environments also in the combined habitat: Our agents are unable to have different sets of parameters for reciprocity and pure equity concerns in ultimatum and dictator games, i.e., they cannot discriminate directly between the games. However, they *indirectly* discriminate based on distinctive features of the games (here: intentionality).

It can be questioned whether the degrees of freedom in the social component of our preferences in reality match the number of different classes of social interaction.[20] Humans seem to adjust behavior to a specific situation only to some extent. It therefore seems interesting and reasonable to limit Nature's freedom in shaping agents' preferences by restricting the possible range of the pure outcome-concern parameter ε which applies in unintentional situations.

One practical possibility is to impose an *exogenous lower bound* $\varepsilon_l > 1/\bar{P}$ (chosen as a multiple of grid size $1/n$) for parameter ε, so that $\varepsilon_l \leq \varepsilon \leq 1$ is required instead of $0 \leq \varepsilon \leq 1$. This situation differs from the above in that a strong concern for reciprocity cannot completely be blanked out in the dictator game by a low ε. So even accounting for indirect discrimination possibilities, an agent's behavior in

---

[20] Biological costs of discrimination by a given agent's (global) preferences would play the central role in a theoretical investigation of this relationship.

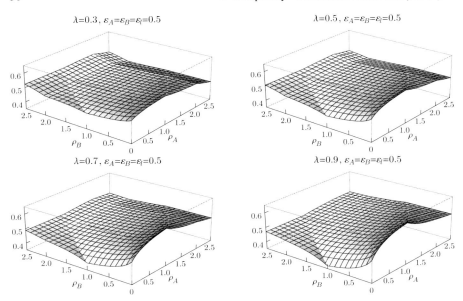

Fig. 3.6 Expected payoff π_A^* of agent A with parameters $\varepsilon_A = \varepsilon_l = 0.5$ and ρ_A in the "game of life" when matched against an agent B with parameters $\varepsilon_B = \varepsilon_l = 0.5$ and ρ_B for several values of λ

dictator realizations of the "game of life" is thus no longer independent from that in ultimatum realizations.

Whenever $\rho \geq 1/\varepsilon_l$, the dictator game induces downward pressure on parameter ε: the smaller ε, the less is given away in the dictator role and hence the greater is own payoff. At the same time, the strategic reaction by ultimatum proposers to responders' reciprocity concern puts persistent upward pressure on parameter ρ. This has the following environment-dependent implications for stable preferences.

For λ not too big, the dictator game is important enough in agents' lives to make "play" of $(1/\varepsilon_l, \varepsilon_l)$ the unique (strict) Nash equilibrium of preference game $\hat{\Gamma}$, which corresponds to an ESS. A payoff positive selection dynamic started at a fully mixed population state can only converge to $(1/\varepsilon_l, \varepsilon_l)$. This results in a zero offer in the dictator game and

$$c^* = \frac{1 + 3\frac{1}{\varepsilon_l} - \sqrt{1 + 6\frac{1}{\varepsilon_l} + \frac{1}{\varepsilon_l^2}}}{4\frac{1}{\varepsilon_l}} \tag{3.7}$$

in the ultimatum game. For example, a value of $\varepsilon_l = 0.25$ implies a split of $(\pi_X, \pi_Y) \approx (0.59, 0.41)$ or $\varepsilon_l = 0.125$ implies $(\pi_X, \pi_Y) \approx (0.55, 0.45)$ in the ultimatum game in the long run. The imposed restriction thus slightly reduces equitableness in ultimatum offers without consequences for selfish behavior in the dictator game.

The influence of parameter λ on the payoffs is illustrated by figure 3.6. The saddle point at $(\rho_A, \rho_B) = (2, 2)$, corresponding to stable preferences with $\rho^* = 1/\varepsilon_l$, is barely visible for $\lambda = 0.7$ and no longer exists for $\lambda = 0.9$. In fact, there is a *critical level* of λ above which $(1/\varepsilon_l, \varepsilon_l)$ is no longer stable, and instead $(\bar{P}, \varepsilon_l)$ becomes the evolutionary prediction. This critical level can be calculated by analyzing expected payoff for values of $\rho > 1/\varepsilon_l$; if it is lower (higher) than for $\rho = 1/\varepsilon_l$ the latter combination is (is not) stable. Constellations $\rho > 1/\varepsilon_l$ belong to case (c) in the ultimatum game and case (IV) in the dictator game (involving positive offers by both agents). The material payoff of agent A in the "game of life" is therefore

$$\pi_A^*(\rho_A, \varepsilon_A, \rho_B, \varepsilon_B, \lambda) = \lambda \left[\frac{3\rho_A + 1 - \sqrt{1 + 6\rho_A + \rho_A^2}}{8\rho_A} + \frac{\rho_B - 1 + \sqrt{1 + 6\rho_B + \rho_B^2}}{8\rho_B} \right]$$

$$+ (1 - \lambda) \left[\frac{1}{2} + \frac{1}{4\varepsilon_A \rho_A} - \frac{1}{4\varepsilon_B \rho_B} \right].$$

The marginal change of agent A's payoff from greater ρ_A is

$$\frac{\partial \pi_A^*(\rho_A, \varepsilon_A, \rho_B, \varepsilon_B, \lambda)}{\partial \rho_A} = \frac{\varepsilon_A \lambda(1 + 3\rho_A) + (2\lambda - 2 - \rho_A \lambda)\sqrt{1 + 6\rho_A + \rho_A^2}}{8\varepsilon_A \rho_A \sqrt{1 + 6\rho_A + \rho_A^2}}$$

and can be analyzed for $\rho_A > 1/\varepsilon_l$ and $\varepsilon_A = \varepsilon_l$ in order to determine at which critical level λ_0 the combination of selfish dictator offers and (moderately) fair ultimatum offers starts to yield smaller payoff than $(\bar{P}, \varepsilon_l)$. The marginal effect of a ρ_A-increase on A's payoff is negative for values of λ up to the critical level

$$\lambda_0(\varepsilon_l) = \frac{2\sqrt{1 + \frac{6}{\varepsilon_l} + \frac{1}{\varepsilon_l^2}}}{3 + \varepsilon_l + (2 - \varepsilon_l)\sqrt{1 + \frac{6}{\varepsilon_l} + \frac{1}{\varepsilon_l^2}}}$$

and then positive. So for $\lambda > \lambda_0(\varepsilon_l)$, $(\bar{P}, \varepsilon_l)$ becomes the unique stable preference.[21] As illustrated in figure 3.7, $\lambda_0(\varepsilon_l)$ is strictly decreasing in the exogenous lower bound on pure equity concern ε_l.[22]

So when the ultimatum game is played very frequently compared to the dictator game, stable preferences involve reciprocity parameter $\rho^* = \bar{P}$ and pure outcome concern $\varepsilon^* = \varepsilon_l$. This implies approximately equal splits in *both* games (becoming exactly equal for $\bar{P} \to \infty$). Loosely speaking, if agents interact in comparatively many "private" situations captured by the ultimatum game compared to few "market" situations reflected by the dictator game, they develop a strong notion of fairness which involves equity concerns but is primarily driven by preference for reciprocity.

---

[21] For $\lambda = \lambda_0(\varepsilon_l)$ all preferences $\hat{s} \in \{(\rho, \varepsilon_l) \in \hat{S}: 1/\varepsilon_l \leq \rho \leq \bar{P}\}$ are NSS.

[22] It falls from $\lambda_0 = 1$ for $\varepsilon_l \to 0$ to a minimum of $\lambda_0 = 2\sqrt{2} - 2 \approx 0.838$ for $\varepsilon_l = 1$.

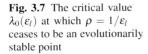

Fig. 3.7 The critical value $\lambda_0(\varepsilon_l)$ at which $\rho = 1/\varepsilon_l$ ceases to be an evolutionarily stable point

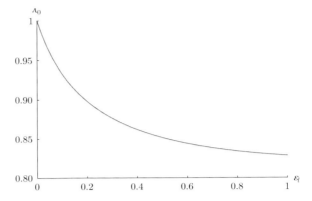

3.3 Comparison with a Model Based on Inequity Aversion

Recall that the crucial difference between this model and that of Güth and Napel (2006) is the considered class of preferences. Agents' sense of fairness is limited to inequity aversion in the paper of Güth and Napel, while we allow intention-based reciprocity.

Results of the separate analysis of ultimatum and dictator game are qualitatively the same. In the *ultimatum game*, agents in the role of the responder benefit from the Fehr-Schmidt type of inequity aversion as well as from reciprocation, because the proposer anticipates that small offers are rejected with positive probability. In the long run, a rather equitable or even equal split is reached (this depends on the precise utility specification).

In the *dictator game*, in contrast, both inequity aversion and reciprocal behavior are detrimental to an agent's average success, as it leads him or her voluntarily to give away part of the pie. In Güth and Napel's investigation as well as this one, agents can be inequity averse to any degree that fails to actually affect proposer behavior. In the analysis by Güth and Napel, this upper bound to stable inequity aversion of dictators is driving results for the mixed environment. Either the long-run level of inequity aversion in the ultimatum game is below this bound, resulting in no behaviorally relevant interaction between the two games, or it is above. In the latter case, the given composition of the stylized "game of life" determines a stable level that, loosely speaking, balances marginal evolutionary benefits and costs of inequity aversion. In our analysis, the situation is complicated by the presence of two free parameters instead of one. The original model of Falk and Fischbacher (2006) allows for both: strong reciprocation and no inequity aversion in unintentional cases. If the possible discrepancy between these two aspects of fairness is not restricted exogenously, agents behave in both games just as if they were independent. This resembles Güth and Napel's case in which agents can directly condition the social component of their utility function—and hence fair behavior—on the game at hand. Here, such a moral discrimination between games is achieved *indirectly*. However, when the "discounting" of fairness in the *unintentional* case is limited, our long-run outcome resembles the one of Güth and Napel's case of game-independent equity aversion.

It is a common result of either analysis that a high share of ultimatum games affects evolutionarily stable preferences. Coincidentally, the minimal level at which the frequency of ultimatum games affects the outcome is similar in both studies, about 80% in Güth and Napel (2006) and around 85% for a wide range of constellations here. So, on the one hand, the explicit consideration of intention-based reciprocity broadly speaking produces results similar to the analytically much simpler case of purely payoff-oriented inequity aversion. On the other hand, we find it interesting that, in a hybrid setting, the former really is the dominant force.

3.4 Concluding Remarks

In general, psychological fairness models explain experimental results better than more tractable equity-based models, which in turn perform better than the default assumption of monetary payoff maximization. This success comes at the expense of more free parameters, which have to be defended against accusations of ad hoc "game fitting." Since parameters *can* be such that an agent, in fact, has traditional materialistic preferences, indirect evolutionary analysis provides a useful theoretical benchmark. If, under plausible modeling assumptions, evolutionary forces select parameters that imply non-degenerate social preferences, this corroborates postexperimental econometric estimations.

The relevance of fairness preference can be expected a priori to vary with the decision situations at hand, even if these are restricted to simple distribution tasks. Our analysis suggests that preference for fair behavior has sound evolutionary reasons, but—in line with experimental observations—more likely plays a significant role in games with punishment opportunities such as the ultimatum game than in what is basically a one-player decision problem such as the dictator game. If Nature permits players to condition the social component of their preferences on different games (as investigated by Güth and Napel 2006) or at least indirectly on differences in games, the same agents can exhibit a pronounced sense of fairness in one type of social interaction, while they are entirely selfish in another one. This is true even though preferences are assumed to evolve simultaneously in a multi-game environment.

If Nature imposes physical or psychological restrictions on the variance in agents' social attitudes across different games and different dimensions of fairness, the precise composition of the stylized "game of life" faced by agents has an impact. When agents most of the time face the more fairness-conducive ultimatum game, they will eventually perceive it in their interest to be generous even as dictators.

We have studied environmental and psychological determinants of material-payoff maximization vs. social preferences in a particularly simple two-game environment. In our view, this is an improvement compared to the usual analysis of preferences in a single game. It highlights the importance of possibly unconscious links between behavioral modes in different classes of interaction. Whether human agents indeed face a binding restriction in their ability to discriminate between the fairness implications of similar play in ultimatum and dictator games, reflected by the reciprocity and pure equity concern parameters ρ and ε in our model, is an empirical question. Experimental evidence on the ultimatum game is consistent with both the unrestricted and restricted evolution of ρ and ε; evidence on the dictator game supports the restricted view (although not the equal splits that would be implied for $\bar{P} \to \infty$).[23]

Finally, it seems desirable to us to extend our stylized "game of life" beyond ultimatum and dictator games. First, an environment with more than two component games would create a natural endogenous restriction on the two parameters of the considered Falk–Fischbacher reciprocal preferences—preventing the full "specialization" observed in section 3.2.3. Second, reciprocal preferences are proposed as explanations for empirical observations of a considerable range of games, including, for example, trust and gift-exchange games, public good games, and variants of the ultimatum game such as the best-shot game. They should hence prove to be evolutionarily stable in an environment including at least these games.

References

Benaïm M, Weibull JW (2003) Deterministic approximation of stochastic evolution in games. Econometrica 71(3):873–903

Berninghaus SK, Güth W, Kliemt H (2003) From teleology to evolution—Bridging the gap between rationality and adaptation in social explanation. J Evol Econ 13(4):385–410

Berninghaus SK, Ehrhart KM, Ott M (2006) A network experiment in continuous time: The influence of link costs. Exp Econ 9(3):237–251

Bolton GE, Ockenfels A (2000) ERC: A theory of equity, reciprocity, and competition. Am Econ Rev 90(1):166–193

Cameron L (1999) Raising the stakes in the ultimatum game: Experimental evidence from Indonesia. Econ Inq 37(1):47–59

Charness G, Rabin M (2002) Understanding social preferences with simple tests. Q J Econ 117(3):817–869

Dekel E, Ely JC, Yilankaya O (2007) Evolution of preferences. Rev Econ Stud 74(3):685–704

Dufwenberg M, Kirchsteiger G (2004) A theory of sequential reciprocity. Games Econom Behav 47(2):268–298

Falk A, Fischbacher U (2006) A theory of reciprocity. Games Econom Behav 54(2):293–315

Falk A, Kosfeld M (2003) It's all about connections: Evidence on network formation, IZA Discussion Paper No. 777, IZA, Bonn, Germany

Falk A, Fehr E, Fischbacher U (2003) On the nature of fair behavior. Econ Inq 41(1):20–26

Fehr E, Gächter S (1998) Reciprocity and economics. The economic implications of homo reciprocans. Eur Econ Rev 42(3–5):845–859

Fehr E, Schmidt KM (1999) A theory of fairness, competition and cooperation. Q J Econ 114(3):817–868

Gale J, Binmore KG, Samuelson L (1995) Learning to be imperfect: The ultimatum game. Games Econom Behav 8(1):56–90

---

[23] Dictator offers in Güth and Napel (2006) continuously rise from zero to moderate positive levels (assuming that marginal disutility of inequality is increasing).

Geanakoplos J, Pearce D, Stacchetti E (1989) Psychological games and sequential rationality. Games Econom Behav 1(1):60–79

Güth W (1995) An evolutionary approach to explaining cooperative behavior by reciprocal incentives. Int J Game Theor 24(4):323–344

Güth W, Napel S (2006) Inequality aversion in a variety of games—An indirect evolutionary analysis. Econ J 116(514):1037–1056

Güth W, Yaari ME (1992) Explaining reciprocal behavior in simple strategic games: An evolutionary approach. In: Witt U (ed) Explaining Process and Change—Approaches to Evolutionary Economics, The University of Michigan Press, Ann Arbor, MI, chap 2, pp 23–34

Güth W, Kliemt H, Napel S (2003) Wie du mir, so ich dir!—Evolutionäre Modellierungen. In: Held M, Kubon-Gilke G, Sturn R (eds) Jahrbuch Normative und Institutionelle Grundfragen der Ökonomik, Band 2: Experimentelle Ökonomik, Metropolis-Verlag, Marburg, Germany, pp 113–139

Henrich J, Boyd R, Bowles S, Camerer CF, Fehr E, Gintis H, McElreath R (2001) In search of homo economicus: Behavioral experiments in 15 small-scale societies. Am Econ Rev 91(2):73–78

Huck S, Oechssler J (1999) The indirect evolutionary approach to explaining fair allocations. Games Econom Behav 28(1):13–24

Napel S (2003) Aspiration adaption in the ultimatum minigame. Games Econom Behav 43(1):86–106

Nowak MA, Page KM (2002) Empathy leads to fairness. Bull Math Biol 64(6):1101–1116

Nowak MA, Page KM, Sigmund K (2000) Fairness versus reason in the ultimatum game. Science 289(5485):1773–1775

Oechssler J, Riedel F (2001) Evolutionary dynamics on infinite strategy spaces. J Econ Theory 17(1):141–162

Oechssler J, Riedel F (2002) On the dynamic foundation of evolutionary stability in continuous models. J Econ Theory 107(2):223–252

Possajennikov A (2005) Cooperation and competition: Learning of strategies and evolution of preferences in prisoners' dilemma and hawk-dove games. Int Game Theory Rev 7(4):443–459

Poulsen A, Poulsen O (2006) Endogenous preferences and social-dilemma institutions. J Inst Theor Econ 162(4):627–660

Rabin M (1993) Incorporating fairness into game theory and economics. Am Econ Rev 83(5):1281–1302

Roth AE, Erev I (1995) Learning in extensive-form games: Experimental data and simple dynamic models in the intermediate term. Games Econom Behav 8(1):164–212

Samuelson L (2001) Introduction to the evolution of preferences. J Econ Theory 97(2):225–230

Sethi R, Somanathan E (2001) Preference evolution and reciprocity. J Econ Theory 97(2):273–297

Slonim R, Roth AE (1998) Learning in high stakes ultimatum games: An experiment in the Slovak Republic. Econometrica 66(3):569–596

Stahl DO, Haruvy E (2008) Level-n bounded rationality in two-player two-stage games. J Econ Behav Organ 65(1):41–61

Weibull JW (1995) Evolutionary Game Theory. The MIT Press, Cambridge, MA

Chapter 4
Fairness Norms in Ultimatum Exchanges

Investigations of fairness in bargaining have been one of the major microeconomic research topics during the last two decades. Countless studies have been published, and various models to explain observed behavior developed (see, e.g., Camerer 2003 for an overview).

One extensive line of research investigates the relevance of reference points for individual behavior. Such a reference point might, for example, resemble a belief about the choice one *should* choose (compare Konow 2000 for a theory based on cognitive dissonance), or the default choice as in models with endowment effects. The literature on reference-dependent preferences can be traced back to the model of Tversky and Kahneman (1991). They base their model on Kahneman and Tversky's (1979) prospect theory and shift the attention from the absolute outcome to the *difference* of an outcome to a given reference level (e.g., the status quo).

Their model is simplified and extended by Munro and Sugden (2003); they also investigate implications of an endogenously determined reference point. Furthermore, Köszegi and Rabin (2006) evaluate a model in which such a reference is based on the decision maker's expectations about outcomes. The question of how subjects develop reference points remains debatable though. For example, Köszegi and Rabin (2006, p. 1143) themselves state that "Our model of how utility depends on expectations could be combined with any theory of how these expectations are formed." Our hypothesis is that in an experimental setting, it highly depends on the framing of the situation at hand, which potential reference point is "activated" by a subject, especially if he or she has no former experience with this situation, from which he or she could otherwise derive a reference.

That the framing of the decision task at hand affects observable behavior is a well-known phenomenon. For example, Hoffman et al. (1994) investigate the effect of framing an ultimatum game as a buyer-seller exchange instead of a pure "splitting the pie" situation, and find that first mover behavior differs significantly between both frames. In the buyer-seller setting, the proposer tends to propose a smaller share, probably due to the notion that it is more legitimate in a market-type exchange to capture as much of the pie as possible. For thorough reviews on various types of framing effects, see Levin et al. (1998), and Handgraaf et al. (2003).

C. Korth, *Fairness in Bargaining and Markets,*
Lecture Notes in Economics and Mathematical Systems, 627
DOI: 10.1007/978-3-642-02252-4_1, © Springer-Verlag Berlin Heidelberg 2009

The literature on negotiations is also full of examples of framing effects; compare, for example, Blount et al. (1996) who investigate reference points based on multiple factors like available information, personal preferences, and budget constraints; or Kristensen and Garling (1997) who successfully affect bargaining behavior by manipulating subjects' reference points by presenting them different initial offers and selecting the buyer's reservation price to be either above or below this initial offer.

Besides reference points and framing effects, preferences based on personal norms offer another promising path to explain experimental results. The central feature of the concept of personal norms originated with Schwartz (1977): individuals that internalized a social norm typically act according to this norm, even in situations where deviations from the norm are not sanctioned or even observed. The driving force behind this behavior would be guilt, shame, or fear if they violated the norm according to Coleman (1990). Potential mechanisms underlying the development of such a norm in a society are, for example, investigated by Savarimuthu et al. (2007). They propose two potential mechanisms—one based on social learning, and one based on role models that members of the society wish to follow.

Bicchieri (2006) examines social norms in detail, including norms for fairness, cooperation, and reciprocity. She focuses on informal norms that develop through the decentralized interaction of subjects and describes the role of fairness in this context. She also develops an explicit utility function that captures such informal norms and demonstrates that this utility function performs well in explaining results from ultimatum bargaining games. When applied to ultimatum bargaining, this utility function resembles a generalized version of the classic fairness preferences proposed by Fehr and Schmidt (1999). Her model has the unique advantage that it can incorporate all of the above-mentioned explanations like reference points and framing effects in one rather simple formal model. References and framing constitute cues to the subjects to initiate the selection of the norm which seems to be most relevant for the situation at hand.

In our study, we are interested in whether we can affect subject's ultimatum game strategies by modifying a payoff-irrelevant detail in the instructions. We aim at shifting subject's reference points, or—in Bicchieri's terms—at triggering different social norms. We expect this to result in subject's strategies in an ultimatum exchange to be shifted relative to the standard setting. Therefore, our study consists of five treatments: three treatments with a market framing, and two reference treatments with a standard "splitting the pie" framing. In the treatments with the market framing, we include a payoff irrelevant reference price in the instructions. This reference price is varied to be either a low price, a medium price, or a high price.

We conjecture that

1. the payoff-irrelevant detail in the instructions has a significant effect on proposer and responder strategies, and
2. the strategies shift towards the induced reference point.

4.1 Experimental Design

Implemented game form: We introduce an exogenous reference point into a variant of the ultimatum game that is presented in a market context as a buyer-seller exchange similar to Hoffman et al. (1994). In any pair of subjects, one subject is assigned the role of a seller with a reservation price of €0 for some fictitious object. The other subject is assigned the role of a buyer with a reservation price of €10 or for the object. First, the seller suggests to the buyer a price $p \in \{€0, €1, €2, \ldots, €10\}$ for which he is willing to sell the object. Second, the buyer either accepts or rejects the price. If the buyer accepts it, there is a trade and the accepted price determines the monetary payoff distribution. Specifically, the seller's payoff is p and the buyer's payoff is $€10 - p$. If the buyer rejects the suggested price, there is no trade and the payoff of either party is zero.

Treatments: In the experiment, we focus on the exogenous reference price ρ as the main treatment variable. We investigate three levels—$\rho \in \{€1, €5, €9\}$—one per treatment. The three treatments differ only in the exogenous reference point ρ at which the seller acquired the object before subjects were assigned roles. Specifically, the instructions include a comment about the circumstance of the fictitious object for sale as follows that was irrelevant to the monetary payoff: "It is a stamp that he (the seller) bought for ρ a while ago."[1] Importantly, the instructions also inform subjects about the determination of individual monetary payoffs, and in these ρ does not affect payoffs.[2]

In addition to the reference point treatments, we also ran two standard ultimatum games as control treatments. Both control treatments only vary in the subject pool used for recruitment. The subjects of the subject pool that participated in one control treatment, UG06, did not participate in the reference point treatments, that is, the subject pool in control treatment UG06 was independent of the pool used for the reference point treatments. Importantly, the composition of both subject pools is similar since both subject pools represent two different cohorts of students who participated in the experiment during the first semester of their undergraduate studies. In the other control treatment, UG07, any subject had the possibility to participate in one randomly assigned reference point treatment four weeks later. The comparison between control treatment UG06 and the reference point treatment with $\rho = 1$ that most closely resembles the standard ultimatum game with no reference point allows us to investigate if the existence of a reference point per se, with a negligible magnitude, affects behavior. Further, by comparing both control treatments we can check if subject pool effects drive the results obtained from the reference point data.

Subjects and procedures: Each subject participated in the reference point treatment once, either in the role of a buyer or in that of a seller. There was no repeated interaction. In total, 1016 students participated in the experiment. It was integrated

---

[1] In the original instructions, the particular treatment value substitutes ρ.

[2] It is possible to interpret the reference price, for example, as sunk cost, but no interpretation was offered to subjects.

into the first-year, first-semester undergraduate course "Economics and Business" as a classroom experiment at Maastricht University. Data were collected in 42 tutorial group classes on October 31, 2007 (UG07, 524 students) and November 30, 2007 (reference point treatments, 417 students). Data for the control treatment UG06 was collected in 39 groups with 492 students on October 31, 2006. On average, there were 12 students per class and no class size exceeded 14. Participation in the experiment was voluntary. In any class, the experimenter read aloud the same set of instructions that was also projected to the screen.[3] All displayed instruction slides were exactly the same across classes except for the value of the reference price. Treatments were randomly assigned to classes; table 4.1 provides details on the number of independent observations by treatment and role. Upon learning instructions, every student received a data collection form informing him or her about the assigned role and the details of the payment procedure.[4]

Table 4.1 Treatment information and independent observations by role

Treatment	Reference price ρ	Presentation	Number of sellers (proposers)	Number of buyers (responders)
Low	€1	Market UG	78	74
Med	€5	Market UG	67	69
High	€9	Market UG	65	64
UG06	None	Standard UG	254	238
UG07	None	Standard UG	269	255

Payment procedure: For each treatment, one seller form and one buyer form were randomly drawn from all forms collected in tutorial group sessions. If the buyer accepted the suggested price, the corresponding students were paid out their payoffs in cash. If the offer was rejected, a new pair was drawn until there was a trade. This procedure was repeated once so that $2 \times$ €10 were allocated as cash payments in any treatment. Those students that earned a cash payoff could choose to either immediately and publicly receive the payment or to privately collect the payment later at the chair's office. All students were informed about this possibility to maintain their anonymity before the experiment.

Strategy method: To collect detailed buyer data and to facilitate the random payment procedure, we employed the strategy method. Any buyer indicated the lowest price that he was willing to pay, instead of either accepting or rejecting a particular price suggested by a particular seller.

Standard equilibrium prediction: When subjects are assumed to simply maximize material payoff, there are two subgame-perfect Nash equilibria in our reference

---

[3] See the appendix for the set of instructions.
[4] See the appendix for the data collection form.

point games (treatments Low, Med, and High) analogously to Roth et al. (1991):[5] ($p = €10$, always accept) and ($p = €9$, reject $p = €10$ and accept otherwise). The first equilibrium requires the seller to extract the maximum surplus of €10 by offering the largest feasible price. This leaves the buyer with zero surplus who accepts this price and also any other price. In the second one, the seller obtains a surplus of €9 by offering the second-largest price, which in turn is the largest price accepted by the buyer, who will thus obtain €1.

4.2 Experimental Results

The following sections describe the results of the classroom experiment. Section 4.2.1 investigates proposer behavior in general, section 4.2.2 analyzes the effect of a small reference price on proposer behavior, and section 4.2.3 evaluates the data that was obtained for responders. Finally, section 4.2.4 briefly explores the effects of reference prices on market efficiency.

4.2.1 Seller Behavior with Reference Points

Figure 4.1 provides the distributions of prices suggested by sellers for each reference point treatment. It is easy to see that the number of observations on the right tail increases as the reference price increases. We define a seller's price as a "high price" if it exceeds €9 (which is the "standard" prediction for ultimatum games). Figure 4.1 reveals that the share of high prices is around 10% in treatment Low ($\rho = €1$); importantly, it increases to 20% in treatment Med ($\rho = €5$), and is above 40% in treatment High ($\rho = €9$).

Therefore, some sellers appear to use higher reference prices as a legitimation to offer higher prices, i.e., to ask for a larger share of the surplus. This impression is confirmed by the results of a Probit regression on treatment indicator variables. As explanatory variables, we use a constant, a variable indicating if the reference price was at least €5, and another variable indicating if the reference price was at least €9. The regression results are provided in table 4.2.

Table 4.2 Influence of reference prices on the probability that sellers offer a high price

Explanatory variable	Coefficient $\hat{\beta}$	σ_β	z	p-value
Constant	−1.342	0.200	−6.72	< 0.001
Reference price $\rho \geq €5$	0.479	0.266	1.80	0.072
Reference price $\rho \geq €9$	0.689	0.235	2.93	0.003

---

[5] Recall that it is always the seller who moves first.

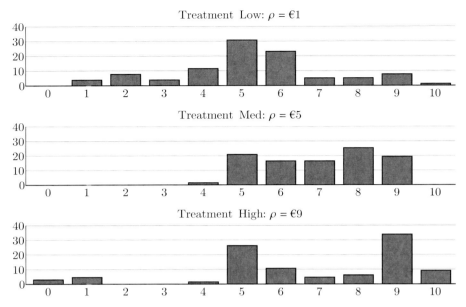

Fig. 4.1 Frequency distributions of price offers by proposers in % by treatment

The results show that the likelihood that a seller offers a high price is significantly larger if the reference price is at least €5. The likelihood of observing high prices increases further if the reference price is even higher. This result is also visible in figure 4.1.

To further investigate how prices offered by sellers respond to a change in reference prices on average, we regress offered prices on reference prices using OLS. The regression results are summarized in table 4.3 and show that the relation between the price offered by sellers and the reference price is strictly positive. If we calculate a hypothetical result based on the regression, sellers ask on average for €5.36 of the surplus for a reference price of €0.[6] However, positive reference prices further increase the prices offered by sellers. Specifically, sellers require an additional €0.20 from buyers for each increase of the reference price by €1.

Table 4.3 Influence of reference prices on price offers

Explanatory variable	Coefficient $\hat{\beta}$	σ_β	t	p-value
Constant	5.357	0.256	20.92	< 0.001
Reference price ρ	0.202	0.044	4.57	< 0.001

---

[6] This is in line with the standard findings for proposers in ultimatum games.

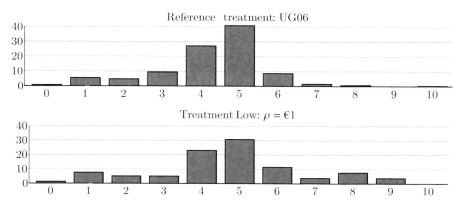

Fig. 4.2 Frequency distributions of surplus offered to responders in % by treatment

Finally, we also test the hypothesis that a higher reference price leads to higher price with non-parametric methods. In particular, we appeal to the Jonckheere-Terpstra test on ranks for ordered alternatives.[7] We find significant evidence ($p <$ 0.001) for ascendingly ordered alternatives, so that the ranks of price offers for our treatment data are systematically varying with the treatment; in particular the ranks of price offers in treatments with higher reference prices are greater than the ranks of price offers in treatments with lower reference prices. Taken together, we can summarize our findings on seller behavior as follows:

Finding 1 *The distribution of proposed prices is not independent of the exogenous reference point as theoretically predicted for subjects that only maximize material payoff. In particular, the average price offered and the probability of a high price offer is positively correlated with the reference price.*

4.2.2 Proposer Behavior: Are Small Reference Prices Negligible?

In this section, we investigate if the existence of reference price per se affects proposer behavior. We also test if subject pool effects might drive our findings with reference prices.

First, we compare proposer behavior observed in reference-price treatment Low to proposer behavior in control treatment UG06. In treatment Low, the reference price is rather small, $\rho = €1$. We use this treatment for comparison since it is much more closely related to a standard ultimatum game with no outside reference points provided by the experimenter than the treatments with larger reference prices.[8] Nevertheless, treatment Low is not identical to a standard ultimatum game. To see the

---

[7] See Terpstra (1952) and Jonckheere (1954) for details on the Jonckheere-Terpstra test.

[8] This is based on the assumption that subjects would perceive a treatment with a reference price of €0 equivalent to a standard ultimatum game.

difference, note that in the standard ultimatum game, there is a pure windfall gain of €10 with no association of cost. In contrast, the entire gain of €10 in treatment Low is associated with a small payoff-irrelevant "seller cost" of €1.

Figure 4.2 depicts the distribution of surplus offered by the proposer to the responder observed in control treatment UG06 and in treatment Low.[9] Obviously, the distributions are quite similar. Formally testing the hypothesis that data for both treatments are drawn from the same distribution using the the non-parametric Kolmogorov-Smirnov-test (two-tailed, $p = 0.113$) reveals no significant differences. However, testing differences on the central location of both distributions using the the non-parametric Mann-Whitney-U-test (two-tailed, $p = 0.080$) and the t-test (two-tailed, $p > 0.040$) reveals differences in median or average which are, however, not large in size.[10]

Finding 2 *The introduction of a small exogenous reference price has a small effect on the distribution of proposer behavior as compared to that in standard ultimatum games.*

As a robustness check, we investigate if there are subject pool differences that drive proposer behavior. Specifically, we compare proposer behavior of our two control studies UG06 and UG07. Importantly, the subject pool for UG07 was the same one as the one for treatments Low, Med, and High. The application of the Mann-Whitney-U-test (two-tailed, $p > 0.422$), the t-test (two-tailed, $p > 0.134$), and the non-parametric Kolmogorov-Smirnov-test (two-tailed, $p = 0.999$), reveals no statistical differences. Therefore, we conclude that it is not subject pool differences that drive our findings.

Finding 3 *Seller behavior in the reference price treatments is not driven by subject pool differences.*

4.2.3 Buyer Behavior with Reference Points

Our experimental results show that sellers offer higher prices when the reference price is higher. Here, we investigate if buyer behavior also responds to exogenous reference prices. Figure 4.3 provides the distributions of the highest prices that buyers are willing to accept for each reference point treatment (their subjective reservation prices). Apparently, a comparison across treatments shows no clear effect of the reference price on the distributions of buyers' reservation prices. The most blatant difference appears to be the amount of maximum prices around the equal split of €5. In treatment Low, 51% of responders accept a maximum price of €4, €5, or €6. However, in treatments Med (42%) and High (39%), this number is some-

---

[9] Note that the distribution for treatment Low is the mirror image of that depicted in figure 4.1 since the latter depicts prices (proposer surplus) and not responder surplus.

[10] The difference between treatment averages is €0.42.

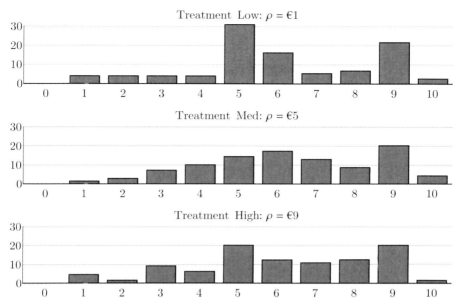

Fig. 4.3 Frequency distributions of highest prices that responders are willing to pay in % by treatment

what smaller and the amount of maximum prices is less concentrated on the fair split of €5.

If buyers were responding to reference prices, then perhaps they would most likely be willing to accept higher price offers for higher reference prices since sellers face a higher (though irrelevant for the material payoff) "cost." In contrast to this intuition, the number of buyers accepting high prices seems independent of the treatment.[11] Specifically, the percentage of buyers that accepts a high price is rather stable across treatments (Low: 24%, Med: 25%, High: 22%). To formally investigate this relation, we regress the instance of a high price on two indicator variables. Regression results are summarized in table 4.4.

Table 4.4 Influence of reference prices on the probability that buyers accept a high price

Explanatory variable	Coefficient $\hat{\beta}$	σ_β	z	p-value
Constant	−0.696	0.159	−4.37	< 0.001
Reference price $\rho \geq$ €5	0.010	0.229	0.04	0.965
Reference price $\rho \geq$ €9	−0.090	0.240	−0.38	0.706

The reference price does not significantly affect the probability that buyers accept high prices. Using an OLS regression to further inquire into possible effects stem-

---

[11] Again, we view a price as high if it is greater or equal to €9.

ming from reference prices reveals no significant findings either. Table 4.5 provides
the regression results. Responders are willing to accept prices of roughly €6 on average while the reference price has no clear effect on their behavior; its coefficient
is not significantly different from zero.

Table 4.5 Influence of reference prices on reservation prices

Explanatory variable	Coefficient $\hat{\beta}$	σ_β	t	p-value
Constant	6.133	0.283	21.66	< 0.001
Reference price ρ	0.009	0.049	0.18	0.860

In view of the accumulated evidence, it is not surprising that the Jonckheere-
Terpstra test does not reject the hypothesis that data on accepted high prices are not
systematically ordered by reference prices in either direction (two-sided, $p = 0.898$).

4.2.4 Efficiency

In this section, we evaluate the effects of the exogenous reference point on efficiency. We have seen that reference prices affect the distribution of prices that sellers
offer. In particular, higher reference prices increase price offers. Since the distribution of responders does not respond much to reference prices, it is straightforward
that efficiency is negatively affected by reference prices.

As a measure of efficiency, we employ the share of feasible transactions out of
all potential transactions where any proposer is matched with any responder for a
given treatment. Table 4.6 summarizes efficiency results by reference point treatment. Clearly, a larger reference price decreases allocative efficiency. For example,
if the reference price is small, equaling €1, then the share of implemented transactions is 68.2% out of all possible seller-buyer encounters. With a reference price
of €9 it drops to just 47.4% of implementable transactions.

Finding 4 *Reference prices are negatively correlated with the share of Pareto-
efficient allocations.*

Table 4.6 Efficiency by treatment

Treatment	Reference price	Share of feasible transactions	Number of matchings
Low	$\rho = 1$	68.2%	5772
Med	$\rho = 5$	49.2%	4623
High	$\rho = 9$	47.4%	4160

4.3 Discussion of Experimental Results

In her book "The Grammar of Society," Christina Bicchieri (2006) introduces a social norm-based model to explain the behavior of subjects in mixed-motive games commonly observed in experimental studies. The model applies to all games with an inherent conflict between selfish and pro-social incentives.

A social norm is defined as a behavioral rule R that exists in a population P for situations of type $\mathscr{S}$ (where $\mathscr{S}$ can be represented as a mixed-motive game) if the following conditions are given for each individual $i \in P_{cf}$ of a "sufficiently large" subset $P_{cf} \subseteq P$ of *conditional followers*:[12]

1) individual i knows that the rule R exists and applies to situations of type $\mathscr{S}$, and
2) individual i prefers to conform to rule R in situations of type $\mathscr{S}$ *on the condition* that:

  2a) individual i believes that a sufficiently large subset of the population P conforms to the rule R in situations of type $\mathscr{S}$, and either
  2b) individual i believes that a sufficiently large subset of the population P expects individual i to conform to the rule R in situations of type $\mathscr{S}$, or
  2b') individual i believes that a sufficiently large subset of the population P expects individual i to conform to the rule R in situations of type $\mathscr{S}$, prefers individual i to conform, and may sanction behavior.

Individuals $i \in P_{cf}$ do not necessarily follow the behavioral rule R. An individual $i \in P_{cf}$ only prefers to conform to behavioral rule R when the conditions 2a), and either 2b) or 2b') are met, which depends on individual i's beliefs. A social norm R is *followed* by population P if a sufficiently large subset $P_f \subseteq P_{cf}$ of "followers" exists, for which each individual $i \in P_f$ believes that conditions 2a), and either 2b) or 2b') are met and, as a result, prefers to conform to rule R in situations of type $\mathscr{S}$.

With this definition, a behavioral rule R can be a social norm in a population P, even if it is currently not followed by any individual $i \in P$. For a social norm to exist, only a sufficiently large subset $P_{cf} \subseteq P$ of conditional followers needs to exist, who would follow the rule if they believed that conditions 2a), and either 2b) or 2b') are met. Social norms are entirely subjective and depend on the individual beliefs of individuals.

The social norms then solve mixed-motive games by *transforming* them into co-ordination games. For a norm to exist, it is necessary that it is an equilibrium of the transformed game, because a subject's belief that other subjects behave according to the norm will be confirmed by experience if and only if it is an equilibrium. A social norm exists for a specific situation. Therefore, which social norm is activated, or if a social norm is activated at all, depends on the framing of the situation and the beliefs and expectations of a subject.

---

[12] The meaning of "sufficiently large" may vary across individuals. One can think of an individual threshold $t_i \in [0, 1]$ that represents the minimum share of population P that individual i regards as sufficiently large.

An activated norm complements a subject's material payoff:[13] A deviation from the norm constitutes a payoff penalty which is weighed with a non-negative factor. This non-negative factor describes the sensitivity towards norm violations for a subject. To determine a player's total payoff, this penalty is subtracted from the material payoff in a similar way as in the model by Fehr and Schmidt (1999) (in the following F&S). The main conceptual difference between the model by F&S and Bicchieri's model is the nature of the reference: In the F&S model, the reference is an equal payoff split, while in Bicchieri's model, the reference is the social norm. And this social norm is not context independent, but depends on the evaluation of the situation by subjects.

Denote the strategy set of player i (for $i \in \{1, \ldots, n\}$) for a n-person normal form game by S_i, and let $\mathbf{S}_{-i} = \prod_{j \neq i} S_j$ be the set of strategy profiles of players other than player i. Then a norm for player i is formally represented by a function $R_i : \mathbf{L}_{-i} \to S_i$, where $\mathbf{L}_{-i} \subseteq \mathbf{S}_{-i}$; it is a function that maps player i's expectations about the behavior of the other players into a strategy for player i. Loosely speaking, a norm regulates behavior conditional on other people's behavior. In a situation for which there is no norm to regulate player i's behavior $\mathbf{L}_{-i}$ could be empty; in a situation in which a norm exists for some strategies of the other players it could be a strict subset of $\mathbf{S}_{-i}$; or in a situation in which a norm exists for any strategies of the other players it could be equal to $\mathbf{S}_{-i}$.

A strategy profile $\mathbf{s} = (s_1, \ldots, s_n)$ *instantiates* a norm for player j if $\mathbf{s}_{-j} \in \mathbf{L}_{-j}$, i.e., if the function R_j is defined at $\mathbf{s}_{-j}$. It *violates* a norm if, for some player j, it instantiates a norm for player j but $s_j \neq R_j(\mathbf{s}_{-j})$. Let π_i be the material payoff function for player i. The norm-based utility function of player i depends on the strategy profile $\mathbf{s}$ and is given by

$$u_i(\mathbf{s}) = \pi_i(\mathbf{s}) - k_i \max_{\mathbf{s}_{-j} \in \mathbf{L}_{-j}} \max_{m \neq j} \{\pi_m(\mathbf{s}_{-j}, R_j(\mathbf{s}_{-j})) - \pi_m(\mathbf{s}), 0\} \, ,$$

where $k_i \geq 0$ is the constant representing player i's sensitivity to the relevant norm. The first (left) maximum operator reflects that a norm may be instantiated by one strategy profile for more that one player simultaneously (for example, in a public-good game). The second maximum operator ranges over all players m with the exception of the norm violator (player j). The maximum is taken of the material payoff loss for player m that results from the violation of norm R_j by player j. The maximum payoff deduction resulting from all norm violations is multiplied with the personal sensitivity to the norm of player i and subtracted from his or her material payoff.

For illustration, take a two-player ultimatum market game as in our experiment, with player 1 being the proposer and player 2 being the responder, a pie size (maximum price) of M, and a price offer of x. The population of agents is assumed to have heterogenous preferences. Assume that a norm R_2 that would prescribe some

---

[13] See Bicchieri (2006, app. chap. 1).

responder behavior is nowhere defined, i.e., no such norm is ever instantiated.[14] However, a given player 1 holds a norm $R_{1,1}$ (with $R_{j,i}$ denoting that player i holds the belief R_j about the norm that applies to the behavior of player j) that he ought to offer the "fair" price N_1. A given player 2 holds the norm $R_{1,2}$ that player 1 ought to offer the "fair" price N_2.[15] In short, N_1 and N_2 denote the price that should be offered by player 1 according to the social norms activated by player 1 and player 2, respectively. Assume further that the norm can only prescribe offering a price smaller than the pie size ($N_i < M$ for $i \in \{1,2\}$).

The utility in case of rejection of player 1's offer by player 2 is zero for both: $u_{1,\text{reject}}(x) = u_{2,\text{reject}}(x) = 0$.[16] In case of acceptance the utility functions for players 1 and 2 are given by:

$$u_{1,\text{accept}}(x) = x - k_1 \max\{x - N_1, 0\}$$
$$u_{2,\text{accept}}(x) = M - x - k_2 \max\{x - N_2, 0\} \ .$$

For the responder to accept an offer, $u_{2,\text{accept}}(x) > 0$ needs to hold, which translates into

$$x < x_{\max} \text{ with } x_{\max} \equiv \frac{M + k_2 N_2}{1 + k_2} \qquad (4.1)$$

as the maximum price the proposer can offer to secure acceptance. Because the proposer utility is increasing in x if $x \leq N_1$, in equilibrium, he will never offer a price below N_1 unless $N_1 \geq x_{\max}$. If the proposer is only mildly sensitive to the norm (with $k_1 < 1$), his utility is increasing in x for all $x \in [0,1]$, so in equilibrium, he would make the most unfair (highest price) offer that is still accepted and offer $x = x_{\max} - \varepsilon$, with ε being the smallest possible decrement. In case he is strongly sensitive to the norm (with $k_1 > 1$), his utility has a maximum for $x = N_1$. Therefore, he would offer $x = N_1$ if $N_1 < x_{\max}$ or $x = x_{\max} - \varepsilon$ otherwise. If $k_1 = 1$, any $x' \in [N_1, x_{\max})$ constitutes an equilibrium if $N_1 < x_{\max}$ and $x = x_{\max} - \varepsilon$ otherwise. This equilibrium offer can be summarized formally:

---

[14] One could think of a norm R_2 that prescribes player 2 to reject certain offers, for example, of prices x of less than $M/2$. But incorporating such a norm into the model would not make any difference to the formal analysis.

[15] $N_1 \neq N_2$ this does *not* imply *wrong* or *inconsistent* beliefs. The model explicitly allows for each individual to hold his individual beliefs about which norms apply to a given situation. Of course, both players could also regard the same price as fair, so that $N_1 = N_2$.

[16] This is based on the following considerations. On one hand, consider a potential norm R_1 that prescribes that the proposer offers a certain price for the case of rejection: in case of rejection, the material payoffs of all players are zero. Therefore, the maximum payoff *reduction* resulting from the violation of such a norm is also zero. On the other hand, consider a potential norm R_2 that prescribes that the responder accepts a certain (e.g., fair) proposal. If the responder violated such a norm, the utility of a player i holding such a norm would be negative (for positive k_i). Nevertheless, in equilibrium the responder never violates the norm because rejection does not increase her utility. Therefore, such a norm is excluded from consideration to simplify the model.

$$x^* = \begin{cases} x_{\max} - \varepsilon & \text{if } k_1 < 1 \\ x_{\max} - \varepsilon & \text{if } k_1 = 1 \ \text{ and } N_1 \geq x_{\max} \\ x' \in [N_1, x_{\max}) & \text{if } k_1 = 1 \ \text{ and } N_1 < x_{\max} \\ \min\{N_1, x_{\max} - \varepsilon\} & \text{if } k_1 > 1 \ . \end{cases} \tag{4.2}$$

If N_2 and k_2, which describe the responder type, are not common knowledge, the proposer's belief about these values figures in his decision, because $x_{\max}$ is a function of N_2 and k_2 (see equation (4.1)). The proposer's belief about the responder type can be represented by a joint probability over N_2 and k_2. In this case, the proposer would, in equilibrium, choose x so that he maximizes his expected utility $\mathrm{E}[u_{1,\text{accept}}(x)]$, which is:

$$\mathrm{E}[u_{1,\text{accept}}(x)] = \mathrm{Prob}(x < x_{\max}) \times u_{1,\text{accept}}(x)$$

$$\Longleftrightarrow \quad \mathrm{E}[u_{1,\text{accept}}(x)] = \mathrm{Prob}(x < \frac{M + k_2 N_2}{1 + k_2}) \times (x - k_1 \max\{x - N_1, 0\}) \ .$$

However, in a typical ultimatum bargaining setting, the proposer could arguably expect that the responder regards the same fairness norm as relevant as he does himself ($N_1 = N_2 \equiv N$). Then, equation (4.1) for $x_{\max}$ is simplified to

$$x_{\max} \equiv \frac{M + k_2 N}{1 + k_2} \ . \tag{4.3}$$

We assumed that the norm can only prescribe offering a price smaller than the pie size ($N < M$). Therefore, $N < x_{\max}$ always holds, which simplifies equation (4.2) for x^* to

$$x^* = \begin{cases} x_{\max} - \varepsilon & \text{if } k_1 < 1 \\ x' \in [N, x_{\max}) & \text{if } k_1 = 1 \\ N & \text{if } k_1 > 1 \ . \end{cases} \tag{4.4}$$

In case the proposer is uncertain about the responder type, the proposer's belief about the responder type can be represented by a probability over k_2. Then, the proposer would, in equilibrium, chose x so that he maximizes his expected utility $\mathrm{E}[u_{1,\text{accept}}(x)]$ for the distribution of k_2 he assumes. The expected utility (for $N_1 = N_2 = N$) is

$$\mathrm{E}[u_{1,\text{accept}}(x)] = \mathrm{Prob}(x < x_{\max}) \times u_{1,\text{accept}}(x)$$

$$\Longleftrightarrow \quad \mathrm{E}[u_{1,\text{accept}}(x)] = \mathrm{Prob}(x < \frac{M + k_2 N}{1 + k_2}) \times (x - k_1 \max\{x - N, 0\}) \ . \tag{4.5}$$

Based on equations (4.3)–(4.5), for any distribution of k_2 the proposer potentially assumes, the following is true with respect to the equilibrium price:[17]

---

[17] Recall that $k_2 \geq 0$ and $N < M$. Therefore, $N < x_{\max} \leq M$ holds.

$$x^* \in [N, M) \text{ if } k_1 \leq 1, \text{ and}$$
$$x^* = N \quad \text{ if } k_1 > 1 .$$

(4.6)

According to Bicchieri, k_i for $i \in \{1, 2\}$ may be a stable characteristic of a subject, but note that the activated social norm N depends on the framing of the situation, and the beliefs of the subject. This is the reason why her theory can explain our experimental findings: The changes in the described context of the situation at hand has the effect that subjects activate different norms. Therefore, they play different games, depending on the given context.

To simplify the analysis of the experimental results we assume that the proposer expects that the responder regards the same fairness norm as relevant as he does himself ($N_1 = N_2 = N$), but we do not limit the behavioral prediction to a specific proposer's belief about the distribution of k_2. If we assumed a specific belief about the distribution of k_2 we would obtain a point-prediction of x^* also for the case of $k_1 \leq 1$ and not only for $k_1 > 1$. Because no specific distribution of k_2 is assumed, equation (4.6) describes a whole *range* of price offers that can be expected for $k_1 \leq 1$.

The framing of our instructions suggests three potential fairness norms: Some subjects (type α) might recognize that the given reference price is irrelevant, and therefore activate the classic "sharing a pie 50–50" norm for the total pie size of €10; thus, for them, $N_\alpha = 5$. Another share of the subjects (type β) might factor in the reference price as a sunk cost to justify their choice of norm. The approach would be to subtract the sunk cost from the pie size and divide the remaining surplus in a 50–50 fashion. For example, if the reference price is given to be $\rho = €5$ as in treatment Med, this norm would prescribe the subject to keep this €5 and split the remaining as evenly as possible, thus taking $N_{\beta A} = \rho + (10 - \rho)/2 = 7.5$ as the fair split or norm. The remaining subjects (type γ) might focus completely on the reference price: they activate a norm that prescribes them to recuperate the price they paid for the good, so for them, $N_\gamma = \rho$. The only treatment where this third type behaves different from the first two types is treatment Low with $\rho = 1$. Overall, we would expect subjects in each treatment to employ one of the three potential fairness norms shown in table 4.7.

Table 4.7 Treatment information and independent observations by role

Treatment	Reference price ρ	Norm of type α	Norm of type β	Norm of type γ
Low	€1	$N_\alpha = 5$	$N_{\beta B} = 5.5$	$N_{\gamma B} = 1$
Med	€5	$N_\alpha = 5$	$N_{\beta A} = 7.5$	$N_{\gamma A} = 5$
High	€9	$N_\alpha = 5$	$N_{\beta C} = 9.5$	$N_{\gamma C} = 9$

According to the prediction given in equation (4.6), a proposer with a k_1-value above unity would offer a price equivalent to the price N his norm prescribes. The price offer made by a proposer with a k_1-value below or equal to unity depends on his assumption about the distribution of responder types (the distribution of k_2).

Whatever his belief about this distribution, the offer will be a price above or equal to the price N his norm suggests. The resulting potential price offers are summarized in table 4.8 (the choice was restricted to full numbers, so proposers of type β had to either round down or up).

Table 4.8 Potential price offers

Treat-ment	Reference price ρ	Norm of type α		Norm of type β		Norm of type γ	
		$k \le 1$	$k > 1$	$k \le 1$	$k > 1$	$k \le 1$	$k > 1$
Low	€1	$x \in \{5,\ldots,9\}$	$x = 5$	$x \in \{5,\ldots,9\}$	$x \in \{5,6\}$	$x \in \{1,\ldots,9\}$	$x = 1$
Med	€5	$x \in \{5,\ldots,9\}$	$x = 5$	$x \in \{7,\ldots,9\}$	$x \in \{7,8\}$	$x \in \{5,\ldots,9\}$	$x = 5$
High	€9	$x \in \{5,\ldots,9\}$	$x = 5$	$x = 9$	$x = 9$	$x = 9$	$x = 9$

If one investigates figure 4.1 in light of these potential price offers, there is a good fit between the theoretical prediction and the observed price offers. The theory might also explain also why the results in treatment Low are so similar to standard ultimatum results: Two of the three norms ($N_\alpha = 5$ and $N_{\beta B} = 5.5$) are equal or close to the norm of $N = 5$ that might typically be activated in a standard ultimatum exchange without any manipulation. The difference between the standard ultimatum results and our results, which is mainly a few price offers below €5, can also be accounted for: they might be the result of some subjects activating a norm of type γ.

The only observed behavior that this theory cannot explain are the 12% of price offers of either €0 or €10 that took place in treatment High, with $\rho = 9$. These might be due to judgement errors of the proposers, who did not understand the implications either for themselves (offering a price of zero, resulting in a zero payoff for them) or for the responder (offering a price of €10, and therefore no incentive to accept).

What does the theory predict for the *responders*, and how does that relate to our observations? Note that the responders potentially activate the same fairness norms as the proposers, which are given in table 4.7. In addition, a fourth norm δ with $N_\delta = 1$ for any treatment can be thought of: as the instructions stated that the good for trade was worthless for the proposer, responders activating norm N_δ might have felt entitled to a lion's share of the gains from trade. This may well be the case, as according to Bicchieri, norms are typically selected with a self-serving bias if there are multiple potential norms to choose from. That is also the reason why proposers are unlikely to adopt this norm—it is a very unfavorable norm from their perspective.

The behavior a norm prescribes for a responder is to accept any offer x that is smaller than $x_{\max}$ given in equation (4.1) above. For any small sensitivity to the norm with $k_2 < 1/(9+N)$, this translates into accepting any price up to €9. For a larger k_2, the maximum acceptable price can decrease to the reference price N that the norm prescribes. For example, the share of about 20% of responders that demanded a share of more than 50% in treatments Med and High can be understood in the light of the fourth norm $N_\delta = 1$. Taken together, the theory can explain the observed responder choices, though the relationship between theory and experimental findings is not as pronounced as for the proposer data.

While Bicchieri's model can overall explain our experimental findings, it does have some problematic aspects. Norms are entirely subjective because they are based on beliefs. In principle, any behavioral rule could be a social norm, and therefore, the theory could explain any behavior. To counter such criticism, Bicchieri explains that a social norm is not arbitrary, but should be linked to the situation at hand in a meaningful way. She devotes an entire chapter of her book to this issue (see Bicchieri 2006, chap. 2), and describes that the interpretation of situational cues leads to the activation of a specific norm. However, she does not provide a formal definition of this link between the situation at hand and the activated norm, and comments herself that "the problem is that we still have quite rudimentary theories of how motives affect behavior."[18]

In this experiment, a meaningful link between the situation at hand and the norm could be a positive relation of the treatment variable and the price that subjects activated to be the price the proposer ought to propose. And indeed, such a positive relation would not be contradicted by our experimental results. Nevertheless, in the above analysis of the experimental results we could only hypothesize which norms the subjects activated based on observed behavior. It would be advisable to repeat the experiment and to elicit the norms which the subjects activate, independent of the observed behavior. Such an elicitation could, for example, follow the approach that was recently proposed by Krupka and Weber (2008): They asked subjects that were *not* those that later actually decided in the decision situation about the social appropriateness of each possible action on a scale from "very socially inappropriate" to "very socially appropriate." These subjects were incentivized to match the responses of others. The additional information about the norms that subjects activate in a given situation would enable us to further validate our theory: we could establish whether subjects' behavior is consistent with those norms that are elicited to be socially acceptable.

4.4 Concluding Remarks

We varied the framing of a standard ultimatum decision situation while holding the payoff structure constant. This affected subject's behavior. One possible explanation for this observation is a theory of social norms as sketched in section 4.3: given that fairness preferences in ultimatum games typically involve a *fair share*, which need not necessarily be an equal split,[19] the instructions were designed to shift the price that subjects might regard as the fair price. Without changing the pecuniary

---

[18] See Bicchieri (2006, p. 105).

[19] Compare also, for example, Kagel et al. (1996), who investigated subject behavior in ultimatum bargaining when bargaining over chips with valuations that differed for proposer and responder, or Schmitt (2004), who focused on the effects of asymmetric payoffs, outside options, and information.

structure of the game, we induced subjects across treatments to behave differently by changing the framing between treatments. We found that the observed differences between treatments correspond to the variation of the treatment variable, as we conjectured in the beginning.

This demonstrates the importance of the framing of a decision situation in the domain of economic decisions that involve a bilateral social interaction. The standard experimental economic approach is to remove as much context as possible from the decision situation in order to analyze subject behavior in a *pure* setting. However, the question of how helpful these studies are to understand real-life economic human behavior arises. Real-life economic decisions are typically very rich in context and are not abstract decisions between payoffs without context. Of course, analysis of any situation is complicated if context needs to be taken into account, but our experiment points out the importance of considering context. One reason for considering context might be that the context triggers a specific norm or reference, which in turn influences subjects' decisions.

Behavior in the light of a given decision context is not random, but a model that relates the context to social norms people activate in order to inform their decision can explain our experimental results. Preferences may be stable in the sense that subjects prefer to stick to social norms in interpersonal bargaining situations. But any such decision situation may trigger one of many potential social or fairness norms, and which norm a subject chooses in a given context depends on framing and subject's character.

Therefore, decision situations involving bilateral bargaining should be considered carefully with regard to the social norms they might trigger and the effects this might have on behavior. The theoretical model developed by Bicchieri (2006) provides a starting point for such analysis. Nevertheless, more experiments are necessary to fully establish and understand the relationship between context and social norms. To address a shortcoming of our analysis it would be advisable to repeat the experiment and elicit the activated norms, as proposed at the end of section 4.3. This would enable us to not only analyze the results based on hypothesized norms, but based on those norms that are activated by the given subject pool in the specific situation at hand.

Appendix: Instructions

In order to introduce the subjects to the experiment, the tutor of the tutorial session presented four slides as an introduction in front of all the students; see figures 4.4 to 4.7. On slides 1 and 3 (figures 4.4 and 4.6), the reference price ρ was mentioned and printed in bold (also bold in the original instructions). The instructions were equivalent in all three treatments, except for this treatment variable ρ. Depending on the treatment, this variable was either €1 (treatment Low), €5 (treatment Med), or €9 (treatment High); see table 4.1.

After listening to the instructions, the subjects had to fill out a paper decision form. The proposers filled out the decision form shown in figure 4.8, and the responders filled out a form like the one in figure 4.9. Again, the treatment variable ρ is mentioned in bold on both decision forms and was varied across treatments according to the setup described above.

Classroom Experiment: Bargaining Game

Instructions

- For this experiment we divided all classrooms into three groups. You are in the first group.
- In this experiment, two individuals in this classroom and any other E+B-classroom of the same group are selected **at random**. Let's call them Steve and Martin.
- Imagine that Steve found a special stamp in his drawer. It is a stamp that he bought for **5 EUR** a while ago. Unfortunately the stamp was valid only for a short time, and cannot be used any more.
- Martin is a stamp trader, and he knows of a collector, who buys the stamp for 10 EUR.

1

Fig. 4.4 Slide 1/4 of instructions for treatment Med

Classroom Experiment: Bargaining Game

Instructions

- Now, Steve suggests stamp trader Martin a price at which he may purchase the stamp.
- Martin can accept or reject the price.
- If Martin accepts the price, Steve receives an amount of money equal to the price, and Martin receives 10 EUR minus the price (Imagine that he immediately sells the stamp to the collector).
- If Martin rejects the price, then no one receives anything: Steve's stamp crumbles to dust and for Martin, there is no other possibility to obtain a stamp that can be sold to the collector.

2

Fig. 4.5 Slide 2/4 of instructions for treatment Med

Classroom Experiment: Bargaining Game

Instructions

- In a minute, you receive a sheet of paper that informs you about the role that you assume (Steve or Martin)
- Please fill in your student number, so that we can later identify you to pay your winnings in cash.
- If you assume the role of Steve, then you indicate for which price between 0 and 10 EUR you would sell the stamp for which you once paid **5 EUR** to Martin.
- If you assume the role of Martin, then you indicate the **highest** price you are willing to pay for the stamp.
- If there is an agreement, Steve receives the price he offered, and Martin receives 10 EUR minus this price.

3

Fig. 4.6 Slide 3/4 of instructions for treatment Med

Classroom Experiment: Bargaining Game

Instructions

- During the lecture, the Bargaining-Game is played with REAL MONEY!
- There is 1x10 EUR: Out of all properly filled in and collected sheets, 1 Steve sheet and 1 Martin sheet of your group is selected at random.
- Then, the bargaining game is played according to the rules and the data on the sheets. The corresponding students will receive the resulting payoffs **DURING THE LECTURE** in **CASH**!

4

Fig. 4.7 Slide 4/4 of instructions for treatment Med

Welcome to the classroom experiment!   **BG- STEVE –GROUP A**

Please fill in your student number: i-_____

You assume the role of STEVE. This means that you suggest the price at which you sell the stamp that you once bought for **5 EUR** to MARTIN if he accepts your suggested price. If he doesn't accept it, you receive nothing. If he accepts, you receive the amount equivalent to the price and MARTIN receives an amount equivalent to 10 EUR minus the price.

Please notice that one pair (Steve/Martin) is randomly matched in the lecture. The result is paid to the corresponding Steve and Martin in **REAL MONEY** in class if the offer is accepted (this is why we need your student number: to identify the lucky ones to give them their money!)

Please check the appropriate checkbox: (check only once!)

I offer MARTIN to buy the stamp for:

0€   ☐

1€   ☐

2€   ☐

3€   ☐

4€   ☐

5€   ☐

6€   ☐

7€   ☐

8€   ☐

9€   ☐

10€   ☐

Fig. 4.8 Proposer form for treatment Med

Welcome to the classroom experiment!   **BG- MARTIN –GROUP A**

Please fill in your student number: i-_____

You assume the role of MARTIN. This means that you decide about the highest price at which you would buy the stamp from STEVE that he once bought for **5 EUR**.

If STEVE suggests a price that is lower or equal to the highest price that you accept, then the transaction is implemented at STEVE's suggested price. Then, STEVE receives the amount equivalent to the price he offered and you receive the amount of 10 EUR minus the price STEVE offered. If STEVE suggests a higher price, then you reject the offer and you both receive nothing.

Please notice that one pair (Steve/Martin) is randomly matched in the lecture. The result is paid to the corresponding Steve and Martin in **REAL MONEY** in class if the offer is accepted (this is why we need your student number: to identify the lucky ones to give them their money!)

Please check the appropriate checkbox: (check only once!)

The highest price I would pay to STEVE is:

0€	☐
1€	☐
2€	☐
3€	☐
4€	☐
5€	☐
6€	☐
7€	☐
8€	☐
9€	☐
10€	☐

Fig. 4.9 Responder form for treatment Med

References

Bicchieri C (2006) The Grammar of Society: The Nature and Dynamics of Social Norms. Cambridge University Press, Cambridge, UK

Blount S, Thomas-Hunt MC, Neale MA (1996) The price is right–Or is it? A reference point model of two-party price negotiations. Organ Behav Hum Decis Process 68(1):1–12

Camerer CF (2003) Behavioral Game Theory: Experiments in Strategic Interaction. Princeton University Press, Princeton, NJ

Coleman JS (1990) Foundations of Social Theory. Harvard University Press, Cambridge, MA

Fehr E, Schmidt KM (1999) A theory of fairness, competition and cooperation. Q J Econ 114(3):817–868

Handgraaf MJJ, Van Dijk E, De Cremer D (2003) Social utility in ultimatum bargaining. Soc Justice Res 16(3):263–283

Hoffman E, McCabe K, Shachat K, Smith VL (1994) Preferences, property rights, and anonymity in bargaining games. Games Econom Behav 7(3):346–380

Jonckheere AR (1954) A distribution-free k-sample test against ordered alternatives. Biometrika 41(1–2):133–145

Kagel JH, Kim C, Moser D (1996) Fairness in ultimatum games with asymmetric information and asymmetric payoffs. Games Econom Behav 13(1):100–110

Kahneman D, Tversky A (1979) Prospect theory: An analysis of decision under risk. Econometrica 47(2):263–291

Konow J (2000) Fair shares: Accountability and cognitive dissonance in allocation decisions. Am Econ Rev 90(4):1072–1091

Köszegi B, Rabin M (2006) A model of reference-dependent preferences. Q J Econ 121(4):1133–1165

Kristensen H, Garling T (1997) The effects of anchor points and reference points on negotiation process and outcome. Organ Behav Hum Decis Process 71(1):85–94

Krupka E, Weber R (2008) Identifying social norms using coordination games: Why does dictator game sharing vary?, IZA Discussion Paper No. 3860, IZA, Bonn, Germany

Levin IP, Schneider SL, Gaeth GJ (1998) All frames are not created equal: A typology and critical analysis of framing effects. Organ Behav Hum Decis Process 76(2):149–188

Munro A, Sugden R (2003) On the theory of reference-dependent preferences. J Econ Behav Organ 50(4):407–428

Roth AE, Prasnikar V, Okuno-Fujiwara M, Zamir S (1991) Bargaining and market behavior in Jerusalem, Ljubljana, Pittsburgh, and Tokyo: An experimental study. Am Econ Rev 81(5):1068–1095

Savarimuthu BTR, Purvis M, Cranefield S, Purvis M (2007) How do norms emerge in multi-agent societies? Mechanisms design, The Information Science Discussion Paper Series, No. 2007/01, University of Otago, New Zealand

Schmitt P (2004) On perceptions of fairness: The role of valuations, outside options, and information in ultimatum bargaining games. Exp Econ 7(1):49–73

Schwartz SH (1977) Normative influence on altruism. In: Berkowitz L (ed) Advances in Experimental Social Psychology, vol 10, Academic Press, New York, NY, pp 222–275

Terpstra TJ (1952) The asymptotic normality and consistency of kendall's test against trend, when ties are present in one ranking. Indagat Math 14:327–333

Tversky A, Kahneman D (1991) Loss aversion in riskless choice: A reference-dependent model. Q J Econ 106(4):1039–1061

Chapter 5
Fairness, Price Stickiness, and History Dependence in Decentralized Trade

Fair behavior in bilateral bargaining situations has been one of the most extensively researched areas in microeconomics—experimentally and theoretically. Whether the robust evidence that people are concerned with fairness in bilateral bargaining (see, e.g., Camerer 2003) has implications for interaction on markets, however, remains unclear. Early studies by Kahneman et al. (1986), followed up by Kachelmeier et al. (1991) and Franciosi et al. (1995), have demonstrated that there are fairness effects on markets. However, they have been observed mainly as a transient phenomenon: the prices in the reported experiments typically approach the standard competitive equilibrium as time passes and unsustainable expectations are unwound. And many experimental studies have failed to find significant fairness effects on markets altogether. In their seminal paper, Fehr and Schmidt (1999, p. 818) summarize that

> ...in competitive experimental markets with complete contracts, in which a well-defined homogenous good is traded, *almost all* subjects behave as if they are only interested in their material payoff. Even if the competitive equilibrium implies an extremely uneven distribution of the gains from trade, equilibrium is reached within a few periods.

The experimental investigations referred to by Fehr and Schmidt mostly concern double-auction settings, and are therefore difficult to interpret: The zero-intelligence trader results of Gode and Sunder (1993) have highlighted the strong built-in tendency of double auctions to reproduce the competitive equilibrium. Whether agents lose their concern for fairness when they interact in market environments or if their social preferences are simply overwhelmed by institutional structure is hard to discern. In fact, Brown et al. (2004) have recently shown that social preferences can play an important role in the presence of contractual incompleteness. Their experimental results complement empirical findings by Young and Burke (2001) which testify to the importance of custom and focal division rules.

Many market forms other than double auctions are of practical interest. The *search* or *matching markets* studied by Diamond and Maskin (1979), Mortensen (1982), or Rubinstein and Wolinsky (1985) are cases in point. They feature promi-

C. Korth, *Fairness in Bargaining and Markets,*
Lecture Notes in Economics and Mathematical Systems, 627
DOI: 10.1007/978-3-642-02252-4_1, © Springer-Verlag Berlin Heidelberg 2009

nently in labor, real estate, and monetary economics.[1] A key property of these markets is that they temporarily involve one-to-one interaction. This establishes a direct social relation and moreover creates leeway for prices to reflect the attitudes towards risk, delay, and possibly fairness of any two trade partners.

This chapter investigates the implications that social preferences have for the stationary strategic equilibrium of such a decentralized market. Agents are supposed to be averse to unfairly unfavorable as well as unfairly favorable deals in the spirit of Fehr and Schmidt (1999),[2] but we stay rather close to standard individualistic preferences: the negative weights on advantageous and disadvantageous deviations from what is considered as the fair benchmark are such that utility remains strictly increasing in own surplus share. And in contrast to the original Fehr-Schmidt model, the fair split need not automatically be a 50–50 division; any price between sellers' cost and buyers' willingness to pay may be the one which—for whatever reasons— is agents' reference point in a given market. This makes it possible to consider a more flexible notion of fairness than is usually done. It is in line with cognitive dissonance theory from psychology and the noteworthy experiments of Binmore et al. (1991; 1993), where subjects who were triggered to play different bargaining equilibria ended up considering very different surplus distributions as "fair."[3]

Apart from agents' concern with fairness, the investigated model is a simple version of the bargaining markets investigated by Rubinstein and Wolinsky (1985), Gale (1986a; 1986b), or Binmore and Herrero (1988): Buyers and sellers are randomly divided into pairs. One randomly selected partner in each match suggests a deal. Rejection dissolves the match and agents wait to be rematched; successful traders leave the market and new ones enter. For simplicity, buyers and sellers are considered to be perfectly homogeneous. And all relevant information—most notably about agents' preferences—is assumed to be common knowledge.

Examples of real world markets in which agents can be thought of as interacting loosely as in our model include housing markets with approximately stationary landlord and tenant populations, similarly stationary labor markets with individual contracting, consumer-to-consumer sales of used cars, or direct procurement of differentiated commodities such as specialty tea, coffee, or wine. Agents in these markets may have an idea about the "right," "fair," or "appropriate" rent, wage, or price which affects their subjective evaluation of a proposal (irrespective of informational imperfections which we completely leave out of our model). We show how already a rather weak concern for fairness can give rise to price stickiness. This fairness effect is predicted to persist over time for the considered market setting. It provides

---

[1] See, for example, Mortensen and Pissarides (1999) or Rogerson et al. (2005) for labor search models, Krainer and LeRoy (2002) or Albrecht et al. (2007) for housing markets, and Shi (2001) or Rocheteau and Wright (2005) for monetary applications.

[2] Prominent related models of social preferences include the ones by Bolton and Ockenfels (2000), Charness and Rabin (2002), Dufwenberg and Kirchsteiger (2004), or Falk and Fischbacher (2006).

[3] An endogenous notion of fairness also features prominently in Binmore's (1994; 1998) theory of distributional justice. It interprets the human sense of fairness as an efficient means to reach agreements quickly; it has evolutionary advantages only if it can adapt to changes in actual bargaining strength.

an explanation for price or wage rigidities that complements the traditional ones based on imperfect information, menu costs, long-term contracts, or money illusion (see, e.g., Woodford 2002 for imperfect information, Golosov and Lucas 2007 for menu cost, Fehr and Tyran 2001 for money illusion, and Ball and Mankiw 1994 or Taylor 1999 for general overviews).

If the fairness benchmark itself is affected by agents' market experience, aversion to deviations from the given reference price gives rise to a continuum of possible self-confirming price conventions. This can explain distinct price levels in fundamentally identical markets. Interestingly, the less friction is associated with the rejection of an offer, the larger the scope of history: friction turns out to erode the effects of fairness concern. Similarly, price stickiness is reduced rather than increased by friction.

We will now introduce the model. The ensuing strategic market equilibrium is studied in section 5.2. We first discuss the market price's response to changes in the ratio of buyers to sellers for a given reference price, and then investigate the implications of endogenizing the latter. Section 5.3 concludes.

5.1 The Model

Our basic market setup mimics that of Rubinstein (1989, Model A): Agents can trade a single indivisible good at discrete points of time indexed by $t = 0, 1, 2, \ldots$. An agent is either a seller endowed with one unit of the good that she wishes to sell, or a buyer with at least one unit of disposable income. The sets of active buyers and sellers have cardinalities B and S, respectively.

In each period, agents are drawn randomly from the current population and matched with an agent of opposite type if there is one. For simplicity, the matching technology is assumed to involve no friction other than delay after the rejection of an offer; that is, all agents on the short side of the market are matched with certainty.[4] Those on the long side of the market each have the same probability of being matched with any specific trade partner, independently of the history of play.

All sellers have a reservation price of zero and all buyers have a reservation price of one. After being matched, each couple engages in a bargaining session in which either the seller or the buyer is selected with equal probability to propose a price $p \in [0, 1]$ that shall be paid by the buyer in exchange for the good. The quoted price amounts to a proposal of how to split the total monetary surplus of size one which is generated by a trade. The responding agent can accept or reject the offer. If it is rejected, then the two agents stop bargaining and both return to the set of active buyers or sellers. If the offer is accepted, then the trade is carried out and both agents leave the market. In this case, a new pair of seller and buyer is assumed to arrive to the market; i.e., the number of active agents in the market is presumed to be constant over time. Intuitively, in case of, for example, a housing market, this

---

[4] Assuming that agents on the short side of the market are matched with probability $\kappa < 1$, the expressions below would be even more cumbersome, without qualitatively different findings.

amounts to positing that new apartments are rented at a rate similar to the one at which agents vacate apartments and start searching for new ones.

All agents of type B or S (buyer or seller) are assumed to have identical von Neumann-Morgenstern utility functions which can reflect a fairness preference as proposed by Fehr and Schmidt (1999). In case that an agent never trades, her utility is zero. If an agent of type $i \in \{S,B\}$ trades, then her utility u_i depends on the period $t \geq 0$ in which the agreement is reached, the accepted price $p \in [0,1]$, and also on an exogenous reference price $p_{\text{ref}} \in [0,1]$. This reference price is assumed to be the same for every agent and meant to capture a common notion of the "fair price" for the good; for example, the average rent per square meter published in municipal housing statistics.[5]

Agents are assumed to be averse towards deviations from the reference price; i.e., a deviation of price and reference price diminishes utility. Positive and negative differences may be judged asymmetrically: deviations to one's own favor (higher price for the seller, lower price for the buyer) are weighted by a parameter $\alpha_i \geq 0$, those to one's disfavor by $\beta_i \geq 0$. This would in principle allow utility functions to have a global maximum at the reference price, leading to an equilibrium in which the agents always agree exactly on that price. To avoid this trivial case we impose that $\alpha_i \in [0,1)$: a seller always prefers a higher price to a lower price, and a buyer always prefers a lower price to a higher one. Note that utility remains strictly monotonic in surplus as in Rubinstein and Wolinsky's original setting, but agents will now prefer a sure payoff to a lottery between two prices with the same expected value if one price deviates from the reference price to their advantage and the other, to their disadvantage.

Agents have stationary time preferences and discount future utility gains—for simplicity, by a common factor $\delta \in (0,1)$. Overall, preferences are assumed to be given by

$$u_S(p,p_{\text{ref}},t) = \delta^t \left(p - \alpha_S (p - p_{\text{ref}})^+ - \beta_S (p_{\text{ref}} - p)^+ \right)$$

for sellers and

$$u_B(p,p_{\text{ref}},t) = \delta^t \left(1 - p - \alpha_B (p_{\text{ref}} - p)^+ - \beta_B (p - p_{\text{ref}})^+ \right)$$

for buyers where $(x)^+ \equiv \max\{0,x\}$. The utility functions are illustrated in figure 5.1 (solid lines) for a trade in the current period. Note that the indicated kinks do not imply kinked aggregate demand or supply curves: Demand is zero for prices which imply negative buyer utility and then jumps to B. Similarly, aggregate supply drops from S to zero.

The considered preferences coincide with those proposed by Fehr and Schmidt (1999) if $p_{\text{ref}} = 0.5$ and fairness concern applies only to the two agents within a match, not those outside. We deem the restriction to one's direct trade partner (as in Brown et al. 2004) a good starting point—in particular, for markets with many buyers and sellers. As an extension of our analysis one might also consider agents

---

[5] For the effects of allowing distinct reference prices amongst buyers and sellers see section 6.2.

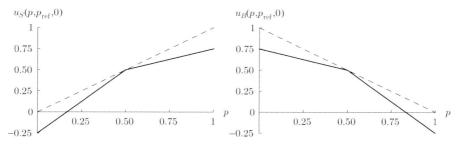

Fig. 5.1 Kinked utility functions of seller and buyer with $\alpha_i = \beta_i = 0.5$ and $p_{\text{ref}} = 0.5$

who compare themselves with, for example, the entire population. As in Ewerhart's (2006) investigation of two-player Rubinstein bargaining, we allow other prices than 0.5 to be considered as fair. We will not construct any detailed model of the "fair price" and initially consider it simply as given. We refer to Bolton et al. (2003) for a discussion of the determining roles played by past prices, competitor prices, and production costs.[6] However, we will later interpret p_{ref} as an endogenous fairness norm, as suggested by Binmore et al. (1993) and Binmore (1998), and require that its distance to the actual market outcome cannot exceed an exogenous threshold, which is interpreted as the maximal tolerated level of cognitive dissonance, in the long run.

5.2 Analysis of the Model

We will consider only symmetric equilibria in which all buyers and all sellers use the same sequentially rational strategy. These strategies may condition agents' actions on the current period t but not the particular history of play or agents' identities. Denote the value (or expected indirect utility) of being a seller in period t by $V_S(t)$, and the value of being a buyer in period t by $V_B(t)$. Let $p_B(t)$ be the price offered in equilibrium by the buyer if he is selected to make the proposal, and $p_S(t)$ the price offered in equilibrium by the seller if she is to make the proposal. Both are selected with equal probabilities, and so $p(t) \equiv 1/2[p_S(t) + p_B(t)]$ is the average price in the market in period t. When there is no danger of confusion we will suppress p_{ref} or t in agents' utility functions.

Whichever equilibrium arises, $\delta V_S(t) + \delta V_B(t) < 1$ must hold because

$$u_S(p, p_{\text{ref}}, 0) + u_B(p, p_{\text{ref}}, 0) \leq 1$$

---

[6] Also see Xia et al. (2004) for a survey of psychological and sociological research on price fairness, and Köszegi and Rabin (2006) for a model of preferences which depend on an endogenous reference point determined by rational expectations about outcomes.

for all $p, p_{\text{ref}}, \alpha, \beta \in [0,1]$ and $\delta < 1$. Therefore, every match must end with a transaction: If this were not the case, then there would be a period t in which at least one proposer quotes a price that is rejected in equilibrium. Now the proposer could gain by making a deviating offer p that satisfies $u_S(p,t) > \delta V_S(t+1)$ and $u_B(p,t) > \delta V_B(t+1)$: any sequentially rational responder strategy would entail acceptance of this offer.

In equilibrium, the buyer will always offer exactly $p_B = u_S^{-1}(\delta V_S(t+1))$ and the seller will always offer $p_S = u_B^{-1}(\delta V_B(t+1))$ in order to render the responder indifferent; these offers will be accepted immediately. Assuming that sellers are on the short side of the market or both types are equally numerous ($S \leq B$), the following equations must hold for all t:

$$u_S(p_B,t) = \delta V_S(t+1) \tag{5.1}$$

$$u_B(p_S,t) = \delta V_B(t+1) \tag{5.2}$$

$$V_S(t) = \frac{1}{2}[u_S(p_B,t) + u_S(p_S,t)] = \frac{1}{2}\left[\delta V_S(t+1) + u_S\left(u_B^{-1}[\delta V_B(t+1)]\right)\right] \tag{5.3}$$

$$\begin{aligned}
V_B(t) &= \frac{S}{B}\frac{1}{2}[u_B(p_S,t) + u_B(p_B,t)] + (1-\frac{S}{B})[\delta V_B(t+1)] \\
&= \frac{S}{2B}\left[\delta V_B(t+1) + u_B\left(u_S^{-1}[\delta V_S(t+1)]\right)\right] + (1-\frac{S}{B})[\delta V_B(t+1)] \tag{5.4}
\end{aligned}$$

$$p(t) = \frac{1}{2}(p_B + p_S) = \frac{1}{2}\left(u_B^{-1}[\delta V_B(t+1)] + u_S^{-1}[\delta V_S(t+1)]\right). \tag{5.5}$$

Analogous expressions characterize the strategic market equilibrium if buyers are on the short side of the market ($S > B$). We refer to Rubinstein (1989) for details.

5.2.1 Equilibrium Price

Equations (5.1)–(5.5) have a unique and time-independent solution $p(t) \equiv p^*$ with three cases that depend on the level of p_{ref} and the other parameters of the model (denote the fraction of buyers in the market by $b \equiv B/(S+B) \in (0,1)$):

$$p^* = \begin{cases}
\frac{(b+[2b(1-\delta)+\delta]\beta_S)p_{\text{ref}}(1-\alpha_B)+b(1-p_{\text{ref}})(1+\beta_S)}{[2b(1-\delta)+\delta](1-\alpha_B)(1+\beta_S)} & \text{if } p_{\text{ref}} \geq \bar{p}, \quad \text{(a)} \\[2em]
\begin{bmatrix} \delta p_{\text{ref}}[\beta_B+(2-\delta)(1+\beta_B)\beta_S+\delta\alpha_S+\alpha_B(1-\alpha_S\delta)] \\ +b[2+2\beta_B p_{\text{ref}}+\beta_S(2-\delta)(1-\delta+[1-2\delta+\beta_B(2-3\delta)]p_{\text{ref}}) \\ -\delta(2+\alpha_B p_{\text{ref}}+3\beta_B p_{\text{ref}}+\alpha_S[1-\delta-p_{\text{ref}}+(2-\alpha_B)\delta p_{\text{ref}}])] \end{bmatrix} \\ \Big/ \begin{bmatrix} 4b(1+\beta_B)(1+\beta_S)+2(1-4b)(1+\beta_B)(1+\beta_S)\delta \\ -\delta^2[2-\alpha_S(1-b)-4b+\alpha_B(\alpha_S-1)(1-b) \\ +(1-3b)(\beta_B+\beta_S+\beta_B\beta_S)] \end{bmatrix} & \text{if } \underline{p} < p_{\text{ref}} < \bar{p}, \text{ (b)} \\[2em]
\frac{(b-[2b(1-\delta)+\delta]\alpha_S)p_{\text{ref}}(1+\beta_B)+b(1-p_{\text{ref}})(1-\alpha_S)}{[2b(1-\delta)+\delta](1-\alpha_S)(1+\beta_B)} & \text{if } p_{\text{ref}} \leq \underline{p} \quad \text{(c)}
\end{cases}$$

with $\bar{p} = \dfrac{b(2-\delta)(1+\beta_S)}{b(2-\delta)(1+\beta_S)+(1-b)\delta(1-\alpha_B)}$ and $\underline{p} = \dfrac{b\delta(1-\alpha_S)}{(2b-3b\delta+\delta)(1+\beta_B)+b\delta(1-\alpha_S)}$. $\tag{5.6}$

p^*, p_B, p_S, p_{ref}, $p^\dagger$

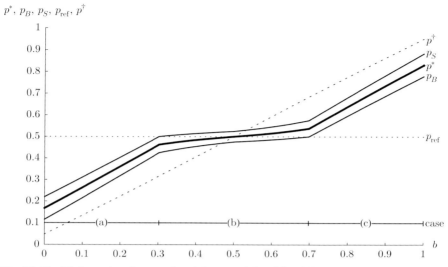

Fig. 5.2 Equilibrium prices for $\alpha_i = \beta_i = 0.3$, $p_{\text{ref}} = 0.5$ and $\delta = 0.95$

This simplifies somewhat if all fairness parameters are equal; for $\alpha_S = \alpha_B = \beta_S = \beta_B \equiv \gamma$ we have

$$p^* = \begin{cases} \dfrac{b(\gamma+1)-\gamma[2b\gamma+(2b-1)(1-\gamma)p]p_{\text{ref}}}{(1-\gamma^2)[2b(1-p)+p]} & \text{if } p_{\text{ref}} \geq \bar{p}, \quad \text{(a)} \\[2ex] \dfrac{\gamma p(-p\gamma+\gamma+2)p_{\text{ref}}+b\left[-p+\gamma\left((1-p)^2+2[\gamma(1-p)^2-2p+1]p_{\text{ref}}\right)+1\right]}{p[(\gamma+1)^2-(\gamma^2+1)p]+2b[(\gamma+1)^2(1-p)^2-\gamma p^2]} & \text{if } \underline{p} < p_{\text{ref}} < \bar{p}, \quad \text{(b)} \\[2ex] \dfrac{b\left(2[p-\gamma(1-p)]p_{\text{ref}}\gamma-\gamma+1\right)-\gamma(\gamma+1)pp_{\text{ref}}}{\left(1-\gamma^2\right)[2b(1-p)+p]} & \text{if } p_{\text{ref}} \leq \underline{p} \quad \text{(c)} \end{cases}$$

with $\qquad \bar{p} = \dfrac{b(2-\delta)(1+\gamma)}{2b(1-\delta+\gamma)+\delta(1-\gamma)} \qquad$ and $\qquad \underline{p} = \dfrac{b\delta(1-\gamma)}{2b(1-\delta-2\delta\gamma+\gamma)+\delta(1+\gamma)}$.

Figure 5.2 visualizes this term.[7] The *thin solid lines* indicate the proposer-specific prices p_S and p_B which give rise to the average market price p^*. Their intersections with the *dotted reference price line* coincide with the case boundaries.

In the first case, case (a), the fair price p_{ref} is so high that $p_B \leq p_S \leq p_{\text{ref}}$. This means that both the seller and the buyer would offer a price below the fair price in equilibrium. In the last case, case (c), the fair price p_{ref} is so low that $p_S \geq p_B \geq p_{\text{ref}}$, and both seller and buyer would offer a price above the fair price in equilibrium. The intermediate case, case (b), with $p_B < p_{\text{ref}} < p_S$ entails that if the seller is to propose

---

[7] The price formulas shown above apply when $S \leq B$, i.e., $b = B/(B+S) \geq 0.5$. The expressions in case of $b < 0.5$ are symmetric (see the left half of figure 5.2). The above term for case (a) becomes relevant under $S \leq B$ only if p_{ref} is very high. In particular, figure 5.2 actually shows the price arising in case (a) of the solution for $S > B$.

a price, she suggests one above the fair price, while if the buyer is to propose a price, this price will be below the fair price.[8]

Figure 5.2 illustrates the key effect of fairness concern in a matching market: in a neighborhood of p_{ref}, the equilibrium price is much less sensitive to changes in the buyer–seller ratio than what would be the case without social preferences; i.e., the price is stickier. More formally, let

$$p^{\dagger} \equiv p^*\Big|_{\alpha_i = \beta_i = 0} = \frac{b}{2b(1-\delta)+\delta}$$

be the associated equilibrium price for standard preferences without fairness concern (*broken line* in figure 5.2).[9] We will focus on markets—as characterized by the preference parameters α_i, β_i, δ and p_{ref}—for which p_{ref} arises as the equilibrium price for *some* fraction of buyers in the market. We denote this buyer share by $\tilde{b}$, i.e., $p^*\big|_{b=\tilde{b}} = p_{\text{ref}}$.[10] Then the following is true:

Proposition 5.1. *The market price is less sensitive to changes in the fraction b of buyers in the market in a neighborhood of $\tilde{b}$ if* $\max\{\alpha_B, \alpha_S, \beta_B, \beta_S\} > 0$ *than if agents have no fairness concern:*

$$0 < \frac{\partial p^*}{\partial b}\Big|_{b=\tilde{b}} < \frac{\partial p^{\dagger}}{\partial b}\Big|_{b=\tilde{b}}.$$

Proof. Buyer shares b in a sufficiently small neighborhood of $\tilde{b}$ pertain to case (b): sellers propose a price above p_{ref} and buyers propose a price below p_{ref}. The derivatives of p^* and $p^{\dagger}$ with respect to b and evaluated at $\tilde{b}$ are therefore

$$\frac{\partial p^*}{\partial b}\Big|_{b=\tilde{b}} = \left\{ \begin{array}{l} \left[(\delta-1)[2p_{\text{ref}}(\beta_B+\beta_S+2)+\beta_S(\delta-2)+\alpha_S\delta-p_{\text{ref}}(-\alpha_B+\alpha_S+3\beta_B+\beta_S+4)\delta-2]^2 \right] \\ /\left[\begin{array}{l} \delta[\beta_S(\delta-2)+\alpha_S\delta-2][2(\beta_B+1)(\beta_S+1)-(\alpha_B(\alpha_S-1)-\alpha_S+\beta_B+\beta_B\beta_S+\beta_S+2)\delta \\ +p_{\text{ref}}((\beta_B+1)\beta_S(\delta-2)-(\alpha_S+\beta_B)\delta+\alpha_B[2\beta_B(\delta-1)+\alpha_S\delta+\delta-2])] \end{array} \right] \end{array} \right.$$

and

$$\frac{\partial p^{\dagger}}{\partial b}\Big|_{b=\tilde{b}} = \frac{[(\delta-2)(p_{\text{ref}}-1)\beta_S+(3\delta-2)p_{\text{ref}}\beta_B+\delta(p_{\text{ref}}-1)\alpha_S+4(\delta-1)p_{\text{ref}}+2]^2}{\delta[2-\delta\alpha_S+(\delta-2)(p_{\text{ref}}-1)\beta_S-2p_{\text{ref}}\alpha_B+\delta p_{\text{ref}}(\alpha_B+\alpha_S+\beta_B)]^2},$$

---

[8] No further cases arise because $p_S \geq p_B$ and $0 \leq \underline{p} \leq \bar{p} \leq 1$. The case boundaries can, of course, also be expressed in terms of b rather than p_{ref}, $\underline{p}$, and $\bar{p}$: case (a) holds if $b \leq \underline{b}$, case (b) if $\underline{b} < b < \tilde{b}$, and case (c) if $\bar{b} \leq b$ with $\underline{b} = [\delta p_{\text{ref}}(1-\alpha_B)]/[(2-\delta)(1-p_{\text{ref}})(1+\beta_S)+\delta p_{\text{ref}}(1-\alpha_B)]$ and $\bar{b} = [\delta p_{\text{ref}}(1+\beta_B)]/[(3\delta-2)p_{\text{ref}}(1+\beta_B)+\delta(1-p_{\text{ref}})(1-\alpha_S)]$.

[9] Again, we only provide explicit expressions for $S \leq B$, but analogous statements apply when $S > B$.

[10] A fraction $\tilde{b}$ of buyers which allows p_{ref} to be an equilibrium price need not exist; for example, when δ is small and p_{ref} is either very high or low. However, one can check that for any given values of α_i, β_i, and δ, there exists an interval of prices p which would arise in equilibrium provided that $p_{\text{ref}} = p$ for some $\tilde{b} \in (0,1)$.

respectively. The range $[\underline{p}_{\mathrm{ref}}, \bar{p}_{\mathrm{ref}}]$ of reference prices p_{ref} for which $\tilde{b}$ exists (see footnote 10) can be identified by solving

$$p^*\Big|_{b=\frac{1}{2},\, p_{\mathrm{ref}}=\underline{p}_{\mathrm{ref}}} = \underline{p}_{\mathrm{ref}} \quad \text{and} \quad p^*\Big|_{b=1-,\, p_{\mathrm{ref}}=\bar{p}_{\mathrm{ref}}} = \bar{p}_{\mathrm{ref}}$$

because p^* is increasing in b. It can then be checked numerically that the claimed inequality holds for any $p_{\mathrm{ref}} \in [\underline{p}_{\mathrm{ref}}, \bar{p}_{\mathrm{ref}}]$. $\square$

The driving force for the decreased sensitivity of prices near p_{ref}[11] is the local increase in concavity of the agents' utility function: Price proposals by buyers and sellers that are below and above the reference price, respectively, ex ante amount to a lottery, towards which both agents are risk-averse. In order to avoid this lottery, they are willing to accept a proposal (and thereby generate a safe return) which is closer to p_{ref} than it would be for agents whose utility is linear everywhere. Importantly, decreased price sensitivity would also be obtained if the baseline utility were already strictly concave rather than linear in price below and above p_{ref}. Moreover, one could also assume an everywhere differentiable utility function without changing our qualitative findings. For example,

$$\tilde{u}_S(p, p_{\mathrm{ref}}, t) = \delta^t \Big[p + \frac{1}{2}(p - p_{\mathrm{ref}}) \big(-\alpha_S + \beta_S - (\alpha_S + \beta_S)\tanh[c(p - p_{\mathrm{ref}})] \big) \Big]$$

is smooth and produces the same stickiness as u_S for large $c > 0$ (it converges uniformly to u_S for $c \to \infty$). The aspect of Fehr-Schmidt preferences which is crucial in our context is that fairness concern increases risk aversion in a neighborhood of the reference price.

When agents have *no* concern for fairness, the market price responds more to changes in the buyer–seller ratio the closer δ is to unity, i.e.,

$$\frac{\partial^2 p^\dagger}{\partial b \partial \delta} = \frac{\delta(2b-1) + 2b}{(2b(1-\delta) + \delta)^3} > 0 \,,$$

and $\lim_{\delta \to 1} \partial p^\dagger / \partial b = 1$. Therefore it is somewhat surprising that the larger the stickiness or decreased sensitivity of prices near p_{ref} in case of $\alpha_i > 0$ or $\beta_i > 0$, the less friction there is: when agents *have* concern for fairness, the larger δ, the less p^* increases in b. This even gives rise to a flat price $p^* \equiv p_{\mathrm{ref}}$ for all buyer–seller ratios pertaining to case (b) in the limit $\delta \to 1$:

Proposition 5.2. *Suppose that* $\max\{\alpha_B, \alpha_S, \beta_B, \beta_S\} > 0$. *Then, first, there exists some* $\delta' \in (0,1)$ *such that the market price's sensitivity to changes in the fraction* b *of buyers in a neighborhood of* $\tilde{b}$ *is decreasing in* δ *for any* $\delta > \delta'$. *Second, the*

---

[11] Whilst the strict inequalities in proposition 5.1 obviously hold on an entire interval around $\tilde{b}$, sensitivity of p^* with respect to the buyer–seller ratio need not be reduced at *every* b: it may locally be greater than for standard preferences near the boundary between cases (a and b), or (b and c). The average slope of p^* over the range of buyer–seller ratios pertaining to case (b) is, however, always smaller for positive α_i or β_i than for $\alpha_i = \beta_i = 0$.

price sensitivity $(\partial p^*/\partial b)\big|_{b=b'}$ *converges to zero as* $\delta \to 1$ *for any* b' *pertaining to case (b) of equation (5.6) (in particular, for* $b = \tilde{b}$).

Proof. The cross-derivative $\partial^2 p^*/(\partial b \partial \delta)$ is very unwieldy, but continuous in δ. It therefore suffices to evaluate its limit as $\delta \to 1$ in order to prove the first claim. One obtains[12]

$$\lim_{\delta \to 1} \left(\frac{\partial^2 p^*}{\partial b \partial \delta} \Big|_{b=\tilde{b}} \right) = - \frac{(1 - p_{\mathrm{ref}})(2 - \alpha_S + \beta_S)}{(b-1)^2(\alpha_B + \alpha_S - \alpha_B \alpha_S + \beta_B + \beta_S + \beta_B \beta_S)} < 0 .$$

To see that the second claim is true, note simply that $\lim_{\delta \to 1} p^* = p_{\mathrm{ref}}$ wherever case (b) applies.   □

The economic intuition for this comparative static result is connected to the different response, as δ increases, of the bargaining advantages conferred by (i) being on the short side of the market and (ii) currently being in the proposer position. To see this, first review the case *without* fairness concern. For concreteness, consider a situation in which buyers are on the short side of the market (i.e., $b < 0.5$). Parameter b directly affects sellers' continuation values, which are associated with rejecting an offer: if the current price is turned down, the seller remains unmatched in the next period with probability $1 - b$. This creates a bargaining advantage for buyers relative to sellers. Because it varies in b, so does p^*. The effect of this advantage is, however, attenuated by the equal distribution of another bargaining advantage: the right to make the first proposal. The value of this temporary "monopoly position" is decreasing in δ. So bargaining outcomes become increasingly driven only by the short side's matching advantage. It is true that this advantage also becomes less important as δ increases: waiting for a rematching bothers sellers less and less in absolute terms. However, the asymmetric matching advantage turns out to vanish more slowly than the symmetrically distributed proposer advantage. Hence, prices become more responsive to the buyers' matching advantage, as parameterized by b.

With fairness concern, the bargaining advantage provided by the right to make the next proposal becomes more pronounced: sellers still hate accepting a low price, but now they are even less attracted by the lottery of getting a more decent price (above p_{ref}) or facing the same proposal (below p_{ref}) again next period than without fairness concern. An analogous statement applies to buyers. Critically, this (still symmetrically distributed) proposer advantage no longer vanishes as $\delta \to 1$: locally risk-averse responders will prefer to accept a price near the benchmark even though there is the chance to almost immediately make a counteroffer. Agents on the long side must, of course, expect a somewhat greater delay until they get to make an offer after rejecting a proposal, and so their continuation value is still lower, the more asymmetric both population sizes are. However, as was also true without fairness concern, not being rematched immediately becomes less and less of a concern for large δ. In the limit, as $\delta \to 1$, the matching advantage becomes negligible relative to the discounting-invariant part of the advantage enjoyed by any agent—from

---

[12] Again, we focus on the case of $b \geq 1/2$, with an analogous expression applying to $b < 1/2$.

the short side or the long side of the market—who has been drawn as the current proposer.

5.2.2 Self-confirming Price Conventions

The reference price was so far treated as exogenously given by, for example, the equal split considered by Fehr and Schmidt (1999), official rental statistics, or perhaps a recommended retail price. In line with a now sizeable economic literature, we presumed that agreements which are not in line with this benchmark entail a subjective penalty. That agents who consider themselves as fair persons attach an additional cost to concluding unfair deals also broadly fits psychologists' view. However, psychological research on *cognitive dissonance* in the tradition of Festinger (1957) (see Nail et al. 2004 or Cooper 2007 for recent overviews and, e.g., Akerlof and Dickens 1982 for an economic perspective on the literature) suggests that agents who stoically bear these costs are not the only possibility. An agent may rather adjust his notion of fairness, and this is particularly likely if deals are not even on average in line with her or his current notion of fairness.[13] We will therefore consider the possibility of the reference price being *endogenous* price and at least partially responsive to economic fundamentals. The reference price could, for instance, plausibly arise as an average of past prices such as official rental statistics, or depend on history in a more complex way. It is meant to capture a broadly shared notion of what constitutes a fair deal, which will plausibly be adapted if it should persistently and noticeably fall out of line with agents' actual experience.

This variation of the above baseline model fits nicely with Ken Binmore's (1994; 1998) theory of distributional justice and the still intriguing experimental findings of Binmore et al. (1993). This study investigates the role of focal points in bargaining and highlights that subjects' notion of a fair division is no universal constant but rather quite path-dependent. Specifically, Binmore et al. first made distinct surplus divisions focal to their subjects by having them bargain with different computer programs in the initial stage of the experiment, one program insisting on 50:50 splits, another one on 75:25 splits, and so on. The subjects switched between the proposer and responder roles in order to become familiarized with both perspectives. Then participants who had played the same program were matched and bargained with each other. The result was that subjects—in fundamentally identical bargaining situations—agreed on different surplus divisions depending on which divisions they had been conditioned to in the initial stage: The bargaining outcomes clustered around the respective induced focal division. And, more surprisingly, most subjects ended up describing the agreements that they had reached as particularly fair. What participants perceived as fair reflected their respective payoff experience (also see Binmore et al. 1991).

---

[13] This is analogous, for instance, to car drivers who are outraged by the common 5–10% gasoline price increase during public holidays with peak demand, but then come to "accept" an altogether higher price level within a few months (think of recent increases above \$3.5/gallon or €1.4/litre).

$p^*, \bar{p}, \underline{p}, p_{\text{ref}}$

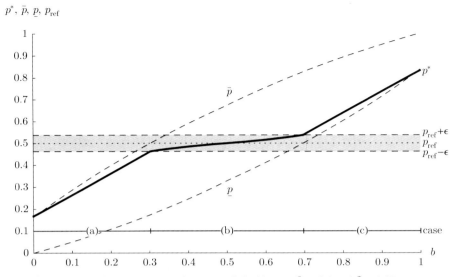

Fig. 5.3 Self-confirming price convention $p_{\text{ref}} = 0.5$ with $\alpha_i = \beta_i = 0.3$ and $\delta = 0.95$

Adjusting one's notion of a fair deal in avoidance of prolonged cognitive dissonance is likely to be subjectively costly itself (see Konow 2000 for a theory of decision making which investigates this assumption in detail). It is worthwhile to incur the adjustment cost only if the dissonance cost associated with the conclusion of deals that are unfair according to the current fairness standard is even higher; i.e., if in our context, the gap between p_{ref} and the average equilibrium price p^* is large enough. Denote by $\varepsilon \geq 0$ the size of the gap between the current reference price and the market price that agents would still tolerate rather than adapting their fairness benchmark in line with cognitive dissonance theory. In other words, agents are assumed to abandon the current reference price p_{ref} at some point in time if $p^* \notin [p_{\text{ref}} - \varepsilon, p_{\text{ref}} + \varepsilon]$. Such prices p_{ref} will be referred to as ε-*unstable*. In contrast, a reference price p_{ref} which gives rise to an average equilibrium price p^* inside the respective ε-neighborhood of p_{ref} would not be changed; it will be referred to as an ε-*stable* price convention. We will assume the cost of adjustment which is indirectly measured by parameter ε to be small but positive; i.e., we consider $\varepsilon > 0$ in the following.

An ε-stable price p_{ref} is *self-confirming* in the following sense: agents regard p_{ref} as fair—this gives rise to an average market price in an ε-neighborhood of p_{ref}, and this in turn confirms p_{ref} as agents' reference price. As illustrated in figure 5.3, the property of a given reference price to be self-confirming can be robust to quite sizeable fluctuations in the buyer–seller ratio. It can be checked that if the tolerable gap between the fair and the equilibrium price is such that

$$\varepsilon \geq \varepsilon_{\min}(p_{\text{ref}}) \equiv \frac{1-\delta}{\delta} \max\left\{ \frac{p_{\text{ref}}}{1-\alpha_S}, \frac{1-p_{\text{ref}}}{1-\alpha_B} \right\}, \tag{5.7}$$

then *any* buyer–seller ratio for which the seller and buyer prices are above and below p_{ref}, respectively, i.e., any market for which case (b) applies, makes the given p_{ref} self-confirming.[14] Fairness concern may thus not only give rise to re-duced short-run sensitivity of prices, but it can cause prices to be sticky; i.e., to be insensitive to variations of b in the long run, too.

One can also look at figure 5.3 from an alternative perspective. Suppose that the buyer–seller ratio is fixed at some level within case (b) and one observes an equilibrium price $p^* \in [0.5 - \varepsilon; 0.5 + \varepsilon]$ as depicted. Then $p_{ref} = 0.5$ would be an ε-stable price convention for the given buyer–seller ratio. However, it is not the only one. If, for instance, ε is so large as to satisfy inequality (5.7) for $p_{ref} = \underline{p}$ and for $p_{ref} = \bar{p}$, then *any* reference price $\tilde{p}_{ref} \in [\underline{p}, \bar{p}]$ would be ε-stable: the monotonic-ity of the two alternative determinants of $\varepsilon_{min}(\cdot)$ in p_{ref} [namely, $p_{ref}/(1 - \alpha_S)$ and $(1 - p_{ref})/(1 - \alpha_B)$] implies that $\varepsilon \geq \varepsilon_{min}(\tilde{p}_{ref})$ holds for any $\underline{p} \leq \tilde{p}_{ref} \leq \bar{p}$. There-fore, recalling ε_{min}'s construction, any such $\tilde{p}_{ref}$ would be self-confirming. Smaller thresholds ε for the subconscious "correction" of cognitive dissonance, of course, imply a smaller range of ε-stable reference prices. However, there must still exist an entire interval of self-confirming price conventions:

Proposition 5.3. *For any $b \in (0,1)$ and $\varepsilon > 0$ there exists a non-empty interval $[\underline{p}, \check{p}] \subseteq [\underline{p}, \bar{p}]$ such that any $p \in [\underline{p}, \check{p}]$ would constitute a self-confirming reference price; i.e.,*

$$p^*\big|_{p_{ref}=p} \in [p - \varepsilon, p + \varepsilon].$$

Proof. Note that for any $b \in (0,1)$, there exists a unique $p^0 \in [\underline{p}, \bar{p}]$ which is 0-stable; i.e., $p^*\big|_{p_{ref}=p^0} = p^0$. This can be evaluated as

$$p^0 = \frac{b(\beta_S(\delta - 2) + \alpha_S\delta - 2)}{(\alpha_B - \beta_B - 2 + b(4 - \alpha_B + \alpha_S + 3\beta_B + \beta_S))\delta - 2b(2 + \beta_B + \beta_S)}$$

from equation (5.6) case (b). It then follows directly from the continuity of p^* in p_{ref} that $p^*\big|_{p_{ref}=p} \in [p - \varepsilon, p + \varepsilon]$ is satisfied for any p in a sufficiently small neigh-borhood of p^0. $\qquad\square$

The only situation which does not create any long-run multiplicity of fair price conventions would be the one in which adjustments of agents' fairness notion entails no costs at all and which therefore involves $\varepsilon = 0$. Leaving this possibility of a perfectly flexible (and then perhaps vacuous) sense of fairness aside, there always exists a *continuum of ε-stable price conventions* for the same market environment. This is an effect of fairness concern that comes on top of reduced short- and long-run sensitivity of prices regarding changes in the buyer–seller ratio, as discussed earlier. Thinking of independent housing markets in city A and city B as an example, the observed price levels could differ by as much as $\bar{p} - \underline{p}$ even though both have exactly the same fundamentals (identical marginal costs and marginal products of housing,

---

[14] Given that p^* is monotone in b, the potential gap between p^* and p_{ref} for case (b) is largest at the case boundaries. So the expression for $\varepsilon_{min}(p_{ref})$ follows from evaluating $|p_{ref} - p^*|$ at $\underline{p}$ and $\bar{p}$.

same numbers of active buyers and sellers, identical parameters α_i, β_i, and δ). The only difference would be that, for instance, because the collection of rental statistics initially had a bias in one but not the other community, cities A and B have different reference prices. These need not necessarily have been self-confirming from the beginning: a very high initial reference rent in city A will presumably give rise to a relatively high initial market price and a long-run equilibrium p_A^* near $\bar{p}$; a low initial one in city B would give rise to p_B^* near $\underline{p}$.[15]

Echoing the comparative static findings in proposition 5.2, the possible history dependence caused by fairness concern does not vanish as $\delta \to 1$; rather, the range of self-confirming reference prices becomes larger as δ increases:

Proposition 5.4. *For any given* $\varepsilon > 0$, *the size of the interval* $[\underline{p}, \check{p}] \subseteq [\underline{p}, \bar{p}]$ *such that* $p^*|_{p_{\mathrm{ref}}=p} \in [p-\varepsilon, p+\varepsilon]$ *holds for every* $p \in [\underline{p}, \check{p}]$ *is increasing in* δ; *i.e.,*

$$\frac{\partial(\check{p}-\underline{p})}{\partial\delta} > 0.$$

Furthermore, $[\underline{p}, \check{p}]$ *converges to* $[\underline{p}, \bar{p}]$ *as* $\delta \to 1$.

Proof. The second part of the proposition follows directly from the fact that

$$\lim_{\delta \to 1} p^* = p_{\mathrm{ref}}$$

for any $p_{\mathrm{ref}} \in [\underline{p}, \bar{p}]$.

The endpoints of interval $[\underline{p}, \check{p}]$ can be computed by solving $p^*|_{p_{\mathrm{ref}}=\check{p}} \equiv \check{p} - \varepsilon$ for $\check{p}$ and $p^*|_{p_{\mathrm{ref}}=\underline{p}} \equiv \underline{p} + \varepsilon$ for $\underline{p}$ in case (b) of equation (5.6). One obtains

$$\check{p} = \left\{ \frac{\left[\begin{array}{l}\delta(2(1+\beta_B)(1+\beta_S)-[2+\alpha_B(-1+\alpha_S)-\alpha_S+\beta_B+\beta_S+\beta_B\beta_S]\delta)\varepsilon+b[2+4(1+\beta_B)\varepsilon-\delta[2+\alpha_S\\ +8(1+\beta_B)\varepsilon]+\delta^2(\alpha_S+[4+\alpha_B(-1+\alpha_S)-\alpha_S+3\beta_B]\varepsilon)+\beta_S(-2+\delta)[-1+\delta+(1+\beta_B)(-2+3\delta)\varepsilon]]\end{array}\right]}{7\left[(-1+\delta)(-2b(2+\beta_B+\beta_S)+[-2+\alpha_B-\beta_B+b(4-\alpha_B+\alpha_S+3\beta_B+\beta_S)]\delta)\right]} \right.$$

and

$$\underline{p} = \left\{ \frac{\left[\begin{array}{l}\delta(-2(1+\beta_B)(1+\beta_S)+[2+\alpha_B(-1+\alpha_S)-\alpha_S+\beta_B+\beta_S+\beta_B\beta_S]\delta)\varepsilon+b[2-4(1+\beta_B)\varepsilon-\beta_S(-2+\delta)\\ [1-\delta+(1+\beta_B)(-2+3\delta)\varepsilon]+\delta(-2+8(1+\beta_B)\varepsilon+(-4+\alpha_B-3\beta_B)\delta\varepsilon+\alpha_S[-1+\delta(1+\varepsilon-\alpha_B\varepsilon)])]\end{array}\right]}{7\left[(-1+\delta)(-2b(2+\beta_B+\beta_S)+[-2+\alpha_B-\beta_B+b(4-\alpha_B+\alpha_S+3\beta_B+\beta_S)]\delta)\right]} \right..$$

The size of the interval therefore equals

$$\check{p} - \underline{p} = \left\{ \frac{\left[\begin{array}{l}2\varepsilon[4b(1+\beta_B)(1+\beta_S)-2(-1+4b)(1+\beta_B)(1+\beta_S)\delta+(-2+\alpha_B+\alpha_S\\ -\alpha_B\alpha_S-\beta_B-\beta_S-\beta_B\beta_S+b[4+\alpha_B(-1+\alpha_S)-\alpha_S+3\beta_S+3\beta_B(1+\beta_S)])\delta^2]\end{array}\right]}{7\left[(-1+\delta)(-2b(2+\beta_B+\beta_S)+[-2+\alpha_B-\beta_B+b(4-\alpha_B+\alpha_S+3\beta_B+\beta_S)]\delta)\right]} \right..$$

---

[15] We do not want to suggest any particular process of adjustment. As long as it is *monotonic* in the sense that the current reference price p_{ref} rises (falls) if it is at least ε below (above) the induced equilibrium price p^* and sufficiently gradual to involve no big overshooting, a price convention will be reached near the corresponding boundary $\underline{p}$ or $\bar{p}$. Note, however, that such dynamics would have to operate on a much larger time scale than the back-and-forth of offers considered in the baseline model. Otherwise, it would be inappropriate to assume that agents behave as in a truly stationary market environment.

p^{**}, $\bar{p}$, $\underline{p}$, p_{ref}, p°

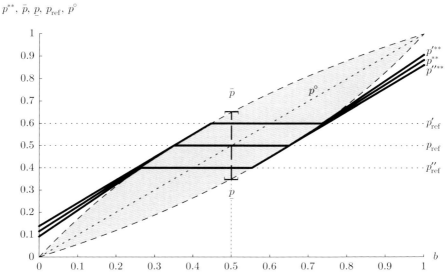

Fig. 5.4 ε-stable range and equilibrium prices for $\alpha_i = \beta_i = 0.3$ and $\delta \to 1$

The partial derivative $\partial(\check{p} - p)/\partial\delta$ is again quite unwieldy, but can be shown to be strictly positive for any b pertaining to case (b) given the restrictions on α_i, β_i, and δ introduced above. $\qquad\qquad\square$

This comparative static result can also be interpreted as saying that the larger the discount factor δ (i.e., the less friction is associated with rejection of an offer), the smaller the tolerable degree of cognitive dissonance ε which suffices to give rise to a *given* interval of ε-stable price conventions. In the limit of $\delta \to 1$, the equilibrium market price p^* is constant for the entire range of buyer–seller ratios pertaining to case (b). Then an arbitrarily small $\varepsilon > 0$ will render the entire interval $[\underline{p}, \bar{p}]$ self-confirming: any reference price $p_{\text{ref}} \in [\underline{p}, \bar{p}]$ implies an equilibrium in which the actual average price happens to be p_{ref}. This is illustrated in figure 5.4. It shows the limit of equilibrium market prices for three different reference prices. For each one, there is a range of buyer shares b which would give rise to it in equilibrium. So any reference price inside the indicated grey intervals $[\underline{p}, \bar{p}]$ would be self-confirming in a robust sense; namely, for an interval of buyer shares.

Note that the difference between the prices proposed in equilibrium by a buyer and by a seller disappears as $\delta \to 1$. They approach

$$p^{**} \equiv \lim_{\delta \to 1} p^* = \begin{cases} b\dfrac{1 - p_{\text{ref}}\alpha_B}{1 - \alpha_B} + (1 - b)\dfrac{p_{\text{ref}}\beta_S}{1 + \beta_S} & \text{if } p_{\text{ref}} \geq \bar{p} \quad \text{(a)} \\[2mm] p_{\text{ref}} & \text{if } \underline{p} < p_{\text{ref}} < \bar{p} \ \text{(b)} \\[2mm] b\dfrac{1 + p_{\text{ref}}\beta_B}{1 + \beta_B} - (1 - b)\dfrac{p_{\text{ref}}\alpha_S}{1 - \alpha_S} & \text{if } p_{\text{ref}} \leq \underline{p} \quad \text{(c)} \end{cases}$$

$$\text{with } \bar{p} = \frac{b(1 + \beta_S)}{b(1 + \beta_S) + (1 - b)(1 - \alpha_B)} \quad \text{and} \quad \underline{p} = \frac{b(1 - \alpha_S)}{b(1 - \alpha_S) + (1 - b)(1 + \beta_B)} \ .$$

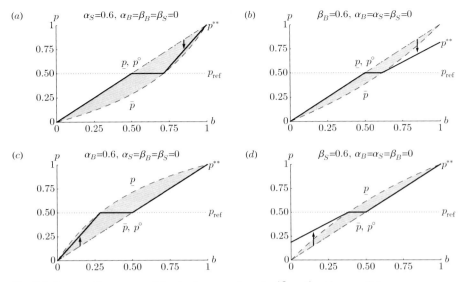

Fig. 5.5 Ranges of approx. sustained reference prices for $(\delta \to 1)$ and $p_{\text{ref}} = 0.5$

This would simplify to[16]

$$p^{**} = b \equiv p^{\circ} \,,$$

for "standard" preferences with $\alpha_i = \beta_i = 0$: the limit market price corresponds exactly to sellers' market power as measured by the relative abundance of buyers. So the *dotted* 45° *line* in figure 5.4 illustrates how aversion to unfairly favorable deals $(\alpha_i > 0)$ and aversion to unfairly unfavorable deals $(\beta_i > 0)$ shifts the equilibrium price p°; for example, a low standard equilibrium price p° is shifted up towards $p_{\text{ref}} = 0.5$ if buyers are scarce and, analogously, is shifted down towards $p_{\text{ref}} = 0.5$ if sellers are scarce.

This qualitative observation does *not* require that both buyers and sellers are concerned about fairness, and neither that there is aversion against both unfairly favorable and unfavorable agreements. As illustrated in figures 5.5(a) and (b), in order for p° to be shifted downwards in a sellers' market, it is sufficient that either $\alpha_S > 0$ or $\beta_B > 0$; i.e., sellers suffer from favorable deals or buyers suffer from unfavorable deals (relative to the current notion of a fair price). Similarly, figures 5.5(c) and (d) illustrate that the standard equilibrium price is shifted upwards in a buyers' market if either buyers subjectively suffer from unfairly favorable deals $(\alpha_B > 0)$ or sellers exhibit aversion to unfavorable deals $(\beta_S > 0)$.

---

[16] Note that equilibrium prices do not violate the tenet that agents on the short side of the market can appropriate all surplus. As first pointed out by Gale, the *flows* rather than the stocks of buyers and sellers need to be considered. Because they are equal in a stationary market, any $p \in [0, 1]$ would be a competitive equilibrium in our setting whilst only p^* as characterized by equations (5.1)–(5.5) is also a strategic equilibrium. See Gale (1986a; 1986b), Rubinstein (1989), Rubinstein and Wolinsky (1990), and Kunimoto and Serrano (2004) for a more detailed discussion.

The equilibrium price curves and ranges of self-confirming prices in figure 5.4 can be understood as the superposition of the four components of figure 5.5: both aversion against unfairly favorable deals by the buyer ($\alpha_B > 0$) and aversion against unfairly unfavorable deals on the part of the seller ($\beta_S > 0$), first, cause price stickiness in a *left* neighborhood of the buyer–seller ratio $b = p_{ref}$; and, second, create an entire interval of prices *above* the standard equilibrium level $p°$ that would remain in place as a self-confirming endogenous reference price. Analogously, positive levels of α_S (seller suffers from unduly favorable deals) and positive levels of β_B (buyer incurs additional subjective costs from paying more than p_{ref}) create price stickiness in a *right* neighborhood of $b = p_{ref}$ and, moreover, allow for ε-stable reference prices below the corresponding level of $p°$. The effects of α_S, α_B, β_S, and β_B complement one another. As can easily be checked, the magnitude of each such effect grows monotonically in the corresponding levels α_i and β_i. For instance, the bigger α_B or β_S,[17] the greater the scope *ceteris paribus* for a price above the standard level $p°$ to be sustained as the self-confirming fair level. Or, for any given current reference price p_{ref}, the bigger α_B or β_S, the greater the downwards stickiness the equilibrium price exhibits, in the sense of responding less when the share of buyers in the market drops from $b = p_{ref}$. The latter effect will show itself in the form of a larger interval of buyer shares b that give rise to $p^{**} = p_{ref}$. For instance,

$$p^{**} = p_{ref} = 0.5 \text{ iff } b \in \left[\frac{1 - \alpha_B}{(1 - \alpha_B) + (1 + \beta_S)}, \frac{1 + \beta_B}{(1 - \alpha_S) + (1 + \beta_B)} \right] ,$$

and it is easily checked that the left endpoint of the interval decreases in α_B and β_S, whilst the right endpoint increases in α_S and β_B.

Returning to the stylized example of a stationary housing market, these comparative static considerations indicate that the more pronounced agents' concern with fairness, the bigger the scope for persistent price differences between two structurally identical cities A and B (in particular, involving the same reference-dependent preferences amongst the respective tenants and landlords). Identical average prices should only be expected to arise if fairness does not matter; i.e., when $\alpha_i = \beta_i = 0$ for $i \in \{B, S\}$.

5.3 Concluding Remarks

We have obtained three main qualitative results from our analysis of fairness in a stylized model of decentralized trade. The first, very broad finding may well be the most significant one: fairness concern can be expected to affect equilibrium market prices in a persistent way, despite the availability of complete contracts and complete information. This prediction contrasts with most of the experimental literature on behavior in markets—presumably because it has mainly looked at double auctions so far.

---

[17] For example, $\frac{\partial \bar{p}}{\partial \beta_S} = \frac{(1-b)b(2-\delta)\delta(1-\alpha_B)}{[(1-b)\delta(1-\alpha_B)+b(2-\delta)(1+\beta_S)]^2} > 0$ for all feasible parameter constellations.

Our second and more specific finding is that fairness concerns are likely to result in a reduced sensitivity of prices in response to variations of market fundamentals. Here, we have studied variations of the buyer–seller ratio, which is a measure of sellers' market power. We conjecture that similar results could also be obtained regarding other supply-and-demand shocks in a more general model, involving, for instance, heterogeneous reservation prices. Somewhat surprisingly, price sensitivity to changes in the relative numbers of buyers and sellers does not increase as the delay between the rejection of an offer and a possible rematching vanishes. On the contrary, the *less* friction there is, the stickier prices may get. The intuitive reason for this is that the bargaining advantage conferred by being on the short side of the market is linked to agents' impatience. It decreases, and eventually vanishes, as agents care less about a given time of delay. In contrast, the symmetrically distributed advantage of facing a responder who dislikes lotteries involving favorable and unfavorable deviations from the reference price is not created by discounting, and therefore does not vanish in the limit.

The third finding of our analysis concerns the possibility that reference prices are subject to psychological adaptation. If we posit, as in Ken Binmore's theory of distributional justice, that agents' notion of a fair deal will ultimately adjust if (and only if) it clashes with their actual, market power-driven bargaining experience in a pronounced way, then different fair price conventions can be associated with the same underlying market fundamentals. We have investigated the stability condition that the considered way of distributing a monetary surplus is close enough to the market outcome which would follow if this way was indeed agents' fair benchmark. Generally, many prices satisfy this requirement for a fixed market configuration. Hence, a sense of fairness which adjusts to cognitive dissonance, that possibly is implied by market fundamentals, will give rise to multiple self-confirming long-run equilibria.

The history dependence and price stickiness predicted for our very stylized stationary market can have important practical implications and provide explanations for several real-world phenomena. In particular, fairness concern creates the potential to influence market prices by "soft" policy measures: non-binding *recommended retail prices* published by producers possibly establish common reference points for consumers and retailers. They can be expected to induce retail market clearing at prices nearby—and moreover to reduce the sensitivity of prices in response to demand or supply fluctuations.[18] Analogously, government policies such as the (lagged) publication of *rent indices*—which is common, for instance, in German municipalities—may have persistent and noticeable effects: even though landlords and tenants are generally free to deviate from the indicated price per area unit, the official figures provide a powerful benchmark; negotiators commonly point out reasons for why a lease should involve different terms. Similarly, compulsory *minimum*

---

[18] Let us emphasize again that we have adopted a rather broad notion of fairness. We understand it as a common benchmark for the participants of a given market, as, for example, the different local crop-sharing conventions in the study of Young and Burke (2001). Consumers may not *consciously* attribute any fairness properties to the recommended retail price of an umbrella—until an opportunistic vendor starts exceeding it during heavy rain.

wages may have an economically relevant effect even after they have ceased to be a binding constraint. This has recently been documented in the laboratory by Falk et al. (2006). Furthermore, in a very recent survey paper also Fehr et al. (2009) discuss the effect of reference-dependent fairness preferences in labor markets.

Of course, our results call for more research. First, the model itself should be varied and generalized, with the goal of evaluating the robustness of our findings. Preliminary attempts to relax the presumption that all agents in the market consider the *same* reference price as their benchmark suggest that the model is very robust at least to some variations. One can, for example, assume that reference prices are identical for all agents on one side of the market (namely, p_{ref}^i for $i \in \{B, S\}$), but different from those on the other side (i.e., $p_{\text{ref}}^B \neq p_{\text{ref}}^S$). This gives rise to the same kind of reduced price sensitivity which we have deduced for the fully homogenous case, except that prices are now sticky around both the buyers' reference price p_{ref}^B and the sellers' reference price p_{ref}^S—corresponding to two disjoint intervals I^B and I^S of buyer–seller ratios with markedly reduced sensitivity to variations of $b \in B^i$. In the limit, as $\delta \to 1$, equilibrium prices again become perfectly flat inside I^B and I^S with a transition zone in between, where p^{**} has a slope close to unity.

Second, it would be desirable to investigate the predictions of the model empirically—in the field or, often allowing sharper targeting, by laboratory experiments. Reflecting the three main qualitative findings, a first testable hypothesis is that different reference prices—induced, for instance, by the framing of the experiment, or by initially allowing prices to settle at some level and then varying the number of buyers and sellers—produce a significant treatment effect. A second one is that the sensitivity of outcomes with respect to sellers' (or buyers') market power varies according to the three qualitative cases captured by equation (5.6) and, moreover, by how close the original price level was to the induced reference price. Finally, provided that stickiness around an induced benchmark can indeed be observed, how does this vary with agents' incentives to avoid delay? Does friction indeed erode the effects of fairness in bargaining markets? Investigation of these issues should require neither a market that is literally stationary, nor particularly large buyer and seller populations. In our view, a lot would already be gained by giving up the double-auction paradigm for market experiments.

References

Akerlof GA, Dickens WT (1982) The economic consequences of cognitive dissonance. Am Econ Rev 72(3):307–319

Albrecht J, Anderson A, Smith E, Vroman S (2007) Opportunistic matching in the housing market. Int Econ Rev 48(2):641–664

Ball L, Mankiw NG (1994) A sticky-price manifesto. Carnegie-Rochester Conference Series on Public Policy 41:127–151

Binmore KG (1994) Game Theory and the Social Contract, vol I: Playing Fair. The MIT Press, Cambridge, MA

Binmore KG (1998) Game Theory and the Social Contract, vol II: Just Playing. The MIT Press, Cambridge, MA

Binmore KG, Herrero MJ (1988) Matching and bargaining in dynamic markets. Rev Econ Stud 55(1):17–31

Binmore KG, Morgan P, Shaked A, Sutton J (1991) Do people exploit their bargaining power? An experimental study. Games Econom Behav 3(3):295–322

Binmore KG, Swierzbinski J, Hsu S, Proulx C (1993) Focal points and bargaining. Int J Game Theor 22(4):381–409

Bolton GE, Ockenfels A (2000) ERC: A theory of equity, reciprocity, and competition. Am Econ Rev 90(1):166–193

Bolton LE, Warlop L, Alba JW (2003) Consumer perceptions of price (un)fairness. J Consum Res 29(4):474–491

Brown M, Falk A, Fehr E (2004) Relational contracts and the nature of market interactions. Econometrica 72(3):747–780

Camerer CF (2003) Behavioral Game Theory: Experiments in Strategic Interaction. Princeton University Press, Princeton, NJ

Charness G, Rabin M (2002) Understanding social preferences with simple tests. Q J Econ 117(3):817–869

Cooper J (2007) Cognitive Dissonance: 50 Years of a Classic Theory. Sage Publications Ltd., London, UK

Diamond PA, Maskin E (1979) An equilibrium analysis of search and breach of contract, I: Steady states. Bell J Econ 10(1):282–316

Dufwenberg M, Kirchsteiger G (2004) A theory of sequential reciprocity. Games Econom Behav 47(2):268–298

Ewerhart C (2006) The effect of sunk costs on the outcome of alternating-offers bargaining between inequity-averse agents. Schmalenbach Bus Rev 58(2):184–203

Falk A, Fischbacher U (2006) A theory of reciprocity. Games Econom Behav 54(2):293–315

Falk A, Fehr E, Zehnder C (2006) Fairness perceptions and reservation wages—The behavioral effects of minimum wage laws. Q J Econ 121(4):1347–1381

Fehr E, Schmidt KM (1999) A theory of fairness, competition and cooperation. Q J Econ 114(3):817–868

Fehr E, Tyran JR (2001) Does money illusion matter? Am Econ Rev 91(5):1239–1262

Fehr E, Goette L, Zehnder C (2009) A behavioral account of the labor market: The role of fairness concerns. Annu Rev Econ (in press)

Festinger L (1957) A Theory of Cognitive Dissonance. Stanford University Press, Stanford, CA

Franciosi R, Kujal P, Michelitsch R, Smith VL, Deng G (1995) Fairness: Effect on temporary and equilibrium prices in posted-offer markets. Econ J 105(431):938–950

Gale D (1986a) Bargaining and competition Part I: Characterization. Econometrica 54(4):785–806

Gale D (1986b) Bargaining and competition Part II: Existence. Econometrica 54(4):807–818

Gode DK, Sunder S (1993) Allocative efficiency of markets with zero-intelligence traders: Market as a partial substitute for individual rationality. J Polit Econ 101(1):119–137

Golosov M, Lucas RE (2007) Menu costs and Phillips curves. J Polit Econ 115(2):171–199

Kachelmeier SJ, Limberg ST, Schadewald MS (1991) Fairness in markets: A laboratory investigation. J Econ Psychol 12(3):447–464

Kahneman D, Knetsch JL, Thaler RH (1986) Fairness and the assumptions of economics. J Bus 59(4):285–300

Konow J (2000) Fair shares: Accountability and cognitive dissonance in allocation decisions. Am Econ Rev 90(4):1072–1091

Korth C, Napel S (2009) Fairness, price stickiness, and history dependence in decentralized trade. J Econ Behav Organ (in press)

Köszegi B, Rabin M (2006) A model of reference-dependent preferences. Q J Econ 121(4):1133–1165

Krainer J, LeRoy SF (2002) Equilibrium valuation of illiquid assets. Econ Theor 19(2):223–242

Kunimoto T, Serrano R (2004) Bargaining and competition revisited. J Econ Theory 115(1):78–88

Mortensen DT (1982) The matching process as a noncooperative bargaining game. In: McCall JJ (ed) The Economics of Information and Uncertainty, The University of Chicago Press, Chicago, IL, pp 233–254

Mortensen DT, Pissarides CA (1999) New developments in models of search in the labor market. In: Ashenfelter O, Card D (eds) Handbook of Labor Economics, vol 3, Elsevier, Amsterdam, Netherlands, chap 39, pp 2567–2627

Nail PR, Misak JE, Davis RM (2004) Self-affirmation versus self-consistency: A comparison of two competing self-theories of dissonance phenomena. Pers Indiv Differ 36(8):1893–1905

Rocheteau G, Wright R (2005) Money in search equilibrium, in competitive equilibrium, and in competitive search equilibrium. Econometrica 73(1):175–202

Rogerson R, Shimer R, Wright R (2005) Search-theoretic models of the labor market: A survey. J Econ Lit 43(4):959–988

Rubinstein A (1989) Competitive equilibrium in a market with decentralized trade and strategic behavior: An introduction. In: Feiwel GR (ed) The Economics of Imperfect Competition and Employment: Joan Robinson and Beyond, Macmillan, London, UK, chap 7, pp 243–259

Rubinstein A, Wolinsky A (1985) Equilibrium in a market with sequential bargaining. Econometrica 53(5):1133–1150

Rubinstein A, Wolinsky A (1990) Decentralized trading, strategic behaviour and the Walrasian outcome. Rev Econ Stud 57(1):63–78

Shi S (2001) Liquidity, bargaining, and multiple equilibria in a search monetary model. Ann Econ Finance 2(2):325–251

Taylor JB (1999) Staggered price and wage setting in macroeconomics. In: Taylor JB, Woodford M (eds) Handbook of Macroeconomics, vol 1, North-Holland, Amsterdam, Netherlands, chap 15, pp 1009–1050

Woodford M (2002) Imperfect common knowledge and the effects of monetary policy. In: Aghion P, Frydman R, Stiglitz J, Woodford M (eds) Knowledge, Information, and Expectations in Modern Macroeconomics: In Honor of Edmund S. Phelps, Princeton University Press, Princeton, NJ

Xia L, Monroe KB, Cox JL (2004) The price is unfair! A conceptual framework of price fairness perceptions. J Market 68(4):1–15

Young HP, Burke MA (2001) Competition and custom in economic contracts: A case study of Illinois agriculture. Am Econ Rev 91(3):559–573

Chapter 6
Generalizations and Extensions of the Decentralized Trade Model

The theoretical analysis of matching markets with bilateral bargaining of chapter 5 is based on a stylized model. Several assumptions are made to enable or simplify analysis and discussion of this model. The results are meant to be relevant for real-life markets like used-car, housing, and labor markets, which closely *resemble* the modeled market. Of course, real-life markets do not exactly match the model's setup, but are different in important regards. For example, the model assumes perfect homogeneity of buyers' and sellers' preferences. However, since the dawn of experimental economics, heterogeneity in subjects' behavior is an established fact. Based on this observation homogenous preferences and beliefs are unlikely to describe real-life agents well.

This led Richard Thaler (2000, p. 136) to make a pointed remark on the relevance of market models based on heterogeneous agents:

> After all, analyses of market interactions between agents of various types is exactly what differentiates economics from other social sciences. Psychologists, sociologists and anthropologists might help us improve our characterizations of economic behavior, but economists are the only social scientists with the tools to analyze what happens in market contexts.

One obvious question that this paper addresses is: how robust are the original findings when homogeneity is dispensed?

Before heterogeneity with respect to several aspects of agent's preferences is investigated, section 6.1 considers the effects of matching friction, which may reduce the likelihood of match formation. Sections 6.2 to 6.6 analyze heterogeneity in the price agents regard as the *fair* or *reference price*, their preference for fairness, and the discounting of future gains. Section 6.7 examines the relevance of the functional form with which these preferences are modeled.

Section 6.8 discusses a model variation concerning the market structure. In the original setup, the number of agents in the markets is constant over time. Section 6.8 investigates a model in which all agents enter the market in the first period, and *no* new agents enter the market subsequently. Finally, section 6.9 considers the effects of incomplete information, and section 6.10 concludes.

In the following, the model as formulated in chapter 5 is referred to as the *original model*, and *original results* refers to the propositions that are given in chapter 5.

C. Korth, *Fairness in Bargaining and Markets,*
Lecture Notes in Economics and Mathematical Systems, 627
DOI: 10.1007/978-3-642-02252-4_1, © Springer-Verlag Berlin Heidelberg 2009

6.1 Matching Frictions

The standard model investigates only one kind of friction in the market, which is the discounting of future gains by a factor of δ. This section extends the analysis to include matching friction. Assume that sellers are on the short side of the market. In the standard model in any given period any seller is then matched for sure in any given period, and any buyer is matched with the likelihood $B/(B+S)$. Denote the probability that such a match potential match is formed by $\vartheta \in (0,1]$. With this matching friction ϑ, the likelihood that any seller is matched in the given scenario (with sellers on the short side of the market) changes to ϑ, and the likelihood that any buyer is matched changes to $\vartheta B/(B+S)$. For $\vartheta = 1$ the model coincides with the original model. To account for ϑ in the market model replace equations (5.3) and (5.4) of the original set of equations leading to the market equilibrium by these new equations (6.1) and (6.2):

$$V_S(t) = \vartheta \frac{1}{2}(u_S(p_B,t) + u_S(p_S,t)) + (1-\vartheta)[\delta V_S(t+1)]$$
$$= \vartheta \frac{1}{2}(\delta V_S(t+1) + u_S(u_B^{-1}(\delta V_B(t+1)))) + (1-\vartheta)[\delta V_S(t+1)] \qquad (6.1)$$

$$V_B(t) = \vartheta \frac{S}{B}\left[\frac{1}{2}(u_B(p_S,t) + u_B(p_B,t))\right] + (1-\vartheta\frac{S}{B})[\delta V_B(t+1)]$$
$$= \vartheta \frac{S}{2B}\left[\delta V_B(t+1) + u_B(u_S^{-1}(\delta V_S(t+1)))\right] + (1-\vartheta\frac{S}{B})[\delta V_B(t+1)] . \qquad (6.2)$$

The following proposition describes the effect of matching friction on equilibrium prices:

Proposition 6.1. *All else equal, the spread between p_S and p_B (recall that $p_S > p_B$ always holds) decreases with matching friction parameterized by $\vartheta \in (0,1]$, and the effect disappears for $\delta \to 1$:*

$$\frac{\partial p_B}{\partial \vartheta} > 0 \text{ and } \frac{\partial p_S}{\partial \vartheta} < 0, \text{ and}$$
$$\frac{\partial p_B}{\partial \vartheta} \to 0, \frac{\partial p_S}{\partial \vartheta} \to 0 \text{ for } \delta \to 1 .$$

Proof. Proof of the first part of the proposition is conducted numerically by analysis of the explicit equilibrium price equation (see equations (6.8)–(6.10) in the appendix), and proof of the second part is obtained by setting $\delta = 1$ in these (equilibrium prices are continuous in δ).   □

The effect of matching friction in a market with discounting is similar to the effect of discounting: With matching friction $\vartheta < 1$ the price spread is larger than without (for $\vartheta = 1$) because of the reduced likelihood of being matched in upcoming periods. In the limit, as $\delta \to 1$, matching friction does not affect prices at all, as agents are infinitely patient and any matching friction simply does not affect the value derived from future periods.

As described in the original analysis, the effect of fairness preferences on equilibrium market prices is due to p_S and p_B circumscribing a reference price. This principle is not affected by the matching friction, thus the original results are sustained.

6.2 Diverging Reference Prices of Buyers and Sellers

Multiplicity of potential sources of reference prices (e.g., past prices, prices for similar goods, prices in other markets) may lead sellers and buyers to adopt different reference prices, so that no common reference p_{ref} may exist. Instead, sellers might hold p_{ref_S} and buyers p_{ref_B} as their reference price; typically with $p_{\mathrm{ref}_B} < p_{\mathrm{ref}_S}$, as, in the spirit of self-serving biases,[1] sellers are likely to adopt a higher reference price than buyers.

Given these distinct reference prices, agents' stationary time preferences are assumed to be:

$$u_S(p, p_{\mathrm{ref}_S}, t) = \delta^t \left(p - \alpha_S (p - p_{\mathrm{ref}_S})^+ - \beta_S (p_{\mathrm{ref}_S} - p)^+ \right) \tag{6.3}$$

for sellers and

$$u_B(p, p_{\mathrm{ref}_B}, t) = \delta^t \left(1 - p - \alpha_B (p_{\mathrm{ref}_B} - p)^+ - \beta_B (p - p_{\mathrm{ref}_B})^+ \right) \tag{6.4}$$

for buyers where $(x)^+ \equiv \max\{0, x\}$.

The original setup in chapter 5 with one common reference price resulted in an equilibrium price equation with three distinct cases, depending on the order of prices p_S, p_B, and p_{ref}. In general, $p_B < p_S$ holds, so the three original cases were $p_B < p_S \leq p_{\mathrm{ref}}$, $p_B \leq p_{\mathrm{ref}} < p_S$ and $p_{\mathrm{ref}} < p_B < p_S$. With now two distinct reference prices, for which $p_{\mathrm{ref}_B} < p_{\mathrm{ref}_S}$ is assumed, there are five cases:[2]

(1) $p_B < p_S \leq p_{\mathrm{ref}_B} < p_{\mathrm{ref}_S}$
(2) $p_B \leq p_{\mathrm{ref}_B} < p_S \leq p_{\mathrm{ref}_S}$
(3) Two alternative intermediate cases
    (3a) $p_B \leq p_{\mathrm{ref}_B} < p_{\mathrm{ref}_S} < p_S$

---

[1] Compare, for example, Babcock et al. (1996) and Babcock and Loewenstein (1997) who conjecture that expectations of adjudicated settlements and in bargaining will be systematically biased in a self-serving manner due to selective evaluation of information in individual judgments of fairness. Or see Kohnz (2006) who analyzes ultimatum bargaining using a formal model that incorporates self-serving biases based on the preferences of Fehr and Schmidt (1999).

[2] Although the case-structure for $p_{\mathrm{ref}_B} > p_{\mathrm{ref}_S}$ (when buyers have a *higher* reference price than sellers) are different, the solution is similar and the results that are given in the following also hold. Note that all equilibrium prices are continuous in all variables and parameters of the model. Therefore, the distinction between strong and weak inequalities does not matter.

(3b) $p_{\text{ref}_B} < p_B < p_S \leq p_{\text{ref}_S}$
(4) $p_{\text{ref}_B} < p_B \leq p_{\text{ref}_S} < p_S$
(5) $p_{\text{ref}_B} < p_{\text{ref}_S} < p_B < p_S$

Of these cases, case (3a) holds whenever the spread $p_S - p_B$ is larger than the difference $p_{\text{ref}_S} - p_{\text{ref}_B}$, and case (3b) holds otherwise. In particular, because $p_S - p_B \to 0$ as $\delta \to 1$, case (3b) is the only relevant subcase in this limit.

Based on these cases an explicit solution for the new equilibrium price $p^*(\cdot)$ can be derived. This equation is stated in the appendix, see equation (6.11).

For all cases in which the offered prices p_S and p_B bracket one or both of the reference prices, so that $p_B \leq p_{\text{ref}_B} < p_S$ and/or $p_B \leq p_{\text{ref}_S} < p_S$ hold, the results of the original analysis with only one common reference price are sustained. Based on the new equilibrium price $p^*(\cdot)$, for example, the original first two propositions translate into the following:

Let

$$p^\dagger \equiv p^*\big|_{\alpha_i = \beta_i = 0} = \frac{b}{2b(1-\delta) + \delta}$$

be the associated equilibrium price for standard preferences without fairness concern. Denote by $\tilde{b}_B$ the market for which $p^*\big|_{b=\tilde{b}_B} = p_{\text{ref}_B}$ and by $\tilde{b}_S$ the market for which $p^*\big|_{b=\tilde{b}_S} = p_{\text{ref}_S}$, if they exist. Then the following is true:

Proposition 6.2. *Relative to a setting in which agents have no fairness concern, the market price is less sensitive to changes in the fraction b of buyers in the market in the neighborhood of $\tilde{b}_B$ if* buyers *have fairness concern, and in the neighborhood of $\tilde{b}_S$ if* sellers *have fairness concern:*

$$0 < \frac{\partial p^*}{\partial b}\bigg|_{b=\tilde{b}_B} < \frac{\partial p^\dagger}{\partial b}\bigg|_{b=\tilde{b}_B} \quad \text{if} \quad \max\{\alpha_B, \beta_B\} > 0, \text{ and}$$

$$0 < \frac{\partial p^*}{\partial b}\bigg|_{b=\tilde{b}_S} < \frac{\partial p^\dagger}{\partial b}\bigg|_{b=\tilde{b}_S} \quad \text{if} \quad \max\{\alpha_S, \beta_S\} > 0.$$

Proposition 6.3. *Suppose that $\max\{\alpha_B, \beta_B\} > 0$. Then, first, there exists some $\delta' \in (0,1)$ such that the market price's sensitivity to changes in the fraction b of buyers in a neighborhood of $\tilde{b}_B$ is decreasing in δ for any $\delta > \delta'$. Second, the price sensitivity $\partial p^*/\partial b\big|_{b=b'}$ converges to zero as $\delta \to 1$ for any b' pertaining to cases (2) and (3a) mentioned above (in particular, for $b = \tilde{b}_B$). Analogous results hold with regard to sellers for $\max\{\alpha_S, \beta_S\} > 0$, $\tilde{b}_S$, and cases (3a) and (4).*

Proof. The proof for both propositions follows the proof for the corresponding results in the original analysis.   □

The underlying principle driving these results is the same as in the original analysis: if agents face a lottery of prices above and below their reference price, the local concavity of $u_i(\cdot)$ around p_{ref_i} kicks in. The resulting equilibrium prices for

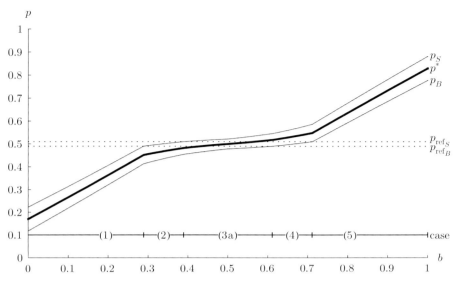

Fig. 6.1 Equilibrium prices for buyers and sellers holding distinct references; example for $p_{\text{ref}_B} = 0.49$, $p_{\text{ref}_S} = 0.51$ with $\alpha_i = \beta_i = 0.3$ and $\delta = 0.95$

a scenario with all cases for which this can be true, i.e., cases (2), (3a), and (4), is depicted in figure 6.1.

If the spread between the two references prices is greater than the spread between the market prices, so that $p_{\text{ref}_S} - p_{\text{ref}_B} > p_S - p_B$, then case (3b) is relevant instead of case (3a). See figure 6.2 for an example. As this example illustrates, the original results then hold for cases (2) and (4), but not for the section belonging to case (3b) in between.

Finally, for $\delta \to 1$ the graph is completely flat for cases (2), (3a), and (4). The slope of case (3b) turns out to be a positive constant:

$$0 < \frac{\partial p^*}{\partial b} = \frac{1 + p_{\text{ref}_B}\beta_B}{1 + \beta_B} - \frac{p_{\text{ref}_S}\beta_S}{1 + \beta_S} < 1.$$

See figure 6.3 for an example.[3] Because the slope is bounded above by unity, the market price never "jumps" between both reference prices, but adjusts gradually.

6.3 Mutant in the Market

In the model designed by Rubinstein and Wolinsky (1985) and in the model described up to here, the market equilibrium was derived as a subgame perfect equi-

---

[3] In this particular example, the slope between the flat sections is $\partial p^*/\partial b \approx 0.815$.

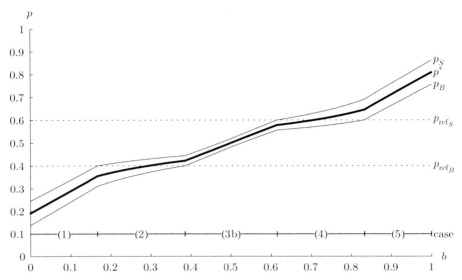

Fig. 6.2 Equilibrium prices for buyers and sellers holding distinct references; example for $p_{\mathrm{ref}_S} = 0.4$, $p_{\mathrm{ref}_B} = 0.6$ with $\alpha_i = \beta_i = 0.3$ and $\delta = 0.95$

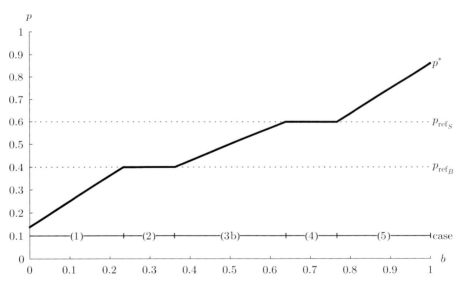

Fig. 6.3 Equilibrium prices for buyers and sellers holding distinct references; example for $p_{\mathrm{ref}_S} = 0.4$, $p_{\mathrm{ref}_B} = 0.6$ with $\alpha_i = \beta_i = 0.3$ and at the limit $\delta \to 1$

librium in stationary strategies; this are strategies that prescribe the same bargaining tactics against all bargaining partners an agent might meet, independent of the period and the bargaining outcomes an agent experienced. In this equilibrium, strategies cannot be conditioned on the identity of the bargaining partner. With this restriction, they cannot be conditioned on the *specific preferences* of the matched bargaining partner as well. So far, this aspect of the original equilibrium concept was not restrictive, because all potential bargaining partners, i.e., all agents on one side of the market, had identical preferences.

In this and the following sections the effects of heterogeneity with regard to agents' preferences will be discussed. Then, allowing for strategies to be conditioned not on the *identity* of the agent, but on the *preferences* of the agent, enables some interesting analysis. Therefore, a slightly adapted equilibrium concept will be used in the following: agents are allowed to condition their strategy on the preferences of the specific agent they face. Because of this, strategies need not prescribe the same bargaining tactics against all bargaining partners. Instead, strategies prescribe the same bargaining tactics against *all* bargaining partners an agent might face *that have the same preferences*.

Consider a market in which all buyers and all sellers are homogenous. With just one exception: a single "mutant" buyer with preferences different from those of the other buyers also enters in this market.[4] How would the price such a mutant buyer pays on average in equilibrium compare with the average price the other buyers pay?

As the number of buyers in the market is large, the presence of this single mutant is assumed not to affect the continuation value of any of the other buyers or sellers. So in case the mutant is matched and selected to propose the price, he or she would offer the same price to the seller as all other buyers do: the price for which the seller's agreement utility is equivalent to the seller's continuation value.[5] However, if the seller is selected to propose a price to the mutant, the situation is less clear and deserves some analysis:

The preferences of the mutant buyer (indexed by B^m) are given by the utility function

$$u_{B^m}(p, p_{\text{ref}_{B^m}}, t) = \delta^t \left(1 - p - \alpha_{B^m}(p_{\text{ref}_{B^m}} - p)^+ - \beta_{B^m}(p - p_{\text{ref}_{B^m}})^+\right)$$

with $(x)^+ \equiv \max\{0, x\}$. Denote the value of being the mutant buyer in period t by $V_{B^m}(t)$. Then, the following equations need to be added to original set of equations to account for the mutant (p_{S^m} denoting the price a seller would offer the mutant buyer in contrast to p_S, the price a seller would offer to all other buyers):

$$u_{B^m}(p_{S^m}, t) = \delta V_{B^m}(t+1)$$

$$V_{B^m}(t) = \frac{S}{B}\left[\frac{1}{2}\left(u_{B^m}(p_{S^m}, t) + u_{B^m}(p_B, t)\right)\right] + \left(1 - \frac{S}{B}\right)\left[\delta V_{B^m}(t+1)\right]$$

$$= \frac{S}{2B}\left[\delta V_{B^m}(t+1) + u_{B^m}(u_S^{-1}(\delta V_S(t+1)))\right] + \left(1 - \frac{S}{B}\right)\left[\delta V_{B^m}(t+1)\right]$$

$$p^m(t) = \frac{1}{2}[p_{S^m} + p_B] = \frac{1}{2}\left[u_{B^m}^{-1}(\delta V_{B^m}(t+1)) + u_S^{-1}(\delta V_S(t+1))\right] .$$

---

[4] The term "mutant" is borrowed from evolutionary game theory. It describes a single agent that may be different from all other agents.

[5] An agent's continuation value in period t is his or her value of being in the market at the beginning of period $t + 1$ discounted by one period, i.e., $\delta V_i(t+1)$.

The solution of the full set of equations including the original ones results in the average price the mutant pays $p^{m*}(t)$ in addition to the regular equilibrium market price $p^*(t)$. Several results can be derived from the analysis of these equilibrium prices; the first is given in the following proposition:

Proposition 6.4. *In case the population of buyers has fairness concern regarding disadvantages ($\beta_B > 0$) and no fairness concern regarding advantages ($\alpha_B = 0$), then a mutant without fairness concern fares strictly worse: in markets belonging to case (1),[6] the average price the mutant pays $p^{m*}(t)$ is equal to the regular price $p^*(t)$, and in all other cases it is strictly higher: $p^{m*}(t) \geq p^*(t)$ with $p^{m*}(t) = p^*(t)$ for case (1), and $p^{m*}(t) > p^*(t)$ for all other cases.*

Proof. As the price p_B all buyers offer is equal and not affected by the mutant, analysis of the prices p_{S^m} and p_S which sellers offer is sufficient; compare equations (6.12) and (6.13) in the appendix for the equilibrium prices in a market with $B \geq S$.[7] Obviously, the price is the same for case (1), and for all other prices it can be shown case by case that $p_S^m(t) > p_S(t)$ holds. For example, for case (2):

$$p_S^m(t) - p_S(t) = -\frac{2\beta_B(-1+\delta)(-(p_{\text{ref}_B} + p_{\text{ref}_B}\beta_S - p_{\text{ref}_S}\beta_S)\delta + b(2 + 2p_{\text{ref}_B}(1+\beta_S)(-1+\delta) - \delta - \beta_S(-2+\delta+p_{\text{ref}_S}\delta)))}{(1+\beta_S)\left((2-\beta_B(-2+\delta)-2\delta)\delta + b\left(4(-1+\delta)^2 + \beta_B\left(4-8\delta+3\delta^2\right)\right)\right)} > 0 .$$

This can be shown numerically to hold for all $\beta_S > 0$.   □

Fair agents dislike being disadvantaged. Therefore, proposing sellers reduce the price they offer in the direction of the fair price for all markets that result in prices above the buyer's reference price p_{ref_B} relative to a scenario in which the buyers have no concern for fairness. This is not necessary for the mutant without fairness concerns. Still, a seller bargaining with a mutant can capture only a smaller share of gains from trade as in a scenario in which no buyer has any concern for fairness. The reason is that the mutant, if matched, faces a fifty percent chance of being in the position to make a price offer. And then he would be able to offer the same relatively low price as any other buyer. Therefore, buyers' concern for fairness is reflected in the mutant's continuation value, even if the mutant him or herself is not concerned about fairness. Figure 6.4 shows this result graphically; the price p_{S^m} is depicted with the *broken thin line* in contrast to the standard p_S, which is the *solid thin line* underneath.

This result is encouraging: In loose terms of a population dynamic in which reproductive fitness is determined solely by material payoff, a population of fair agents that are averse to being disadvantaged ($\beta > 0$, $\alpha = 0$) is robust regarding an invasion of a mutant without fairness concern. The fair agents fare better (get more favorable market prices) than the mutant. The only case when this is not true is when agents in the population are averse towards being overly advantaged ($\beta = 0$, $\alpha > 0$). In this case, a mutant receives lower prices in markets that result in market prices below the reference price of the buyers.

---

[6] See section 6.2 for the case definition.

[7] The proof for $B < S$ is symmetric.

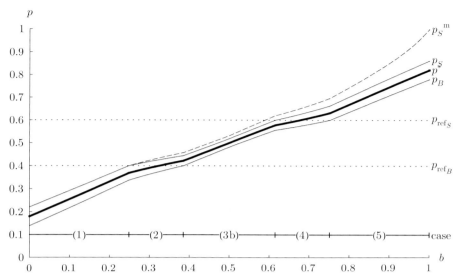

Fig. 6.4 Equilibrium prices when a mutant without fairness concern is in the market; example for $p_{\text{ref}_S} = 0.4$, $p_{\text{ref}_B} = 0.6$ with $\alpha_i = 0$, $\beta_i = 0.3$ and $\delta = 0.95$

A similar result, that a population of agents without fairness concerns is *not* robust against intrusion of fair-minded mutants, is given in proposition 6.5:

Proposition 6.5. *In case the population of buyers has no fairness concern regarding disadvantages ($\beta_B = 0$) and no fairness concern regarding advantages ($\alpha_B = 0$), then a mutant with fairness concern ($\beta_{B^m} > 0$, $\alpha_{B^m} = 0$) fares strictly better: for all markets resulting in market prices below the mutant's reference price $p_{\text{ref}_{B^m}}$, the mutant price is equal to the regular price, and otherwise it is strictly* lower: $p^{m*}(t) \leq p^*(t)$ *with* $p^{m*}(t) = p^*(t)$ *for* $p^* \leq p_{\text{ref}_{B^m}}$ *and* $p^{m*}(t) < p^*(t)$ *otherwise.*

Proof. The proof is comparable to the approach for proposition 6.4. □

Proposing sellers have to discount their price offers towards the fair price to accommodate the mutant's concern for fairness, in case the price is above the mutant's reference price. This results in lower prices for the mutant relative to those agents without fairness concern.[8]

Furthermore, the results hold in general for any values of β_{B^m} and β_B and also with regard to the reference prices $p_{\text{ref}_{B^m}}$ and p_{ref_B}:

Proposition 6.6. *Given any population of buyers, a mutant buyer with the same utility function as the other buyers,* except

---

[8] Proposing sellers do not discount the price unboundedly, but only to the point where they are indifferent between rejection of the offer and acceptance. In case the mutant's utility for accepting this price was negative, he or she would not trade at all.

(a) a higher degree of fairness concern regarding disadvantages, so $\beta_{B^m} > \beta_B$, or

(b) a lower reference price $p_{\mathrm{ref}_{B^m}} < p_{\mathrm{ref}_B}$, or

(c) both, (a) and (b),

receives strictly lower *prices than a "standard" agent in a market with $p_S^* > p_{\mathrm{ref}_{B^m}}$. Formally, for any market with $\alpha_{B^m} = \alpha_B$ and $p_S^* > p_{\mathrm{ref}_{B^m}}$:*

$$\beta_{B^m} \geq \beta_B \wedge p_{\mathrm{ref}_{B^m}} \leq p_{\mathrm{ref}_B} \wedge \beta_{B^m} - p_{\mathrm{ref}_{B^m}} > \beta_B - p_{\mathrm{ref}_B} \implies p^{m*} < p^*.$$

A symmetric case also holds: Given any population of buyers, a mutant buyer with the same utility function as the other buyers, except

(a) a lower degree of fairness concern regarding disadvantages, so $\beta_{B^m} < \beta_B$, or

(b) a higher reference price $p_{\mathrm{ref}_{B^m}} > p_{\mathrm{ref}_B}$

(c) both, (a) and (b), or

receives strictly higher *(worse) prices than a "standard" agent, in any market for which $p_S^* > p_{\mathrm{ref}_{B^m}}$. Formally, for any market with $\alpha_{B^m} = \alpha_B$ and $p_S^* > p_{\mathrm{ref}_{B^m}}$:*

$$\beta_{B^m} \leq \beta_B \wedge p_{\mathrm{ref}_{B^m}} \geq p_{\mathrm{ref}_B} \wedge \beta_{B^m} - p_{\mathrm{ref}_{B^m}} < \beta_B - p_{\mathrm{ref}_B} \implies p^{m*} > p^*.$$

Proof. The proof is conducted numerically by evaluating the equilibrium prices.
□

The intuition behind this result with regard to the reference prices is that the smaller the buyer's reference price, the greater the "utility discount" for any price above this reference price. And a greater "utility discount," which reflects a greater effect of fairness concern, results in a greater price concession the sellers have to give in order to achieve price acceptance by buyers.

The original paper discusses the limit case ($\delta \to 1$) in detail. The result including the mutant buyer is straightforward:

Proposition 6.7. *The difference between mutant and standard prices vanishes for $\delta \to 1$:*

$$\delta \to 1 \implies p^{m*} \to p^*$$

for any mutant and standard population.

Proof. For $\delta \to 1$ one can directly show $p_S^m(t) - p_S(t) \to 0$ by setting $\delta = 1$ in the equilibrium price equations (equilibrium prices are continuous in δ). □

Given that waiting for the next period is without cost, a seller matched with the mutant would never offer a lower price than he could get otherwise, and a mutant would never accept a higher price than other buyers, knowing that he or she could wait without cost until he or she may propose this "standard" price. Therefore, prices coincide in the limit.

As the model is symmetric for buyers and sellers, all results of this section also apply analogously for a mutant *seller*.

6.4 Two Types of Agents

If the mutant is not a single agent, but there is a whole set of mutants, one aspect of the above analysis changes: the continuation value of sellers is affected, as they face a mutant with a positive probability. Denote by $\lambda \in [0, 1]$ the share of mutants of the total buyer population B^m and by $1 - \lambda$ the share of standard buyers B. To accommodate this in the model, the equation denoting the value of a seller needs to be adopted. The original equation is:

$$V_S(t) = \frac{1}{2} \left(u_S(p_B, t) + u_S(p_S, t) \right)$$
$$= \frac{1}{2} \left(\delta V_S(t+1) + u_S(u_B^{-1}(\delta V_B(t+1))) \right)$$

This needs to be changed to:

$$V_S(t) = \frac{1}{2} \left(u_S(p_B, t) + \lambda u_S(p_{S^m}, t) + (1 - \lambda) u_S(p_S, t) \right)$$
$$= \frac{1}{2} \left(\delta V_S(t+1) + \lambda u_S(u_{B^m}^{-1}(\delta V_{B^m}(t+1))) + (1 - \lambda) u_S(u_B^{-1}(\delta V_B(t+1))) \right) .$$
$$(6.5)$$

This model change implies that not only are the prices offered to mutants by sellers affected, but that *all* prices in the model are dependent on the mutant group's preferences. Price offers by both types of buyers to a seller are equal (denoted by p_B), but price offers of sellers towards buyers are differentiated between standard agents (p_S) and mutants (p_{S^m}).

Following the structure above, first a scenario is investigated in which standard buyers B have a concern for fairness (with $\beta_B > 0$), and a mutant group B^m without fairness concern ($\beta_{B^m} = 0$) is also present in the market. First and foremost, as the single mutant was offered higher prices, the mutant group also receives higher price offers in any market that results in prices above the buyer's reference price. As these higher price offers also shift up the continuation value of the sellers, this affects all offered prices, as well as those prices offered from buyers to the sellers, and the prices offered by sellers to the "standard" buyers. All prices shift upwards, and this shift is increasing in the share λ of mutants, which is described in proposition 6.8 and visualized in figure 6.5, which is comparable with figure 6.4 for the single mutant:[9]

Proposition 6.8. *Assuming* $\lambda \in (0, 1)$, $\alpha_B = \alpha_{B^m}$, $\beta_B > 0$ *and* $\beta_{B^m} = 0$:

$$p^{m*} \geq p^* \text{ and } \frac{\partial p^*}{\partial \lambda} \geq 0 \text{ and } \frac{\partial p^{m*}}{\partial \lambda} \geq 0 \text{ hold for any } b \in (0, 1) ,$$

---

[9] In this scenario, the number of "cases" of the equilibrium price equation increases even more, as not only the intersections of p_S and p_B with the reference prices are relevant, but also the intersection of p_{S^m} with the seller's reference price. For simplicity of exposition, the cases are therefore not denoted in the graph.

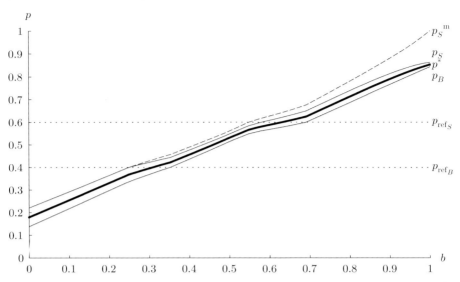

Fig. 6.5 Equilibrium prices when a share of mutant buyers without fairness concern is in the market; example for "unfair" mutant share $\lambda = 0.5$ and $\alpha_i = 0$, $\beta_i = 0.3$ and $\delta = 0.95$

and they hold with strict inequalities for all b for which $p_S^* > p_{\mathrm{ref}_B}$.

Proof. Proof is conducted numerically as above.   □

Another interesting effect is that the spread between prices p_S and p_B is smaller, when such mutants are present in the market. The intuition behind this is that the proposer advantage for the buyers is worth less, because the sellers' continuation value is higher due to the mutants' presence. There may even be a tipping point b^m, at which sellers' continuation value due to potential sales to a mutant buyer is so high that "standard" buyers are not interested in offering more, as this would result in a negative utility for them. At the tipping point $u_B(p_S) = u_B(p_B) = 0$ holds (so p_B and p_S coincide), and it is given by:

$$b^m = \frac{(\beta_B p_{\mathrm{ref}_B} + 1)\delta}{(3\delta + \beta_B \lambda \delta) + \beta_B p_{\mathrm{ref}_B}(3\delta - \lambda \delta - 2) - 2} .$$

This b^m is only relevant if it is smaller than one ($b^m < 1$). For example, if $\beta_B = 0.3$, $p_{\mathrm{ref}_B} = 0.4$ and $\delta = 0.95$ as in the depicted examples, $b^m < 1 \Longleftrightarrow \lambda > 0.654971$, which implies that this tipping point is relevant for a mutant share of more than 65.5%, though only for markets with b close to unity. If, for example, $\lambda = 90\%$, then this is true for all markets with $b > b^m = 0.962112$.

In markets for which $b > b^m$ holds fair buyers do not participate any more: sellers can obtain such high prices from mutant buyers, that prices they would expect from fair buyers are so high that these would result in a negative utility for these fair buyers.[10] So every match between sellers and fair buyers results in disagreement, and both agents remain in the market for the next period.[11] Only mutant buyers, when matched with a seller, will agree on a price. Sellers, if on the short side of the market, therefore only face a likelihood of λ of being matched with a buyer *and* being able to trade with this agent in any given period. This is similar to a *one-sided* matching friction (see section 6.1) with $\vartheta_S = \lambda$ which only affects the sellers. To account for this in the model, equation (6.5) needs to be adjusted in a like manner to the equation (6.1) for markets with $b > b^m$:

$$V_S(t) = \lambda \frac{1}{2} \left(u_S(p_B,t) + u_S(p_{S^m},t) \right) + (1-\lambda) \left[\delta V_S(t+1) \right]$$
$$= \lambda \frac{1}{2} \left(\delta V_S(t+1) + u_S(u_{B^m}^{-1}(\delta V_{B^m}(t+1)))) \right) + (1-\lambda) \left[\delta V_S(t+1) \right] .$$

The resulting equilibrium price is continuous at b^m; see figures 6.6 and 6.7.

In the limit, as $\delta \to 1$, the prices sellers offer to all buyers coincide; compare the case of a single mutant. Of course, the presence of mutants without concern for fairness does affect the market price: it reduces the range of markets, for which the market price coincides with buyers' reference price, and shifts prices upwards. For an example of this effect, see figure 6.6, in which the *lower bold line* denotes the market price in a homogenous market with only fair-minded buyers, and the *upper bold line* depicts the market price for a market in which half of the buyers are without fairness concern. The presence of a significant share of buyers without fairness concern does not *eliminate* the effects of fairness concern, but it *reduces* the effects. This does not come surprising, as for $\lambda \to 1$ the market price is exactly the same as for a market full of buyers without fairness concern, and prices are continuous in λ. At the same time as the market price is increasing in λ, the tipping point b^m is decreasing in λ. In figure 6.6 the *dashed lines* show how to derive b^m for $\delta \to 1$: it is the share b, for which the equilibrium price p^* for any $\lambda > 0$ (for example, the *upper bold line* for $\lambda = 0.5$) equates the limit equilibrium price p^* for $\lambda = 0$ and $b \to 1$.

The results for a mutant group with a positive fairness parameter $0 < \beta_{B^m} \neq \beta_B$ are similar, and, therefore, not discussed in detail.

Another interesting case, in which the two groups of buyers hold distinct reference prices, is considered in the following: Imagine the mutant buyer group holds $p_{\text{ref}_{B^m}} \neq p_{\text{ref}_B}$ as their reference price, while for simplicity, all other fairness parameters are equal. Now, for any $\lambda \in (0,1)$, both buyers' reference prices are relevant for the market price, and the effect they each have depends on the share of buyers holding this reference. For obvious reasons, for $\lambda = 0$ only p_{ref_B} is relevant, and for $\lambda = 1$ only $p_{\text{ref}_{B^m}}$ is relevant. Otherwise, both are relevant, with a continuous transition in λ. Figure 6.7 displays an example with $p_{\text{ref}_B} = 0.3$, $p_{\text{ref}_{B^m}} = 0.5$, and

---

[10] Recall that the utility for perpetual disagreement is normalized to zero for all agents, i.e., they can obtain a zero payoff by staying in the market indefinitely.

[11] As "fair" agents cannot gain positive utility from trading in markets with $b > b^m$, they would not enter in the first place if they had a choice, and if getting to the markets involved some small cost. Then, only shares $b \leq b^m$ are relevant.

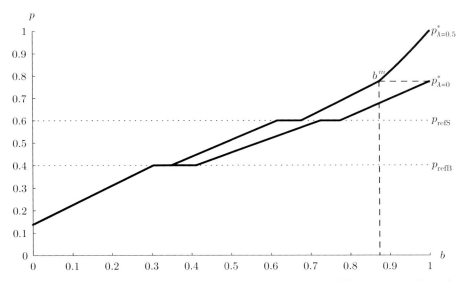

Fig. 6.6 Equilibrium prices when a share of mutant buyers without fairness concern is in the market at the limit $\delta \to 1$; example for $\alpha_i = 0$, $\beta_S = 0.3$, and $\beta_B = 0.6$

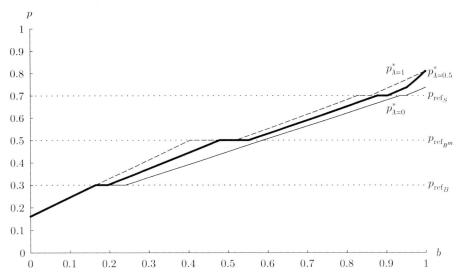

Fig. 6.7 Equilibrium prices when a share of mutant buyers without fairness concern is in the market at the limit $\delta \to 1$; example for $\alpha_i = 0$, and $\beta_i = 0.6$

$p_{\mathrm{ref}_S} = 0.7$, in which equilibrium prices are shown for $\lambda \in \{0, 0.5, 1\}$: for $\lambda = 0$ as a *thin solid line*, for $\lambda = 0.5$ as a *thick solid line*, and for $\lambda = 1$ as a *thin dashed line*. One can well see that three "flat" sections exist for $\lambda = 0.5$; one for each of the three reference prices held by some agents in the market.

The range of markets (with regard to b) for which the market price for $\delta \to 1$ is exactly equal to the reference price of one of the two agent groups is increasing in the share of this group. This is formulated in the following proposition:

Proposition 6.9. *Assume that there exist mutant buyers holding $p_{\mathrm{ref}_{B^m}} \neq p_{\mathrm{ref}_B}$ as their reference price and $\beta_{B^m} > 0$. Then, for $\delta \to 1$ the range $b \in [\underline{b}, \bar{b}]$ for which $p^*(b) = p_{\mathrm{ref}_{B^m}}$ holds (if it exists) is increasing in the share λ of mutants:*

$$\frac{\partial(\bar{b} - \underline{b})}{\partial \lambda} \geq 0 \, .$$

Proof. Proof is conducted numerically by setting $\delta = 1$ (recall that equilibrium prices are continuous in δ) and evaluating the partial derivatives of the relevant case limits of the equilibrium price function for $p^*(b)$. $\square$

6.5 Multiple Agent Types

To further generalize the above results, consider a market in which n types of buyers exist; their respective masses denoted by $B^1, B^2, \ldots, B^n$ with $\sum_{x=1}^{n} B^x = B$. Analogous, there are m types of sellers, their amount each denoted by $S^1, S^2, \ldots, S^m$ with $\sum_{y=1}^{m} S^y = S$.

In this market, the proposed prices depend on the specific type of the matched trading partner. Denote by p_{B^y} the price that any buyer proposes to a seller of type y, and denote by p_{S^x} the price proposed by any seller to a buyer of type x. The market equilibrium (for $B \geq S$) is then defined by the following set of equations (where $(z)^+ \equiv \max\{0, z\}$):[12]

For each $x \in \{1, \ldots, n\}$:

$$
\begin{aligned}
u_{B^x}(p_{S^x}, t) &= \delta^t \left(1 - p_{S^x} - \alpha_{B^x}(p_{\mathrm{ref}_{B^x}} - p_{S^x})^+ - \beta_{B^x}(p_{S^x} - p_{\mathrm{ref}_{B^x}})^+\right) \\
&= \delta V_{B^x}(t+1) \\
V_{B^x}(t) &= \frac{S}{B}\left[\frac{1}{2}\left(u_{B^x}(p_{S^x}, t) + \frac{1}{S}\sum_{y=1}^{m} S^y u_{B^x}(p_{B^y}, t)\right)\right] + \left(1 - \frac{S}{B}\right)(\delta V_{B^x}(t+1)) \\
&= \frac{S}{2B}\left(\delta V_{B^x}(t+1) + \frac{1}{S}\sum_{y=1}^{m} S^y u_{B^x}(u_{S^y}^{-1}(\delta V_{S^y}(t+1)))\right) + \left(1 - \frac{S}{B}\right)(\delta V_{B^x}(t+1)),
\end{aligned}
$$

and for each $y \in \{1, \ldots, m\}$:

---

[12] These equations hold when all agents participate in the market. In case $b^{\max} < 1$ with $u_{B^x}(p_{S^x}(b)) < 0 \; \forall \; b > b^{\max}$ for some $x \in \{1, \ldots, n\}$ exists, or a $b^{\min} > 0$ with $u_{S^y}(p_{B^y}(b)) < 0 \; \forall b < b^{\min}$ for some $y \in \{1, \ldots, m\}$ exists, then the equations need to be adjusted: Agents with an otherwise negative utility would not participate in the market. This adjustment would be according to the example given in section 6.4 for a case of two buyer types.

$$u_{S^y}(p_{B^y}, t) = \delta^t \left(p_{B^y} - \alpha_{S^y}(p_{B^y} - p_{\text{ref}_{S^y}})^+ - \beta_{S^y}(p_{\text{ref}_{S^y}} - p_{B^y})^+ \right)$$
$$= \delta V_{S^y}(t+1)$$

$$V_{S^y}(t) = \frac{1}{2}\left(u_{S^y}(p_{B^y}, t) + \frac{1}{B}\sum_{x=1}^{n} B^x u_{S^y}(p_{S^x}, t) \right)$$
$$= \frac{1}{2}\left(\delta V_{S^y}(t+1) + \frac{1}{B}\sum_{x=1}^{n} B^x u_{S^y}(u_{B^x}^{-1}(\delta V_{B^x}(t+1))) \right) .$$

The average equilibrium market price turns out to be constant over time and is given by:

$$p^* = \frac{1}{2}\left(\frac{1}{B}\sum_{x=1}^{n} B^x p_{S^x} + \frac{1}{S}\sum_{y=1}^{m} S^y p_{B^y} \right) .$$

We conjecture that the results of the above sections carry over to this setup: For example, for any reference price held by any agent type, the sensitivity of the market price with respect to b is decreased for markets that result in equilibrium prices around this reference price and in which the agent type participates, see footnote 12. Of course, the smaller the fraction of agents with this reference price, the smaller the effect; i.e., the smaller the range of markets with regard to b for which this holds, and the smaller the reduction in sensitivity of the market price with regard to changes in b. In the limit, as $\delta \to 1$, all prices coincide, then $p_{S^x} = p_{B^y} = p^*$ for any x and any y. And again, the equilibrium price function is flat in b, i.e., $\partial p^*/\partial b = 0$ for p^* equal to any reference price held by any fairness-minding agent that participates in the market. In section 6.4 this was proved numerically for a scenario with two types of buyers, and as the principle is the same for more agent types, we conjecture without proof that the results carry over to the case of n buyers and m sellers in general.

6.6 Heterogeneous Discount Factors

So far, all buyers and sellers were assumed the have the same discount factor. In the following, buyers and sellers are allowed to hold *distinct* discount factors, denoted by δ_B and δ_S. Also buyer and seller populations that hold *heterogeneous* discount factors are considered.

The effects of distinct discount factors are best understood from a relative perspective: Imagine, for example, a "base" scenario 1, in which $\delta_{B_1} = \delta_{S_1}$, and a "new" scenario 2 in which $\delta_{B_2} > \delta_{B_1} = \delta_{S_2}$. In scenario 2, the buyers have a higher discount factor and are more patient than the sellers, and the buyers in scenario 1. The effect on the equilibrium price is simple: the more patient buyers can capture a higher share of gains than the less patient buyers. The logic behind this result is that any price offer is equivalent to the continuation value of the agent that receives the offer. This continuation value in period t is his or her value of being in the market at the

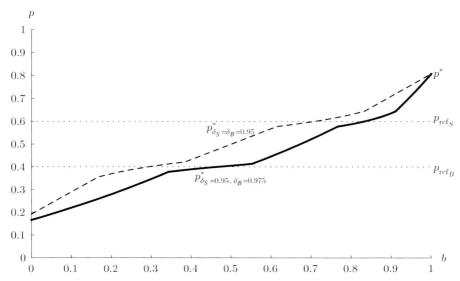

Fig. 6.8 Equilibrium prices when buyers and sellers hold distinct discount factors; example for $\alpha_i = \beta_i = 0.3$ and different discount factors

beginning of period $t + 1$ discounted by one period. The smaller the discount, the more attractive the price offer needs to be to make the responder indifferent between accepting and rejecting. Or from a different perspective: patience increases bargaining power; therefore, more patient agents get the better price offer. Figure 6.8 shows scenario 1 with $\delta_{B_1} = \delta_{S_1} = 0.95$ (which is exactly the same as in figure 6.2) marked by the *dashed line*, while scenario 2 with $\delta_{B_2} = 0.975 > \delta_{B_1}$ and $\delta_{S_2} = \delta_{S_1} = 0.95$ is marked by the *solid line*. Formally:

Proposition 6.10. *Everything else constant,*

$$\frac{\partial p^*}{\partial \delta_B} < 0 \quad and \quad \frac{\partial p^*}{\partial \delta_S} > 0 \quad for\ any \quad b \in (0,1)\,.$$

Proof. Proof is conducted by numerical analysis of the partial derivatives of p^*, see equations (6.14) and (6.15) in the appendix.   □

All results from the original analysis carry over: For example, a range of markets may exist in which the sensitivity of the market price with regard to the buyer–seller ratio is reduced, and the equilibrium price function may be partially flat in the limit as δ_B and δ_S simultaneously approach unity. Only the relevant ranges of b are shifted.

Note one interesting effect: if the discount factor approaches unity only for one side of the market, that is, only for the sellers or only for the buyers, this side appropriates the possible maximum, and leaves the trading partners without a positive payoff. Formally:

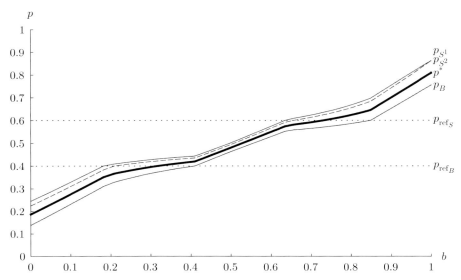

Fig. 6.9 Equilibrium prices when buyers hold heterogenous discount factors; example for $\alpha_i = \beta_i = 0.3$, $\lambda = 0.5$, $\delta_S = \delta_{B^1} = 0.95$ and $\delta_{B^2} = 0.96$

Proposition 6.11. *Denote by $p_{B_{max}}$ the price for which buyer utility equals zero, that is, $u_B(p_{B_{max}}) = 0$, and by $p_{S_{min}}$ the price for which $u_S(p_{S_{min}}) = 0$. Then, for any fixed $\delta_0 \in (0, 1)$ the following two statements hold:*

$$For\ \delta_S = \delta_0\ and\ \delta_B \rightarrow 1:\ p^* \rightarrow p_{S_{min}},\ and$$

$$for\ \delta_B = \delta_0\ and\ \delta_S \rightarrow 1:\ p^* \rightarrow p_{B_{max}},$$

$$with\ p_{S_{min}} = \frac{\beta_S p_{ref_S}}{1 + \beta_S}\ and\ p_{B_{max}} = \frac{1 + \beta_B p_{ref_B}}{1 + \beta_B}\ .$$

Proof. Proof is conducted by setting $\delta_B = 1$ or $\delta_S = 1$ in p^* (equilibrium prices are continuous in δ_i). For p^* see equation (6.16) in the appendix. □

The intuition behind this result is: if one side of the market is completely patient while the other side is not, then the patient side is in a very strong bargaining position and can capture the maximum possible gains from trade, consistent with the other side participating in the market; that is, the limit price is the price for which the utility of the impatient trading partner is zero.

When homogeneity on each side of the market is dispensed with, the findings are more differentiated. For simplicity of exposition, assume that all sellers are homogenous, and that there are two types of buyers. Type B^1 holds a low discount factor of δ_{B^1}, while buyers of type B^2 have a higher discount factor denoted by $\delta_{B^2} > \delta_{B^1}$. The share of buyers with type B^2 is given by λ. Figure 6.9 displays an example with $\delta_{B^1} = 0.95$ and $\delta_{B^2} = 0.96$ in a scenario with $\lambda = 0.5$. Both buyer types in this market offer the same price p_B to the sellers, but the sellers differentiate their offers by buyer type, with $p_{S^1} > p_{S^2}$. In figure 6.9, the price p_{S^1} is marked by the upper *thin solid line*, while p_{S^2} directly underneath is marked with the *thin broken line*. All prices (including p_B) are shifted downwards relative to the case of a homogenous buyer population of type B^1 only, as, for example, in figure 6.2. This is formally described in proposition 6.12:

Proposition 6.12. *For any given* $b \in (0,1)$ *and for any buyer of type* B^x *with* $x \in \{1,2\}$, *the following inequalities hold:*

$$\frac{\partial p_{S^x}}{\partial \delta_{B^x}} < 0 \,, \quad \frac{\partial p_B}{\partial \delta_{B^x}} < 0 \text{ and therefore also } \frac{\partial p^*}{\partial \delta_{B^x}} < 0 \,.$$

Proof. The proof is conducted by numerical analysis of the partial derivatives. □

If only one agent type, for example, B^2 is infinitely patient (so $\delta_{B^2} \to 1$) and $\lambda < 1$, then these agents do *not* appropriate the full gains from trade (as described by $p_{S_{\min}}$, see proposition 6.11), in contrast to the case above for a homogenous buyer population. The reason is that sellers face a positive likelihood of being matched with a less patient type of buyer going forward, so they do not give in completely; however they retain some bargaining power. Of course, this bargaining power then diminishes with λ, and for $\lambda \to 1$, the result is the same as above.

6.7 Shape of the Utility Function

The utility functions of buyers and sellers can be split into two parts, the first being the baseline utility as a function of the price, which is $u_S(p) = p$ for the sellers and $u_B(p) = 1 - p$ for the buyers. The second part is the "fairness" part, in which some utility is subtracted for deviations from the reference price. This section investigates the relevance of the linearity of both parts by allowing for alternative forms.

Denote by $f_B(p)$ and $f_S(p)$ two functions $f_B, f_S \colon \mathbb{R}_+ \to \mathbb{R}_+$ that are strictly monotone, continuous, differentiable, and satisfy $f_B(0) = f_S(0) = 0$. These can be applied to the first baseline part of the utility function. The utility functions for buyers and sellers are then given by:

$$u_B(p, p_{\text{ref}_B}, t) = \delta^t \left(f_B(1 - p) - \alpha_B (p_{\text{ref}_B} - p)^+ - \beta_B (p - p_{\text{ref}_B})^+ \right) \text{ and}$$
$$u_S(p, p_{\text{ref}_S}, t) = \delta^t \left(f_S(p) - \alpha_S (p - p_{\text{ref}_S})^+ - \beta_S (p_{\text{ref}_S} - p)^+ \right) .$$

When agents hold no fairness concern (so that $\alpha_i = \beta_i = 0$ for $i \in \{B, S\}$), then the function $f(p)$ does affect market prices, but the resulting equilibrium price $p^*(\cdot)$ is still strictly monotone, continuous, and differentiable for any $b \in (0,1)$. Figure 6.10 shows four different exemplary functions, each for the case of discounting with $\delta = 0.95$, and figure 6.11 the same functions, but at the limit ($\delta \to 1$). In both figures the "standard" prices for $f_B(p) = f_S(p) = p$ are marked with a *dashed line* for comparison.

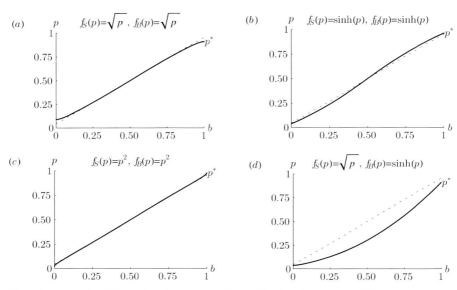

Fig. 6.10 Prices for different functional forms of the utility functions without fairness concern and for $\delta = 0.95$

The interesting question is whether this change to the utility function affects the effects of fairness concern on market prices discussed before. Prices for the same four exemplary functions as above, but for agents with fairness concern ($p_{\text{ref}_i} = 0.5$, and $\alpha_i = \beta_i$ for $i \in \{B,S\}$) are illustrated in figures 6.12 and 6.13; in figure 6.12 for the case of discounting with $\delta = 0.95$, and in figure 6.13 for $\delta \to 1$.

These graphs demonstrate visually that the results that were derived for $f_B(p) = f_S(p) = p$ are in principle sustained, at least for the given functions. Only the range of markets with reduced sensitivity of the equilibrium price $p^*(\cdot)$ with regard to changes in b may be shifted and affected in size. To date, we could prove this numerically for different specific functions as those given here, but not in general for any function. Nevertheless, so far we could not identify any function for which the results do *not* hold. Therefore we conjecture that the results hold for any function that is strictly monotone, continuous, differentiable, and satisfies $f(0) = 0$.

The second part of the utility function describes the reduction in utility for a deviation from the reference price. In the standard setup, this is assumed to be piecewise linear and with a kink in the utility function. Here, this assumption is relaxed by smoothing the kink with a differentiable function. This is, for example, possible with the hyperbolic tangent $\tanh(\cdot)$ or the exponential function $\exp(\cdot)$. As the results are qualitatively the same for any such design, the hyperbolic tangent is used in the following exposition. Define the utility functions of buyers and sellers by

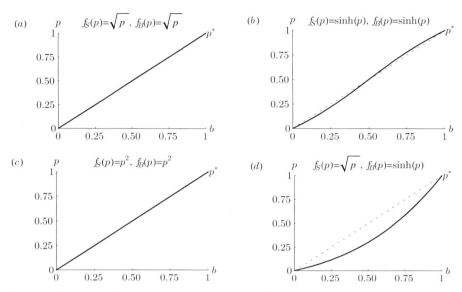

Fig. 6.11 Prices for different functional forms of the utility functions without fairness concern at the limit $\delta \to 1$

$$u_B(p, p_{\text{ref}}, t) = \delta^t \left(1 - p + \frac{1}{2}(p_{\text{ref}} - p)\left(\beta_B - \alpha_B - (\alpha_B + \beta_B)\tanh(c(p_{\text{ref}} - p))\right) \right)$$
(6.6)

$$u_S(p, p_{\text{ref}}, t) = \delta^t \left(p + \frac{1}{2}(p - p_{\text{ref}})\left(\beta_S - \alpha_S - (\alpha_S + \beta_S)\tanh(c(p - p_{\text{ref}}))\right) \right).$$
(6.7)

These utilities given in equations (6.6) and (6.7) are smooth and converge uniformly to $u_B(\cdot)$ and $u_S(\cdot)$, respectively, of the linear setup as $c \to \infty$. Figure 6.14 displays these utility functions for different values of c; for comparison, linear utility is marked with the *dashed line*. The resulting price functions for the same utility functions are shown in figure 6.15.

Obviously, the equilibrium price converges to the obtained for piecewise linear utility functions as $c \to \infty$. If c is rather small, the effects of fairness concern on the equilibrium price are significantly reduced, as is easily seen from figure 6.15. Nevertheless, the effects can in principle be sustained with a differentiable utility function as given here. Only the result for $\delta \to 1$ of a partially *completely flat* equilibrium price holds only in the limit, as $c \to \infty$; this is illustrated in figure 6.16.

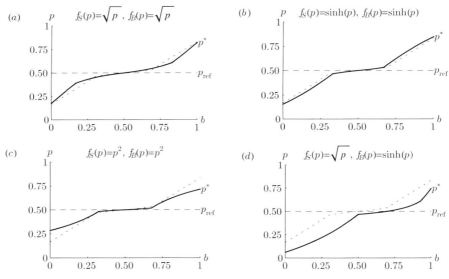

Fig. 6.12 Prices for different functional forms of the utility functions with fairness concern; example for $\alpha_i = \beta_i = 0.3$, $\delta = 0.95$

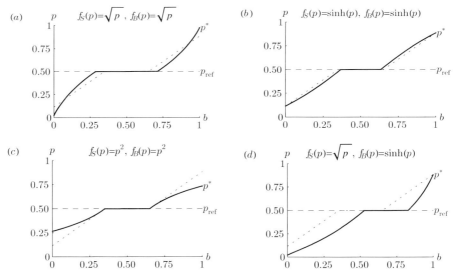

Fig. 6.13 Prices for different functional forms of the utility functions with fairness concern at the limit $\delta \to 1$; example for $\alpha_i = \beta_i = 0.3$

6.8 A Model with One-Time Entry

In his overview paper paper, Rubinstein (1989) contrasts a model with one-time entry (Model B) with the steady state model (Model A) that was the basis of our

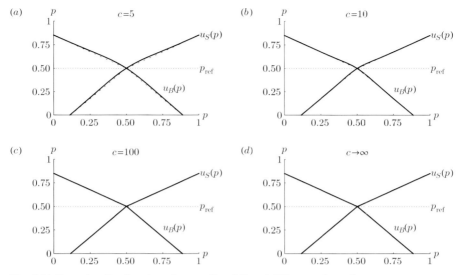

Fig. 6.14 Smooth utility functions for $\alpha_i = \beta_i = 0.3$, and different values of c

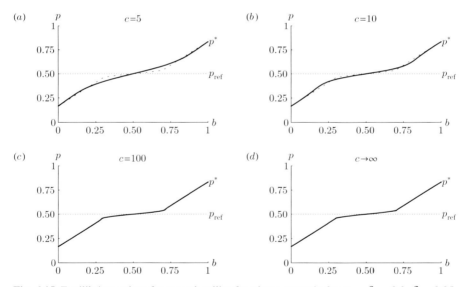

Fig. 6.15 Equilibrium prices for smooth utility functions; example for $\alpha_i = \beta_i = 0.3$, $\delta = 0.95$, and different values of c

analysis so far. In Model B, all agents enter the market before the first matching and trading period, and stay in the market until they make an agreement with a trading partner. No new agents enter the market in subsequent periods. For the case of one seller ($S = 1$) and more than one buyer ($B > 1$), the market equilibrium is characterized by the following set of equations:

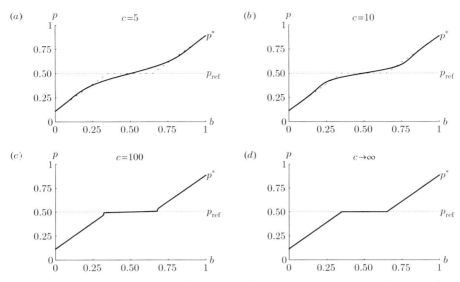

Fig. 6.16 Equilibrium prices for smooth utility functions at the limit $\delta \to 1$; example for $\alpha_i = \beta_i = 0.3$, and different values of c

$$u_B(p_S,t) = \delta V_B(t+1)$$
$$u_S(p_B,t) = \delta V_S(t+1)$$
$$V_S(t) = \frac{1}{2}(u_S(p_B,t) + u_S(p_S,t))$$
$$= \frac{1}{2}(\delta V_S(t+1) + u_S(u_B^{-1}(\delta V_B(t+1))))$$
$$V_B(t) = \frac{1}{2B}(u_B(p_S,t) + u_B(p_B,t))$$
$$= \frac{1}{2B}(\delta V_B(t+1) + u_B(u_S^{-1}(\delta V_S(t+1))))$$
$$p(t) = \frac{1}{2}[p_B + p_S] = \frac{1}{2}\left[u_B^{-1}(\delta V_B(t+1)) + u_S^{-1}(\delta V_S(t+1))\right] .$$

The equilibrium price in the standard setup without fairness concern converges towards unity ($p^* \to 1$) for $\delta \to 1$ and $b = B/(B+S) > 1/2$.

This result is only affected in one regard when preferences that allow for fairness concern are taken into account (compare equations (6.3) and (6.4)): in the standard setup with $\alpha_i = \beta_i = 0$ for $i \in \{B,S\}$, buyer utility is zero for a price of one. This changes with fairness concern. Denote the price that results in a utility of zero for the buyers by $p_{B_{max}}$, i.e., $u_B(p_{B_{max}}) = 0$. With fairness concern, the equilibrium market price does not converge to unity, but $p^* \to p_{B_{max}}$ for $\delta \to 1$ and $b = B/(B+S) > 1/2$. Figure 6.17 shows an example with $\delta = 0.95$ (*thick line*) and for $\delta \to 1$ (*thin line*).

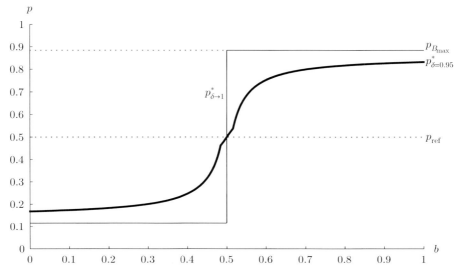

Fig. 6.17 Equilibrium prices for a model with one-time entry; example for $\alpha_i = \beta_i = 0.3$ with $\delta = 0.95$, and for $\delta \to 1$

The effect that fairness concern has on prices around the reference price is rather limited as one can see from the example, and therefore not investigated in further detail.

6.9 Some Thoughts on Incomplete Information

This section explores some implications of incomplete information for the model's equilibrium. Assume that agents do not know the specific utility functions of their trading partners; they only know the distribution of utility functions in the population. This distribution is assumed to be common knowledge.

In this scenario, agents are not able to condition their actions on the specific preferences of their matched trading partner. As a result, strategies can only prescribe the same bargaining tactics against all potential trading partners, regardless of their type. An agent's utility of accepting such a price offer depends on his or her specific utility function and may thus vary across the population. If the utility of accepting an offer is below his or her continuation value, an agent would reject the offer.

We did not succeed in extending our analysis to a general case of n types of buyers and m types of sellers. The fact that continuation values are dependent on each other could give rise to multiple equilibria in case of two-sided incomplete information. Nevertheless, a simple example for one-sided incomplete information is discussed in the following.

Consider a market in which all sellers have the same preferences, and there are two types of buyers, indexed by 1 and 2. In this market, there is only one-sided incomplete information; all buyers are assumed to know the preferences of the sellers. However, a matched seller cannot tell with which type of buyer he or she is matched. Denote the utility function of buyers of the type 1 with $u_{B1}(\cdot)$, and that of buyers of type 2 with $u_{B2}(\cdot)$. The share of buyers of each type is common knowledge, because the distribution of utility functions is known. The share of type 1 is parameterized by $\lambda \in (0,1)$, and the resulting share for type 2 is $1 - \lambda$. Due to the different preferences of both buyer types, the continuation values of both buyer types may also be different. Denote these continuation values by δV_{B1} for buyers of type 1 and by δV_{B2} for buyers of type 2. For buyers of type 1 to be indifferent between accepting or rejecting an offer, the utility of the offered price p_{S1} needs to be equal to the continuation value, so that $u_{B1}(p_{S1}) = \delta V_{B1}$. For type 2, accordingly, $u_{B2}(p_{S2}) = \delta V_{B2}$. If these prices differ, i.e., $p_{S1} \neq p_{S2}$, then the seller could offer a low price that reflects the lower of the two with $p_S^{\text{low}} = \min\{p_{S1}, p_{S2}\}$ or he could offer a high price with $p_S^{\text{high}} = \max\{p_{S1}, p_{S2}\}$. p_S^{low} would be accepted by both buyer types, while p_S^{high} would be accepted only by one of the two. In the latter case, the seller would face a lottery between $u_S(p_S^{\text{high}})$ and rejection of his offer. In equilibrium, all sellers propose either p_S^{high} or p_S^{low}, depending on which strategy yields the higher expected utility in the given market. All matched buyers face the same type of seller and would therefore offer the same price p_B, regardless of their type—unless their utility for a trade at that price is negative. If the latter was the case, they would resign from trading and the equilibrium would change accordingly (see section 6.4). Note that if a buyer's utility for trade at price p_B is positive, this buyer participates in the market, even if sellers choose not to offer him or her acceptable prices. In equilibrium, these buyers would still make price offers, that are in turn accepted by the sellers.

Denote by B^{high} the mass of agents for which p_S^{high} is an acceptable price offer (with $u_{B^{\text{high}}}(p_S^{\text{high}}) \geq 0$). The average market price in the equilibrium in which the sellers offer p_S^{high} is then:[13]

$$p^{*,\text{high}} = \frac{B}{B + B^{\text{high}}}\left[p_B + \left(\frac{B^{\text{high}}}{B}\right)p_S^{\text{high}}\right],$$

and in the equilibrium in which the sellers offer p_S^{low} the average market price is

$$p^{*,\text{low}} = \frac{1}{2}\left[p_B + p_S^{\text{low}}\right].$$

Sellers choose the strategy that maximizes their expected utility. Therefore, in equilibrium for any given market configuration, the continuous equilibrium price is

---

[13] For any given market configuration of this type, there is only one unique equilibrium. See equations (6.17) and (6.18) in the appendix for the equilibrium market price as a function of the parameters of the model.

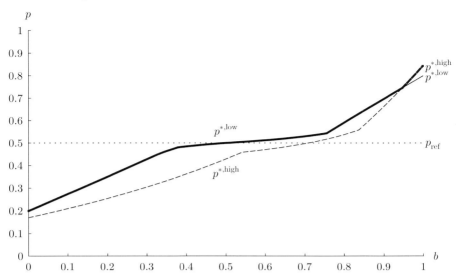

Fig. 6.18 Equilibrium prices with one-sided incomplete information; example for $p_{\text{ref}_S} = p_{\text{ref}_B} = p_{\text{ref}} = 0.5, \delta = 0.95, \alpha_S = \alpha_{B^1} = 0.4, \alpha_{B^2} = 0, \beta_S = \beta_{B^1} = 0.4, \beta_{B^2} = 0$, and for the share $\lambda = 0.5$

$$p^* = \max\{p^{*,\text{high}}, p^{*,\text{low}}\} .$$

This is visualized in figure 6.18 for an example: $p^{*,\text{low}}$ is plotted with a *solid line*, and $p^{*,\text{high}}$ with a *dashed line*; the equilibrium price p^* is plotted as the *thick part* of these two lines.

As in above sections, the effects of fairness concern on this equilibrium price are sustained when price offers are made to *and accepted* by agents with a preference for fairness that have a reference price between p_S and p_B (with $p_S = p_S^{\text{high}}$ or $p_S = p_S^{\text{low}}$ depending on the equilibrium strategy of the sellers). This need not be the case, even if agents with such preferences are in the market. For example, in a market with only a few fair-minded buyers and many buyers without a concern for fairness, it may be that sellers propose prices that are only acceptable for those buyers without fairness concern. In this case, the reference price of the fair-minded buyers would not affect the equilibrium market price.

6.10 Concluding Remarks

The preceding sections clarified the robustness of the original model's results in various aspects. A different, additional type of friction was analyzed in section 6.1, that considered matching friction. This type of friction was not modeled in the original analysis, which focused only on friction in the form of discounting of future gains. Comparable to discounting, matching friction increases the spread between the prices offered by both sides of the market but does not render our general results invalid.

Section 6.2 addressed reference prices that were originally considered to be equal for all agents in the market. However, there are good reasons why buyers and sellers might not hold the same reference price: The reference price resembles an agent's belief about the "fair" price. Given the natural human inclination for self-serving biases, the likelihood that buyers and sellers adopt the same reference price seems small. Nevertheless, even if they adopt distinct reference prices, effects of fairness concern on equilibrium market prices around these reference prices are sustained.

In sections 6.3 to 6.5, this analysis of diverging reference prices was extended to markets in which not all agents on one side of the market (buyers or sellers) hold a common reference price. Agents were allowed to hold heterogeneous, but commonly known, reference prices—and again, the effects of fairness concern on equilibrium market prices are sustained: For example, whenever a positive mass of agents holds a certain reference price, the price sensitivity of the market price to changes in the buyer–seller ratio is still reduced for market prices around that reference. Naturally, the effect depends on the share of agents holding this reference. If it is just a single agent who adopts a certain reference price, the effect in a market with many agents is negligible. The larger the share of agents that hold a specific reference, the more pronounced the effect. Parallel results were found with regard to the fairness parameters. In a market in which, for example, some agents care a lot about fairness (high fairness parameters), some agents care less, and some agents do not care at all, the general results are sustained. Again, the larger the share of fair-minded agents, the greater the effect of fairness concern on equilibrium market prices. An interesting additional result is that fair agents in most cases receive higher payoffs than less fair-minded agents.[14]

These results regarding mixed agent populations are also interesting with respect to evolutionary stability. As Güth and Napel (2006) and chapter 3 of this book demonstrate with an indirect evolutionary approach, fairness in terms of *inequity aversion* or *reciprocity* is evolutionary stable in a "game of life" consisting of ultimatum and dictator games, when evolutionary fitness of agents is determined solely by material success. With this reasoning the results given here lead to a parallel insight for matching markets: fairness concern results in higher payoffs, and would therefore prove to be evolutionary stable.

Section 6.6 investigated heterogeneity with regard to discount factors, and found that if an agent discounts future gains less, he or she takes away a higher payoff from the bargaining table. This is a typical result for settings that involve bargaining processes and discounting over time, because discounting less than others improves an agent's bargaining position. Still, the effects of fairness concern on equilibrium market prices are sustained when different discount factors prevail in the population. They only disappear in the limit if the discount factor of a whole market side

---

[14] Here, *fair* refers to fairness concern with regard to being *disadvantaged*. Agents receive higher payoffs only in *most* cases and not in all cases, because there is one exception: when fair agents are in a minority position, *and* less fairness-concerned agents trade at prices that are completely unattractive to fair agents. In this case, fair agents resign from trading.

(all buyers or all sellers) approaches unity while it does not for the other. In this unbalanced case, the infinitely patient side of the market appropriates so much of the gains from trade, that the other side gets no positive utility out of the trade.

A final robustness check concerning agent's preferences was conducted in section 6.7. There, different functional forms which could represent agents' preferences were compared. Most notably, the results of the model do not fully depend on the kink of the utility function at the reference price.[15] Effects of fairness concern on equilibrium market prices are sustained with a differentiable approximation. Nevertheless, the sharper the "bend" around the reference price, the more pointed the effect of fairness on prices. If a sharp kink in the utility function is interpreted as a sharp notion of the reference price, then this finding has an important interpretation: There are little effects of fairness concern on equilibrium prices in a market if agents hold only a diffuse notion of what they regard as a fair price. A clear idea of the reference price is a prerequisite for fairness to be significantly reflected in market prices. As mentioned above, not *all* agents necessarily need to have this clear idea about their reference price; it is sufficient that *some* agents have this notion. And not all agents need to have the same reference price—only if nobody in a market had a sharp notion of what the reference price is, then there would be no effect of fairness on market prices.

Section 6.8 applied fairness preferences to a modified version of the market model: Instead of a market with steady numbers of buyers and sellers, a market in which all agents enter at the first period and no agents enter the market subsequently was investigated. The standard result is, loosely speaking, that the short side of the market appropriates all gains from trade. Here, fairness preferences do not qualitatively change this aspect of the equilibrium.

Finally, section 6.9 considered the role of information and found that dispensing perfect information not only complicates analysis; it may also lead to multiplicity of equilibria. For a simple scenario of one-sided incomplete information with two different buyer types, the results for fairness concern may be sustained for a range of markets and the equilibrium may still be unique; but we were unable to further generalize these findings. This would require analysis beyond the scope of this book. We consider this an interesting area of potential future research.

---

[15] Only the result of partially *completely* "flat" equilibrium prices in the limit, as the discount factor of all agents approaches unity, depends on the kink in preferences. Prices can only be *approximately* flat with differentiable preferences.

Appendix: Price Formulas

For matching friction ϑ the equilibrium prices are given by (for simplicity given for $\beta_S = \beta_B = \beta$, and $\alpha_S = \alpha_B = 0$):

$$
p_S = \begin{cases}
\dfrac{b\left((\vartheta-2)\delta^2+(\vartheta-2)\delta+\beta\left(\vartheta\,p_{\mathrm{ref}}+\vartheta-2\right)\delta^2+(\vartheta+2)\delta-2\right)-\delta\vartheta(\delta(\vartheta-2)+1)\beta(\delta(p_{\mathrm{ref}}+\vartheta-2)+2)\delta-2)}{(\beta+1)\left(\delta\vartheta(-\vartheta\delta+\delta-2)+b\left((\vartheta-1)\vartheta\delta^2+(\vartheta+2)\delta-2\right)\right)} & \text{for } b < b^{1,2} \\[2ex]
\dfrac{\delta(-\delta-2)(\delta(\vartheta-2)+2)\beta^2-2(\delta-2)(\beta-2)(\delta(\vartheta-1)+2)p_{\mathrm{ref}}-\delta+b(p_{\mathrm{ref}}(\vartheta\delta^2-2(\vartheta+1)\delta-2)\beta+b(p_{\mathrm{ref}}(\vartheta\delta^2-\delta-1)-(\delta-1)(\delta\delta-1))\beta-2(\delta-1)\beta-2(\delta-1))}{(p_{\mathrm{ref}}\beta+1)(\delta\vartheta-2)+2)(b(\delta\vartheta-1)-\delta\vartheta)} & \text{for } b^{1,2} \le b \le b^{2,3} \\[2ex]
\dfrac{}{(p_{\mathrm{ref}}\beta+1)(\delta\vartheta-2)+2)(b(\delta\vartheta-1)-\delta\vartheta)} & \text{for } b > b^{2,3}
\end{cases}
\tag{6.8}
$$

$$
p_B = \begin{cases}
\dfrac{b\delta(\beta+1)\delta\vartheta(\delta\vartheta-1)-p_{\mathrm{ref}}\beta(-\vartheta\delta^2+2(\vartheta+1)\delta-2))-\delta\vartheta((\beta+1)\delta\vartheta-p_{\mathrm{ref}}\beta(\delta-2))}{(\beta+1)(\delta\vartheta(-\vartheta\delta+\delta-2)+b((\vartheta-1)\vartheta\delta^2+(\vartheta+2)\delta-2))} & \text{for } b < b^{1,2} \\[2ex]
\dfrac{\delta\vartheta(-p_{\mathrm{ref}}\beta(\delta-2)+\beta(\delta(\vartheta-2)+2)(\beta(\delta(\vartheta-2)+2)+2\delta(\vartheta-1)+2))+b(2(\delta-1)\delta\vartheta-2(\delta-1)+p_{\mathrm{ref}}\beta(\vartheta\delta^2+2(\vartheta+1)\delta-2))}{(p_{\mathrm{ref}}\beta+1)\delta\vartheta(b(\delta\vartheta-1)-\delta\vartheta)} & \text{for } b^{1,2} \le b \le b^{2,3} \\[2ex]
\dfrac{}{(p_{\mathrm{ref}}\beta+1)\delta\vartheta(b(\delta\vartheta-1)-\delta\vartheta)} & \text{for } b > b^{2,3}
\end{cases}
\tag{6.9}
$$

$$
p^* = \begin{cases}
\dfrac{b((\vartheta-1)\vartheta\delta^2+\delta+p_{\mathrm{ref}}(\vartheta\delta(\delta-1)-1)-1)-\delta\beta(p_{\mathrm{ref}}\vartheta\delta(\vartheta-1)+1)+1)\vartheta}{(\beta+1)(\delta\vartheta(-\vartheta\delta+\delta-2)+b((\vartheta-1)\vartheta\delta^2+(\vartheta+2)\delta-2))} & \text{for } b < b^{1,2} \\[2ex]
\dfrac{\delta(-p_{\mathrm{ref}}(\delta\vartheta(-\vartheta\delta+\delta-2)+b(p_{\mathrm{ref}}(\vartheta+1)\vartheta\delta^2-2\delta-2))}{(\beta+1)(\delta\vartheta(-\vartheta\delta+\delta-2)+b((\vartheta-1)\vartheta\delta^2))} & \text{for } b^{1,2} \le b \le b^{2,3} \\[2ex]
\dfrac{}{(p_{\mathrm{ref}}\beta+1)(\delta\vartheta-1)+b((\vartheta-1)\vartheta\delta^2-(\vartheta+2)\delta-2))} & \text{for } b > b^{2,3}
\end{cases}
\tag{6.10}
$$

with

$$
b^{1,2} = \frac{\delta\left(p_{\mathrm{ref}}\left(\beta(\delta(\vartheta-2)+2)+\delta(\vartheta-1)+2\right)-(\beta+1)(\delta(\vartheta-2)+2)\right)\vartheta}{p_{\mathrm{ref}}\left((\vartheta-1)\vartheta\delta^2+(\vartheta+2)\delta+\beta((\vartheta-2)\vartheta\delta^2+(\vartheta+2)\delta-2)-2)-(\beta+1)((\vartheta-2)\vartheta\delta^2+(\vartheta+2)\delta-2)\right)}
$$

$$
b^{2,3} = \frac{\delta\vartheta(\delta\vartheta-1)+p_{\mathrm{ref}}\left(\beta(\delta(\vartheta-2)+\delta-\delta\vartheta-2)\right)}{\delta\vartheta(\delta\vartheta-1)+p_{\mathrm{ref}}\left(-(\vartheta-1)\vartheta\delta^2-(\vartheta+2)\delta+\beta(\vartheta\delta^2-2(\vartheta+1)\delta+2)\right)}.
$$

For two distinct reference prices the resulting equilibrium price is (for simplicity given for $\beta_S = \beta_B = \beta$, and $\alpha_S = \alpha_B = 0$):

$$
p^* =
\begin{cases}
\dfrac{b(\delta+\beta(2\delta p_{\mathrm{ref}_S}-p_{\mathrm{ref}_S}+\delta-1)-1)-(p_{\mathrm{ref}_S}\beta+\beta+1)\delta}{(\beta+1)(b)(3\delta-2)-2\delta} & \text{for } b \le b^{s,b} \\[4ex]
\dfrac{\splitfrac{\delta(\delta-2)\big((p_{\mathrm{ref}_B}+p_{\mathrm{ref}_S}-p_{\mathrm{ref}_S}\delta)\delta(\delta^2-6\delta+2)\beta^2+(2\delta-1)(2\delta p_{\mathrm{ref}_S}-p_{\mathrm{ref}_S}-\delta+1)\beta-2(\delta-1)+p_{\mathrm{ref}_S}(\delta^2-4\delta+2)\big)\delta}{-b\big((p_{\mathrm{ref}_B}+p_{\mathrm{ref}_S})\delta(\delta^3-6\delta^2+10\delta-4)-(\beta\delta-2)^2-4\delta+1)^2-(\beta\delta-2)^2-4\delta+1)\delta\big)}}{\splitfrac{(\beta+1)\big(b(-6\delta^2+10\delta-4)\beta^2-2\big(p_{\mathrm{ref}_B}\beta(\delta^2-4\delta+2)-(\delta-1)(\delta^2-6\delta^2+10\delta-4)\beta^2+(p_{\mathrm{ref}_S}+p_{\mathrm{ref}_B}\beta+p_{\mathrm{ref}_S}\beta+1)\delta}{}}} & \text{for } b^{s,b} < b \le b^{s,s} \wedge b \le b^{b,b} \\[4ex]
\dfrac{2\big(b\big(\delta^3-6\delta^2+10\delta-4\big)\beta^2-2\big(p_{\mathrm{ref}_B}\beta(2\delta-1)-1\big)-(p_{\mathrm{ref}_B}\beta+p_{\mathrm{ref}_S}\beta+1)\delta}{(\beta+1)(b)(3\delta-2)-2\delta} & \text{for } b^{s,s} < b \le b^{b,b} \\[4ex]
\dfrac{b\big(p_{\mathrm{ref}_B}\beta(\delta-1)+\delta+p_{\mathrm{ref}_S}\beta(2\delta-1)-1\big)-(p_{\mathrm{ref}_B}\beta+p_{\mathrm{ref}_S})\beta+1)\delta}{(\beta+1)(b)(3\delta-2)-2\delta} & \text{for } b^{b,b} < b \le b^{s,s} \\[4ex]
\dfrac{\splitfrac{b\big((\delta-2)\big(p_{\mathrm{ref}_B}\beta(\delta-1)^2+p_{\mathrm{ref}_S}\delta-2p_{\mathrm{ref}_B}\delta(\delta-1)^2\big)\beta-2\delta(\delta-1)^2\big)\beta-2(\delta-2)-1\big)\beta^2-(\delta-2)\delta+2\beta\big(\delta-2)^2-4\delta+4\big)\delta}{-\delta\big((\delta-2)(\delta p_{\mathrm{ref}_B}-p_{\mathrm{ref}_B})\beta^2+(-(p_{\mathrm{ref}_S}-\delta+1)(\delta-2)-2p_{\mathrm{ref}_B}(\delta-1)\beta-2\delta-2\big)\delta}}{(\beta+1)\big(b(-6\delta^2+10\delta-\beta\big(\delta^3-6\delta^2+10\delta-4\big)\big)-(\beta\delta-2)^2-4\delta+4\big)\delta} & \text{for } b^{b,b} < b \le b^{b,s} \wedge b^{s,s} < b \\[4ex]
\dfrac{(p_{\mathrm{ref}_B}\beta+1)(b)(\delta-1)-\delta)}{(\beta+1)(b)(3\delta-2)-2\delta} & \text{for } b^{b,s} < b
\end{cases}
$$

$$(6.11)$$

with

$$
b^{s,b} = \frac{\delta\big(2p_{\mathrm{ref}_B}(\beta+1)+\delta+\beta(-p_{\mathrm{ref}_S}\delta+\delta-2)-2\big)}{\delta^2-3\delta+p_{\mathrm{ref}_B}(\beta+1)(3\delta-2)+\beta\big(-p_{\mathrm{ref}_S}\delta^2+\delta^2-3\delta+2\big)+2}
$$

$$
b^{s,s} = \frac{\delta\big((\beta+1)\big(p_{\mathrm{ref}_B}\beta(\delta-2)+2(\delta-1)\big)(\delta-2)-p_{\mathrm{ref}_S}\big(\beta^2(\delta-2)^2-4\delta+\beta(3\delta^2-10\delta+8)+4\big)\big)}{(\beta+1)(2(\delta-1)^2+p_{\mathrm{ref}_B}\beta(\delta^2-4\delta+2))+p_{\mathrm{ref}_S}\big(-(\delta^3-6\delta^2+10\delta-4)\beta^2-(\delta-2)^2(3\delta-2)\beta+6\delta^2-10\delta+4\big)}
$$

$$
b^{b,b} = \frac{\delta\big(-p_{\mathrm{ref}_S}^2-p_{\mathrm{ref}_S}\beta(\beta+1)\big(\delta^3-6\delta^2+10\delta-4\big)\beta^2+2(\delta-1)\delta+p_{\mathrm{ref}_B}\big(\big(\delta^3-6\delta^2+10\delta-4\big)\beta^2+(3\delta^3-16\delta^2+22\delta-8)\beta-6\delta^2+10\delta-4\big)\big)}{2\delta(\delta-1)^2-p_{\mathrm{ref}_S}\beta(\beta+1)\big(\delta^3-6\delta^2+10\delta-4\big)\beta^2+2(\delta-1)\delta+p_{\mathrm{ref}_B}\big(\big(\delta^3-6\delta^2+10\delta-4\big)\beta^2+(3\delta^3-16\delta^2+22\delta-8)\beta-6\delta^2+10\delta-4\big)}
$$

$$
b^{b,s} = \frac{\delta\big(-2p_{\mathrm{ref}_S}(\beta+1)+p_{\mathrm{ref}_B}\beta\delta+\delta\big)}{(p_{\mathrm{ref}_B}\beta+1)(\delta-1)\delta-p_{\mathrm{ref}_S}(\beta+1)(3\delta-2)}.
$$

Equations underlying proof of proposition 6.4:

$$
p_S = \begin{cases}
\dfrac{-Pref_S\,\beta_S\,\delta + b\left(-2+\delta+\beta_S(-2+\delta+Pref_S\,\delta)\right)}{(1+\beta_S)(2b(-1+\delta)-\delta)} & \text{for case (1)} \\[2ex]
\dfrac{-\left(Pref_B\,\beta_B(1+\beta_S)(-2+\delta)+2Pref_S\,\beta_S(-1+\delta)\right)\delta+b\left(Pref_B\,\beta_B(1+\beta_S)(4-8\delta+3\delta^2)+2(-1+\delta)(-2+\delta+\beta_S(-2+\delta+Pref_S\,\delta))\right)}{(1+\beta_S)\left((2-\beta_B(-2+\delta)-2\delta)\delta-b(4(-1+\delta)^2+\beta_B(4-8\delta+3\delta^2))\right)} & \text{for case (2)} \\[2ex]
\dfrac{\delta\left(-2+\beta_S(-2+\delta)+\beta_B(1+\beta_S)(-2+\delta)+2\delta-\alpha_S\,\delta\right)-b\left(4-6\delta+2\delta^2-Pref_S\,\alpha_S\,\delta^2+\beta_S(-2+\delta+Pref_S\,\beta_B\,\delta)\right)}{(1+\beta_B)\beta_S\,\delta+b(-2+Pref_B\,\beta_B(1+\beta_S)(-2+\delta)+\delta+\beta_S(-2+\delta+Pref_S\,\beta_B\,\delta))} & \text{for case (3a)} \\[2ex]
\dfrac{-Pref_S(1+\beta_B)\beta_S\,\delta+b(-2+\delta)+\beta_S(-2+\delta)-Pref_S\,\alpha_S\,\delta^2}{(1+\beta_B)(1+\beta_S)(2b(-1+\delta)-\delta)} & \text{for case (3b)} \\[2ex]
\dfrac{-Pref_S(1+\beta_B)\delta(\beta_S(-2+\delta)+b(4-6\delta+2\delta^2-Pref_S\,\alpha_S\,\beta_B\,\delta^2+\beta_S(-2+\delta)+(-2+\alpha_S)\delta)+b(4+8\delta-(-4+\alpha_S)\delta^2+\beta_S(4-8\delta+3\delta^2))}{(1+\beta_B)(\delta(2-\beta_S(-2+\delta)+(-2+\alpha_S)\delta)+b(4+8\delta-(-2+\alpha_S)\delta^2+\beta_S(4-8\delta+3\delta^2))} & \text{for case (4)} \\[2ex]
\dfrac{-Pref_S\,\alpha_S(1+\beta_B)\delta+b(-(1+Pref_B\,\beta_B)(-2+\delta)+\alpha_S(-2+\delta+Pref_S\,\delta+Pref_S\,\beta_B\,\delta))}{(-1+\alpha_S)(1+\beta_B)(2b(-1+\delta)-\delta)} & \text{for case (5)}
\end{cases}
$$

$$(6.12)$$

$$
p_{S^n} = \begin{cases}
\dfrac{-Pref_S\,\beta_S\,\delta+b(-2+\delta+\beta_S(-2+\delta+Pref_S\,\delta))}{(1+\beta_S)(2b(-1+\delta)-\delta)} & \text{for case (1)} \\[2ex]
\dfrac{\delta(-2Pref_S(1+\beta_B)\beta_S(-1+\delta)+Pref_B\,\beta_B(1+\beta_S)\delta)+b(2(-1+\delta)(-2+\delta+\beta_S(-2+\delta+Pref_S\,\delta))+Pref_B\,\beta_B(1+\beta_S)\delta)+b(2(-1+\delta)^2+Pref_B\,\beta_B(4-8\delta+3\delta^2))}{(1+\beta_S)((2-\beta_B(-2+\delta)-2\delta)\delta-b(4(-1+\delta)^2+\beta_B(4-8\delta+3\delta^2)))} & \text{for case (2)} \\[2ex]
\dfrac{\delta(-1+\alpha_S)\beta_B\,\delta-Pref_S(1+\beta_B)\beta_S(-2+\delta)-\alpha_S\,\delta)-b(-6\delta+2\delta^2-Pref_S\,\alpha_S\,\delta^2+\beta_S(-2+\delta)-Pref_S(-2+\delta)+\beta_B(1+\beta_S)\delta-Pref_B(-2+\delta+Pref_S\,\delta))}{\delta(2-\beta_S(-2+\delta)-\beta_B(1+\beta_S)(-2+\delta)+(-2+\alpha_S)\delta)+b(-8\delta+4\delta^2-\alpha_S\,\delta^2+\beta_S(4-8\delta+3\delta^2)-\beta_B(1+\beta_S)(-2+\delta)+\beta_B(1+\beta_S)\delta-2+3\delta))} & \text{for case (3a)} \\[2ex]
\dfrac{2b(1+\beta_B)(-1+\delta)(4b(1+\beta_S)-2(-1+4b)(1+\beta_S)\delta+b(4-\alpha_S+3\beta_S)\delta^2)-(-1+b)\delta-Pref_S(1+\beta_B\beta_B(-2-\delta)+\alpha_S\delta-b(2(-1+\alpha_S)(1+Pref_B\,\beta_B)(-1+\delta)\delta+Pref_S(1+\beta_B)(-2+3\delta)\beta_S(-2-\delta)-\alpha_S\delta)))}{(1+\beta_B)(b(2-3\delta)-\delta)(4b(1+\beta_S)-2(-1+4b)(1+\beta_S)\delta+(-1+\alpha_S)\beta_S\delta-(-1+\alpha_S)-\beta_S+b(4-\alpha_S+3\beta_S)\delta^2)} & \text{for case (3b)} \\[2ex]
\dfrac{2b(1+\beta_B)(-1-\delta)(4b(1+\beta_S)-2(-1+4b)(1+\beta_S)\delta+(-2+\delta)-\alpha_S\delta)(1+\beta_B)\delta+b(-(-1+\alpha_S)(1+Pref_B\,\beta_B)\delta+Pref_S\,\alpha_S(1+\beta_B)(-2-3\delta)))}{(1+\beta_B)(b(2-3\delta)-\delta)(4b(1+\beta_S)-2(-1+4b)(1+\beta_S)\delta+(-1+\alpha_S)-Pref_B\,\beta_B\delta+Pref_S\,\alpha_S(1+\beta_B)(-2-3\delta))} & \text{for case (4)} \\[2ex]
\dfrac{2b(-1+\alpha_S)(1+\beta_B)(2b(-1+\delta)-\delta)(-1+\delta+b(-(-1+\alpha_S)\delta-Pref_B\,\beta_B\delta+Pref_S\,\alpha_S(1+\beta_B)(-2-3\delta)))}{(-1+\alpha_S)(1+\beta_B)(2b(-1+\delta)-\delta)(b(2-3\delta)+\delta)} & \text{for case (5)} .
\end{cases}
$$

$$(6.13)$$

For distinct discount factors of buyers and sellers the equilibrium price is (for simplicity given for $\beta_S = \beta_B = \beta$, $\alpha_S = \alpha_B = 0$, and $p_{\mathrm{ref}_S} = p_{\mathrm{ref}_B} = p_{\mathrm{ref}}$):

$$p^* = \begin{cases} \dfrac{b\left((\delta_B-1)^2 + \beta\left(\delta_B-1\right)^2 + p_{\mathrm{ref}}\left(2\delta_B-1\right)\left(\delta_S-1\right)\right) + \delta_S\left(-\delta_B + \beta\left(-\delta_S p_{\mathrm{ref}} + p_{\mathrm{ref}} - \delta_B + 1\right) + 1\right)}{(\beta+1)\left(b\left(\delta_B^2 + 2\left(\delta_S-2\right)\delta_B - \delta_S + 2\right) - \delta_B\left(\delta_B + \delta_S - 2\right)\right)} & \text{for } b < b^{1.2} \\[2em] \dfrac{\delta_B\left(-p_{\mathrm{ref}}\left(\delta_B-2\right)\delta_S-2\right)\beta^2 + \left(-p_{\mathrm{ref}}\left(\delta_B+\delta_S-4\right)-\left(\delta_B-1\right)\left(\delta_S-2\right)\right)\beta + 2\left(\delta_B-1\right)\right) + b\left(p_{\mathrm{ref}}\left(\delta_B^2 - 4\delta_B + 2\right)\delta_S - 2\beta^2 + \left(\delta_S-2\right)\beta^2 + p_{\mathrm{ref}}\left(-\delta_B^2 - 2\delta_S\delta_B + 8\delta_B + 8\delta_S - 4\right)\beta - 2\left(\delta_B-1\right)^2\right)}{(p_{\mathrm{ref}}\beta+1)\left(b\left(\delta_B^2 - 4\delta_B + 2\right)\delta_S - 2\right)\delta_B - \delta_S+2\right) + b\left(-\left(\delta_B-2\right)\left(\delta_S-2\right)\beta - 2\left(\delta_B-2\right)\beta - 2\left(\delta_B-2\right)\beta^2 - 2\left(\delta_B-2\right)\beta - 2\left(\delta_B-\delta_S-2\right)\right)} & \text{for } b^{1.2} \leq b \leq b^{2.3} \\[2em] \dfrac{\left(p_{\mathrm{ref}}\beta+1\right)\left(b\left(\delta_B-1\right)-\delta_B\right)\left(\delta_B-1\right)}{(\beta+1)\left(b\left(\delta_B^2+2\left(\delta_S-2\right)\delta_B-\delta_S+2\right)-\delta_B\left(\delta_B+\delta_S-2\right)\right)} & \text{for } b < b^{2.3} \end{cases}$$

$$(6.14)$$

$$\dfrac{\partial p^*}{\partial \delta_S} = \begin{cases} \dfrac{\left((p_{\mathrm{ref}}-1)\beta-1\right)\left(\delta_B-1\right)\left(\left(2\delta_B^2 - 3\delta_B + 1\right)b^2 + \left(2-3\delta_B\right)\delta_B b + \delta_B^2\right)}{(\beta+1)\left(b\left(\delta_B^2 + 2\left(\delta_S-2\right)\delta_B - \delta_S+2\right) - \delta_B\left(\delta_B+\delta_S-2\right)\right)^2} & \text{for } b < b^{1.2} \\[2em] \dfrac{\left(2 - \beta\right)\left(\delta_B-2\right)\delta_B + b\left(\delta_B^2 - 4\delta_B + 2\right)\left(\delta_S-2\right)\beta^2 - 2\left(\delta_B^2 - 4\delta_B + 2\right)\beta + 2\right)\left(-p_{\mathrm{ref}}\left(\delta_B-2\right)\delta_B + 1\right)\beta - 2\delta_B + 1\right)\beta-2\delta_B\delta_S-2\right)\beta + \delta_B\left(\delta_B^2-2\left(\delta_S-2\right)\delta_B-\delta_S+2\right)\right)}{(p_{\mathrm{ref}}\beta+1)\left(b\left(\delta_B^2-4\delta_B+2\right)\delta_S-2\right)\delta_B-\delta_S+2\right) + b\left(-\left(\delta_B-2\right)\left(\delta_S-2\right)\beta\right)^2} & \text{for } b^{1.2} \leq b \leq b^{2.3} \\[2em] \dfrac{\left(p_{\mathrm{ref}}\beta+1\right)\left(b\left(\delta_B-1\right)-\delta_B\right)\left(\delta_B-1\right)b^2 + \left(2-3\delta_B\right)\delta_B b + \delta_B^2}{(\beta+1)\left(b\left(\delta_B^2+2\left(\delta_S-2\right)\delta_B-\delta_S+2\right)-\delta_B\left(\delta_B+\delta_S-2\right)\right)^2} & \text{for } b < b^{2.3} \end{cases}$$

$$(6.15)$$

$$\dfrac{\partial p^*}{\partial \delta_B} = \begin{cases} -\dfrac{(b-1)\left(p_{\mathrm{ref}}-1)\beta-1\right)\left(2b\left(\delta_B-1\right)-\delta_B\right)\delta_B\left(\delta_S-1\right)}{(b-1)\left(2b\left(\delta_B-1\right)-\delta_B\right)\delta_B\left(\delta_S-1\right)-\delta_B\left(\delta_B+\delta_S-2\right)\right)^2} & \text{for } b < b^{1.2} \\[2em] \dfrac{\left(b\left(\delta_B^2-4\delta_B+2\right)\delta_S-2\right)\beta^2 + 2\left(\delta_B^2-4\delta_B+2\right)\delta_S-2\right)\beta + \left(\delta_B^2+2\left(\delta_S-2\right)\delta_B-\delta_S+2\right)\right) + \delta_B\left(-\left(\delta_B-2\right)\delta_S-2\right)\beta^2 - 2\left(\delta_B-2\right)\beta - 2\delta_S+2\right)\right) + b\left(\left(p_{\mathrm{ref}}-1\right)\left(\delta_S-2\right)\beta^2-2\left(\delta_S-2\right)\beta - 2\delta_S+2\right)}{(b-1)\left(2b\left(\delta_B-1\right)-\delta_B\right)\delta_B\left(\delta_S-1\right)\right)^2} & \text{for } b^{1.2} \leq b \leq b^{2.3} \\[2em] \dfrac{\left(b\left(\delta_B^2-4\delta_B+2\right)\delta_S-2\right)\beta^2+2\left(\delta_B^2-4\delta_B+2\right)\delta_S-2\right)\beta+\left(\delta_B^2+2\left(\delta_S-2\right)\delta_B-\delta_S+2\right)\right)}{(b-1)\left(p_{\mathrm{ref}}\beta+1\right)\left(2b\left(\delta_B-1\right)-\delta_B\right)\delta_B\left(\delta_S-1\right)\right)^2} & \text{for } b < b^{2.3} \end{cases}$$

$$(6.16)$$

with

$$b^{1.2} = \dfrac{\delta_B\left(p_{\mathrm{ref}}\left(-\delta_B + \beta\left(\delta_B-1\right)\left(\delta_S-2\right) - \delta_S+2\right) - \left(\beta+1\right)\left(\delta_B-1\right)\left(\delta_S-2\right)\right)}{p_{\mathrm{ref}}\left(\beta\left(\delta_S-2\right)\left(\delta_B-1\right)^2 - \delta_B^2 - 2\delta_B\left(\delta_S-2\right) + \delta_S-2\right) - \left(\beta+1\right)\left(\delta_B-1\right)^2\left(\delta_S-2\right)}$$

$$b^{2.3} = \dfrac{\delta_B\left(p_{\mathrm{ref}}\left(-\delta_B + \beta\left(\delta_B-2\right)\left(\delta_S-1\right) - \delta_S+2\right) + \left(\delta_B-1\right)\delta_S\right)}{\delta_S\left(\delta_B-1\right)^2 + p_{\mathrm{ref}}\left(-\delta_B^2 - 2\delta_S\delta_B + 4\delta_B + 2\right) + \beta\left(\delta_B^2 - 4\delta_B + 2\right)\left(\delta_S-1\right) + \delta_S-2\right)}.$$

Equilibrium prices with one-sided incomplete information and two types 1 and 2 of buyers with $\beta_{B1} > \beta_{B2}$ are (for simplicity given for $\alpha_S = \alpha_{B1} = \alpha_{B2} = 0$, $p_{\mathrm{ref}_S} = p_{\mathrm{ref}_{B1}} = p_{\mathrm{ref}_{B2}} = p_{\mathrm{ref}}$):

$$
p^{*,\mathrm{high}} =
\begin{cases}
\dfrac{p_{\mathrm{ref}}\beta_S\delta(\lambda+1)+b((\beta_S+1)(\delta+b(\delta(\lambda-3)-2))(\lambda-1)+2)\lambda-p_{\mathrm{ref}}\beta_S(\delta(\lambda+3)-2))}{(\beta_S+1)(\delta+b(\delta(\lambda-3)-2))(\lambda+1)} & \text{for } b < b^{1,2} \\[2ex]
\dfrac{b(2(\delta-1)(\beta_S(\delta(\lambda-2)-2)+\delta(\lambda-1)+2)\lambda-p_{\mathrm{ref}}\beta_{B2}^2(3\delta-2)(\delta(\lambda-1)-2)\lambda-\beta_S(\delta(\lambda-2)+2)(\beta_{B2}(3\delta-2)(\delta(\lambda-1)+2)\lambda+(\beta_{B2}+1)\beta_S(\delta(\lambda-2)+2)(\lambda+1))-p_{\mathrm{ref}}\delta(\beta_{B2}(\delta(\lambda-1)+2)\lambda+3)-2)}{(\beta_{B2}^2+1)(\delta+b(\delta(\lambda-3)+2))(\lambda+1)} & \text{for } b^{1,2} \le b \le b^{2,3} \\[2ex]
\dfrac{b(p_{\mathrm{ref}}\beta_{B2}+1)(\delta(\lambda-1)+2)\lambda}{(\beta_{B2}+1)(\delta+b(\delta(\lambda-3)+2))(\lambda+1)} & \text{for } b < b^{2,3}
\end{cases}
$$

$$(6.17)$$

with

$$
b^{1,2} = -\frac{p_{\mathrm{ref}}\delta}{p_{\mathrm{ref}}(\beta_S(\delta(\lambda-2)+2)+\delta(\lambda-3)+2)-(\beta_S+1)(\delta(\lambda-2)+2)}
$$

$$
b^{2,3} = \frac{p_{\mathrm{ref}}\delta}{\delta\lambda+p_{\mathrm{ref}}(-\lambda\delta+3\delta+\beta_{B2}(3\delta-2)-2)}
$$

$$
p^{*,\mathrm{low}} =
\begin{cases}
-\dfrac{p_{\mathrm{ref}}\beta_S\delta+b(\beta_S(-2\delta p_{\mathrm{ref}}+p_{\mathrm{ref}}+1))}{(\beta_S+1)(2b(\delta-1)-\delta)} & \text{for } b < b^{1,2} \\[2ex]
\dfrac{p_{\mathrm{ref}}\delta(2\beta_S\beta_{B1}-\beta_S\delta\beta_{B1}+\beta_{B1}+2\beta_S-\beta_S\delta+b((\beta_S(\delta-2)-2)(\delta-1)+p_{\mathrm{ref}}(\beta_{B1}(\beta_S(\delta-2)-1)(3\delta-2+\beta_S(2\delta^2-5\delta-2))))}{b(4(\delta-1)^2+\beta_S(3\delta^2-8\delta+4)+\beta_{B1}(\beta_S+1)(3\delta^2-8\delta+4))-(\beta_S(\delta-2)+\beta_{B1}(\beta_S-2)+\delta(\delta-2)+2(\delta-1))\delta} & \text{for } b^{1,2} \le b \le b^{2,3} \\[2ex]
-\dfrac{b(p_{\mathrm{ref}}\beta_{B1}+1)}{(\beta_{B1}+1)(2b(\delta-1)-\delta)} & \text{for } b < b^{2,3}
\end{cases}
$$

$$(6.18)$$

with

$$
b^{1,2} = \frac{p_{\mathrm{ref}}\delta}{p_{\mathrm{ref}}(\beta_S(\delta-2)+2(\delta-1))-(\beta_S+1)(\delta-2)}
$$

$$
b^{2,3} = \frac{p_{\mathrm{ref}}\delta}{\delta+p_{\mathrm{ref}}(3\delta\beta_{B1}-2\beta_{B1}+2\delta-2)}.
$$

References

Babcock L, Loewenstein G (1997) Explaining bargaining impasse: The role of self-serving biases. J Econ Perspect 11(1):109–126

Babcock L, Wang X, Loewenstein G (1996) Choosing the wrong pond: Social comparisons in negotiations that reflect a self-serving bias. Q J Econ 111(1):1–19

Fehr E, Schmidt KM (1999) A theory of fairness, competition and cooperation. Q J Econ 114(3):817–868

Güth W, Napel S (2006) Inequality aversion in a variety of games—An indirect evolutionary analysis. Econ J 116(514):1037–1056

Kohnz S (2006) Self-serving biases in bargaining: Explaining impasse, Discussion Paper 2006-09, Department of Economics, LMU Munich, Germany

Rubinstein A (1989) Competitive equilibrium in a market with decentralized trade and strategic behavior: An introduction. In: Feiwel GR (ed) The Economics of Imperfect Competition and Employment: Joan Robinson and Beyond, Macmillan, London, UK, chap 7, pp 243–259

Rubinstein A, Wolinsky A (1985) Equilibrium in a market with sequential bargaining. Econometrica 53(5):1133–1150

Thaler RH (2000) From homo economicus to homo sapiens. J Econ Perspect 14(1):133–141

Chapter 7
Price Rigidity in an Experimental Market

Experimental evidence of fair behavior in bilateral bargaining situations is well known, and the ultimatum game dominates publications in this domain.[1] In contrast to studies of bilateral interactions, studies of market games mostly find limited or no effects of fairness, which leads many to cast doubt on the relevance of fairness in market settings. For example, Camerer (2003, p. 115) notices that fairness is hard to express in markets:

> The effects of multiple players and limited information suggest a general conjecture about bargaining and markets. In two-person games with perfect information about how much each side is earning, fairness concerns loom largest. As players are added, competition can create very lopsided allocations. And, as the Responder's knowledge about the Proposer's gain becomes hazier, Responders become more tolerant of low offers (since they aren't sure how unfair the Proposers is being). The concern for fairness evident in two-player perfect information games therefore disappears in large markets. That does *not* mean traders in such markets do not care about fairness per se. They may care, but they behave self-interestedly because they aren't sure whether others are being fair and can't easily punish unfairness. A competitive market is simply a place in which it is hard to express your concern for fairness because buying or selling (or refusing to do so) will not generally change your inequality much. This does not mean that 'fairness doesn't matter much in important situations'; it just means that people will then express social preferences about unfair market outcomes through 'voice' (protest, newspaper editorials), regulations, and laws. For example, many states that are disaster prone have laws prohibiting 'gouging,' which is defined as raising prices of basic commodities such as water and gasoline after a shortage due to a disaster. These laws codify a social norm of fairness.

Most experimental studies of markets find that market prices converge quickly to the competitive equilibrium, even if as a result the gains from trade are split very unevenly (see, e.g., Fehr and Schmidt 1999, p. 818). These findings mostly concern double-auction settings or multi-proposer ultimatum games.[2] A key question is whether agents dispense with fairness considerations in market-like settings, or if their fairness preferences are simply suppressed by some specific types of institutions as Camerer suggested. This latter explanation seems plausible for the case

---

[1] See, for example, Roth (1995) and Camerer (2003) for good reviews.

[2] See, for example, Kachelmeier and Shehata (1992) and Smith and Williams (1982).

C. Korth, *Fairness in Bargaining and Markets,*
Lecture Notes in Economics and Mathematical Systems, 627
DOI: 10.1007/978-3-642-02252-4_1, © Springer-Verlag Berlin Heidelberg 2009

of double auctions or multi-proposer games. As noted by Fehr and Schmidt, rejecting an unfair offer induces a negligible cost on the proposer in such settings due to fierce competition and minimal frictions. Thus, even fair types may resign themselves to accepting unfair offers, because the alternative is low income without the satisfaction of punishment.

However, some notable exceptions exist—for example, Brown et al. (2004) find rent sharing in an experimental labor market in which contracts are incomplete and workers can credibly threaten to impose a punishment by shirking, Young and Burke (2001) find empirically that custom and focal division rules play an important role in agricultural crop-sharing, and Arai (2003) shows that rents are shared between employer and employee in any institutional setting of the wage determination. Also Fehr et al. (1998) address social norms in the context of labor markets and do find wage agreements above the competitive level when there is room for efficiency gains through reciprocity.

The aforementioned papers are also examples of settings in which the market institution is not necessarily a double auction. The markets that are often consulted in labor and monetary economics are the *matching markets* which were originally considered by Diamond and Maskin (1979), Mortensen (1982), or Rubinstein and Wolinsky (1985), amongst others.[3] In these market models, agents are randomly matched and engage in bilateral bargaining. If an offer is rejected, both parties remain in the market, and with some probability are matched with a new partner, but otherwise remain idle that period. Real-life examples include labor markets with bilateral wage negotiations or used-car markets.

In labor economics, research typically revolves around search frictions and the search and matching function, while the standard Mortensen-Pissarides framework assumes straightforward Nash bargaining for the splitting of gains from trade.[4] In calibrated models using the Nash bargaining solution, a fixed share of the gains from trade is assumed to be captured by each side of the bargaining table. In contrast, the focus of Rubinstein and Wolinsky (1985) is less the search and matching, but rather the actual bargaining, which is modeled strategically. This is also the focus of the work at hand: on which split of the gains from trade do bargainers actually agree on in such a market setting?

We hypothesize that in this market institution fairness affects the market outcome because a rejected proposer does not automatically find a new partner and thus suffers a potentially significant punishment.[5] As discussed below in section 7.1, fairness concern might therefore induce price stickiness with regard to changes in the market conditions, which would not be predicted by standard theory, i.e., assuming simple material payoff maximization.

---

[3] See, for example, Mortensen and Pissarides (1999) or Rogerson et al. (2005) for labor search models, Krainer and LeRoy (2002) or Albrecht et al. (2007) for housing markets, and Shi (2001) or Rocheteau and Wright (2005) for monetary applications.

[4] Therefore the label "search theory" is typically used to describe these models.

[5] However, the strategic situation in a matching market is complex; when deciding to accept or reject, agents must, for instance, take into account market conditions and the resulting probability of future matches.

Our experiment will implement a simple version of the aforementioned strategic *matching market* investigated by Rubinstein and Wolinsky (1985). Our key treatment variable is the ratio of buyers to sellers, which determines the probability of being re-matched in the case of a rejection. Beyond shedding light on the interaction of fairness and market institutions, the results will be informative for the large literature on matching markets. We are not aware of any previous experimental investigation of how individuals actually behave in such a strategic environment, despite the existence of sharp theoretical predictions.

Experimental investigations of market institutions in general have a long history dating back at least to Plott and Smith (1978). Still, there are only few experimental papers about bargaining markets. One example is the comparison between a bargaining or "haggling" market with a more classic market institution like a double-auction or a posted-offer market by Cason et al. (2003). They compare a posted-offer market with a haggling setting, and find that efficiency is lower in the latter market due to volume losses. Sellers obtain a larger share of gains in the bargaining setting, and prices are stickier.

Fairness in markets also received some attention. For example, fairness in a market with *posted bids* was investigated by Kachelmeier et al. (1991), while Kujal and Smith (2008) examined the robustness of their results using *posted offers*. In both studies self-interested behavior dominates fairness in the long run. This suggests that fairness is best described as affecting agents' expectations. In contrast, Fehr et al. (1998) demonstrate that in an experimental labor market involving a setting with complete contracts and competition, wages are kept well above the rather inequitable competitive equilibrium. This observation can be explained with inequity aversion effects.

We conjecture that a bargaining market involving *matching* is the market institution with the most pronounced fairness effects, given the experimental evidence of bargaining experiments in general and the evidence above. It combines bargaining, which generally fosters fairness concerns, with the possibility to reject "unfair" offers because by the means of the matching process another—possibly more generous—trading partner can be found thereafter.

7.1 Theoretical Background and Experimental Design

Our analytical model is based on augmenting the original baseline model of Rubinstein and Wolinsky (1985) with utility functions that reflect a concern for fairness in the sense of Fehr and Schmidt (1999). For a detailed discussion of this model see chapter 5.

Agents' interaction in this study amounts to a particular version of strategic matching markets: Buyers and sellers are randomly divided into pairs. One randomly selected partner in each match suggests a deal. Rejection resolves the match and agents wait to be rematched; successful traders leave the market and new ones enter, so that the number of agents on each side of the market remains constant.

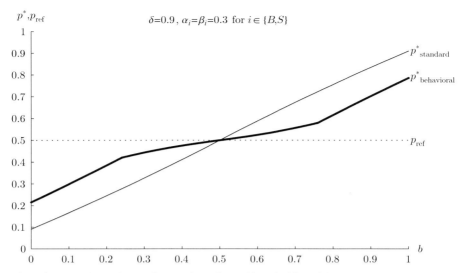

Fig. 7.1 Comparison of exemplary market prices with and without fairness concern

As shown by Rubinstein and Wolinsky (1985) the equilibrium[6] market price depends on agents' discount factor and the ratio of buyers to sellers in the market. The larger the share of buyers, the larger the share of gains from trade the sellers can capture. The model described in chapter 5 enriches the model of Rubinstein and Wolinsky: Agents have information about the "typical" or "fair" rent, wage, or price and this enters their subjective evaluation of a proposal, which we will, for simplicity, in the following refer to as the *fair price*. Prices that deviate from this fair price result in a reduced utility relative to the case without fairness concern, which is comparable to the modeling of deviations from the even split in the model of Fehr and Schmidt (1999). The analysis in chapter 5 finds that such fairness concern results in a predictable shift of equilibrium market prices towards the fair price. Furthermore, fairness concern reduces the sensitivity of prices in response to variations of the ratio of buyers to sellers in the market relative to the predictions of the original model without fairness considerations.

This is illustrated in figure 7.1: The horizontal axis represents the ratio b of buyers to total agents (buyers and sellers) in the market.[7] The *thin line* labeled with $p^*_{standard}$ denotes the price without fairness considerations, while the *thick line* labeled $p^*_{behavioral}$ depicts the predicted price when agents do have a concern for fair-

---

[6] This refers to the solution concept of a subgame perfect equilibrium in semi-stationary strategies. These are strategies that prescribe the same bargaining tactics against all bargaining partners an agent might meet, independent of the period and the number of unsuccessful bargaining processes an agent has experienced.

[7] The share b of buyers is given by $b = B/(B + S)$, with B being the number of buyers and S the number of sellers.

ness.[8] In a neighborhood of the fair price p_{ref}, the equilibrium price is much less sensitive to changes in the buyer–seller ratio than it would be without social preferences; i.e., the price is *stickier*. The driving force is a local increase of concavity of the agents' utility function: Price proposals that are below or above the reference price ex ante amount to a lottery, towards which agents are risk-averse. In order to avoid this lottery, they are more willing to accept proposals (generating a sure return) that are close to p_{ref} than they would be in the case of linear preferences.

With this model the expected magnitude of price shifts and the degree of price stickiness induced by non-standard preferences on the bargaining outcomes relative to the standard prediction based on pecuniary payoff maximization can be estimated. This is the prediction we want to test in this laboratory study. We conjecture that the relationship between the market-defining variables and market outcomes is different than standard theory predicts—we expect the outcome to be shifted towards a fair split of the gains from trade.

Implementing such a matching market in a laboratory environment is not straightforward, as the laboratory as an environment imposes some restrictions. One constraint in our case is time: in the model discussed above, the market never ends, while agents discount future gains by a factor δ. To facilitate laboratory implementation, we need to take a different perspective on this aspect of the model: for expected utility maximizers a continuation probability δ is analytically equivalent to discounting of future gains by a factor δ in this model. So we may alter the interpretation of this variable for our design without changing the model's predictions.

A second constraint emerges with regard to the random matching: The model is based on the premise that agents are matched with a new trading partner each time, and do not encounter the same trading partner twice. Given that the subject pool is limited, we cannot guarantee this, but we can set everything up so that the probability that two subjects are matched more than once is minimized.[9] We deem this sufficient, especially given that the interaction of subjects remains anonymous: subjects have no way to tell with whom they are matched when they bargain. Nevertheless, this also implies that we cannot use distinct matching groups to increase the number of independent observations generated by one experimental session, as we need to be able to match all subjects of the subject pool with each other.

A final difficulty is that in the model each agent enters the market only once, thus has only one opportunity to earn a profit. If we implemented it in exactly that manner in the laboratory, we would need a huge subject pool to generate just a few market prices. Our solution is to allow that subjects enter markets multiple times during the session, but we select by random just one of their payoffs for payout.

---

[8] The assumed parameters for this example are: $\delta = 0.9$, $\alpha_i = \beta_i = 0.3$ for $i \in B, S$, and $p_{\text{ref}} = 0.5$, see chapter 5 for details.

[9] The experiment is programmed and the trial session was conducted with the software z-Tree (Fischbacher 2007). We programmed this software to select those subjects from the pool, which have been least active in the market, to enter the market first. By using a simulation we were able to determine the minimum number of subjects we needed to approximately guarantee that no two agents would meet more than once in the same market. We found that under a wide range of assumptions twenty subjects would be a sufficient pool size for our setup.

This way a subject has little incentive to strike an agreement quickly and by this means increase the number of times he or she can enter a market, because there is no direct benefit from multiple agreements.

7.2 Experimental Procedures

To test for the main predictions of the behavioral theory that prices are shifted towards the fair reference and respond less to changes in the buyer–seller ratio than one expects based on pure material payoff maximization, we employ three treatments: one treatment with five buyers and five sellers, one with three buyers and seven sellers, and a third with two buyers and eight sellers. Across treatments we hold the discount factor δ constant, and as mentioned above, we implement this as a continuation probability of δ or, in other terms, a termination probability of $1 - \delta$. Each treatment is run in one session with twenty subjects that lasts about one hour and consists of several markets of the same setup to be run sequentially, and each market in turn consists of multiple periods.

To induce a common fair reference across treatments the paid treatment is preceded by a "training" phase, in which subjects bargain a few periods against the computer in order to practice the usage of the user interface. At the same time the computer guides them towards proposing and accepting a 50/50 split, and we expect that this experience leads most subjects to accept this 50/50 split as the reference or fair price.[10] Furthermore, we expect that at least some subjects stick to this reference for the rest of the session. In case these first three treatments deliver results that support our theory, we would subsequently investigate treatments in which a different split is induced as the reference price at the beginning. Because the model that is analyzed in chapter 5 allows for *any* reference or fair price, we would also have a testable theoretical prediction. We chose to first employ the 50/50 split as we assumed that it is easiest to induce.

To enable a richer analysis of the results, we first run a paid elicitation of fairness and risk preferences of all subjects. This way we are later able to differentiate the subjects by type. Then, the twenty subjects of each session are randomly divided into buyers and sellers, and they keep their role for the whole experiment. All subjects receive written instructions according to their role with detailed explanations about the experiment that include screenshots of the actual user interface. At the end of the instructions they have to answer some questions in writing, that we use to check the understanding of the instructions and the payoff effects of different actions. We take the time and explain wrong answers to the individual subjects to make sure all subjects are well prepared. See the appendix for a copy of these instructions.

During the main treatment only 10 of the 20 subjects in the session are in a market at any time; the remaining 10 subjects are "off-market," waiting to enter

---

[10] Compare Binmore et al. (1993) and Binmore et al. (1991) who showed that an actually experienced payoff may lead a subject to accept this payoff as the *fair* payoff for the bargaining situation at hand.

one. At the beginning of each period subjects are randomly selected to enter the market. All subjects that enter a market are informed about this and the number of buyers and sellers in this market. Next they are asked about the price they expect to obtain in the market (in the following referred to as *expected price*). This question is for evaluation purposes only and not payoff relevant.

After this, buyers and sellers in the market are randomly matched into trading couples. If there are more sellers than buyers in the market, some sellers in the market remain unmatched. After being informed about whether they are successfully matched, the matched subjects engage in a simple bargaining game. A proposer is determined at random for each couple, both subjects (buyer/seller) are equally likely to be selected for this role. The selected proposer then enters a price offer (*proposed price*), and the other party enters their *reservation price*. If the other party thereby accepts the proposed price, both trading partners earn a profit according to the agreed-on *trade price* and leave the market. If the offer is rejected, both trading partners remain in the market. At the end of each period an information screen informs each subject about the outcome: it displays (if the subject made a proposal or entered his reservation value) if he or she made a deal, and if so, what the profits from this deal are for the involved buyer and seller.

A market can continue or end after each period. If the market continues, each couple that agreed and therefore leaves the market is replaced with a new couple from the "off-market" pool of subjects at the beginning of the next period, so that the number of buyers and sellers remains constant. Those couples who did not agree stay in the market, and are potentially matched with a new partner in the next period. If the market terminates, all subjects still in the market receive a payoff of zero. In any case an information screen informs all subjects about the events.

Since we can schedule only a limited amount of time for a lab session, we determine the number of periods a market lasts beforehand based on a constant termination probability of 10% per period, as discussed above. We do not communicate these numbers to the subjects, but instead inform them, that we have determined the number of rounds beforehand, and that we have chosen these so that they can assume that the market will end after each round with a fixed termination probability of 10%. We chose the sequence of lengths so that subjects are not able to reject this hypothesis in any period during the session using statistic reasoning for standard confidence levels. For another example in which this method was employed, see, e.g., Binmore et al. (1991, p. 301f).

From observed market lengths a confidence interval of the actual termination probability can be calculated in the following way: The distribution function of market lengths is given by the exponential distribution $F_X(t) = 1 - e^{-\lambda t}$ for $t \in \{1, 2, \ldots, \infty\}$ with parameter $\lambda = -\ln(1 - 10\%) \approx 0.105$. For this distribution $F_X(1) = 0.1$, $F_X(2) = 0.19$ and so on. After n observed market lengths, the confidence interval to the confidence level of $1 - \alpha$ is given by

$$\left[\frac{\mathscr{X}^2_{2n;\alpha/2}}{2\sum_{i=1}^n x_i} ; \frac{\mathscr{X}^2_{2n;1-\alpha/2}}{2\sum_{i=1}^n x_i} \right]$$

with x_i denoting the market length of market number i. Table 7.1 contains the market lengths we chose and the resulting confidence intervals for λ. It demonstrates that the subjects cannot reject the hypothesis that the termination probability is smaller or larger than 10% down to a confidence level of $1 - \alpha = 0.9$.

Table 7.1 Confidence intervals for λ after i observations, announced $\lambda \approx 0.105$

Market no. i	Length of market x_i	Confidence interval for $1 - \alpha = 0.95$	Confidence interval for $1 - \alpha = 0.90$
1	7	[0.004;0.527]	[0.007;0.428]
2	5	[0.020;0.464]	[0.030;0.395]
3	2	[0.044;0.516]	[0.058;0.450]
4	1	[0.044;0.351]	[0.055;0.310]
5	3	[0.058;0.366]	[0.070;0.327]
6	4	[0.069;0.365]	[0.082;0.329]
7	4	[0.078;0.363]	[0.091;0.329]
8	2	[0.091;0.380]	[0.105;0.346]
9	9	[0.088;0.335]	[0.100;0.307]

Each time a subject enters and subsequently leaves a market, he or she receives a payoff: if both agree on a trade price, the seller receives a payoff equivalent to this trade price, and the buyer receives a payoff equivalent to the pie size minus the trade price. Subjects receive a payoff of zero if the market terminates while they are unmatched or if it terminates after a disagreement.

In case a subject gains more than one payoff (zero or positive) during the treatment, just one of these payoffs is randomly selected for payout at the end of the treatment. When the treatment ends, the subjects are informed about this event, shown their payoffs, and which one of them was chosen to be paid out.

During the experiment the subjects bargain in terms of "points," which resemble an artificial currency that is later converted to euro using a fixed exchange rate. This is clarified in the instructions. The pie size the subjects negotiate about is set to be 1000 points, and the exchange rate is 100 points equal €1. So effectively subjects bargain about how to split €10 each time.

At the end of all three treatments the subjects are shown a summary of all their gains including the show-up fee of €5 and their earnings of the pre-study. To conclude the session they are called one by one into the neighboring room and paid their earnings in cash.

To generate the amount of data necessary for robust results, we would need a data set of at least twelve sessions[11] with 20 participants each, with an average duration of 60 minutes.

---

[11] Twelve sessions would be sufficient for the first two described treatments. To implement all three treatments, we would run 18 sessions.

7.3 Trial Setup

Before running the full set of sessions we devised a trial session with twenty paid subjects, which we invited for two hours into the laboratory. We used the extra hour relative to the setup described above to integrate all three treatments into one single session. Of course we did not generate independent observations for each treatment with this approach, but the observed behavior per treatment would be indicative of what to expect during the regular sessions that would encompass only one of the three treatments each.

We planned the three treatments in this trial session in the following order: first, five buyers and five sellers; then, three buyers and seven sellers; and finally, two buyers and eight sellers. As we expected most subjects to gravitate towards an equal split during the first treatment, we excluded the "training phase" from the session and rather used the time to extend the number of periods the subjects could interact with each other in the markets. We expected that the first treatment would be sufficient to induce a 50/50 split as the reference or fair price. Each treatment then consisted of several markets of the same setup to be run sequentially, and each market consisted of multiple periods. As discussed above, we determined the number of periods a market would last beforehand (compare table 7.2), and ran a total of three markets in each treatment.

Table 7.2 Treatments and number of periods each market lasted

Treatment no.	Number of buyers (B)	Number of sellers (S)	Share of buyers $b = B/(B+S)$	Sequence of market lengths in periods
1	5	5	0.5	$\{7,5,2\}$
2	3	7	0.3	$\{11,3,4\}$
3	2	8	0.2	$\{4,2,9\}$

To account for the multiple treatments in one session, we organized the payout so that subjects would receive one randomly determined payoff per treatment based on their actual payoffs. Given that the session encompassed three treatments, each subject was paid out three payoffs after the experiment, one for each treatment. Overall the trial session lasted two hours and subjects were paid €19.67 on average. The average earning for the main experiment was €13.10, the average payout for the short pre-study was €1.57, and the show-up fee was set to be €5.00.

7.4 Trial Results

Figure 7.2 displays the average trial results per treatment (*circles*) in comparison to the standard prediction where subjects are motivated only by material self-interest

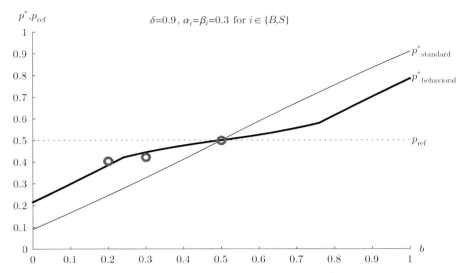

Fig. 7.2 Trial results in comparison with standard and behavioral predictions

(*thin line*) and the prediction based on fairness preferences[12] (*thick line*); see table 7.3 for the data. The x-axis shows the treatment variable b (share of buyers), while the y-axis indicates the predicted and observed market prices. If we ignored the dependence of observations and performed t-tests within treatments, we would find that the market price is significantly higher than the predictions of the standard model in treatment 2 with three buyers and seven sellers ($p < 0.002$), and treatment 3 with two buyers and eight sellers ($p < 0.001$). The price would not be significantly different from the prediction of 0.5 for treatment 1 with five buyers and five sellers ($p < 0.958$).

Table 7.3 Observed prices in the experimental market relative to standard prediction

Treatment no.	Number of observations	Standard prediction	Average observed price	Standard deviation	t-test statistic	p-value
1	41	0.500	0.501	0.119	0.052	0.958
2	37	0.327	0.423	0.175	3.338	<0.002
3	21	0.245	0.402	0.168	4.293	<0.001

This aggregated view can of course be separated by subject, period, and action of each subject. See figures 7.4 and 7.5 for all details. These figures show the trade prices that were agreed on as well as the reservation prices and price offers the subjects entered. This is complemented by the expected price they mentioned whenever

---

[12] Parameters in this example are a discount factor of 10% ($\delta = 0.9$), and the behavioral prediction is based on fairness parameters $\alpha = \beta = 0.3$, $p_{\text{ref}} = 0.5$.

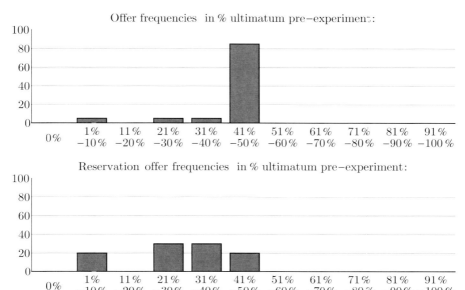

Fig. 7.3 Ultimatum game results of the pre-experimental stage

they entered a market. *Thin vertical lines* mark the end of markets and *bold vertical lines* the ends of the treatments. A glance at these figures reveals that behavioral patterns vary by subject, and that some subjects seem to gravitate towards a *fair* split, while others show a more *adaptive* behavior regarding the market conditions and their personal history of play.

Recall that we started the experimental session with a paid elicitation of fairness preferences. We ran a simple one-shot paid ultimatum experiment as part of the pre-experimental study, so we are able to compare the behavior of our subject pool with one of other experimental investigations of the ultimatum game. Furthermore, we can identify subjects that demonstrate a concern for fairness during this initial part of the experiment.

All subjects made one ultimatum offer and also stated the minimum offer they are willing to accept.[13] Figure 7.3 shows the proposer and responder behavior of all subjects. It reveals that we had a relatively large share of subjects in our subject pool that made generous ultimatum offers. Typically around 30%–40% of subjects offer between 41% and 50% of the pie to the responder,[14] while in our subject pool 85% of subjects made offers in this range. In the following we will refer to these 85% of our subjects as "fair ultimatum proposers." Compare table 7.4 for subjects' ultimatum offers and the column "Classification based on pre-experiment" for our categorization of fair ultimatum proposers.

---

[13] We used the strategy method to elicit subjects' responder behavior.

[14] Compare, for example, Camerer (2003) for an overview of ultimatum experiments.

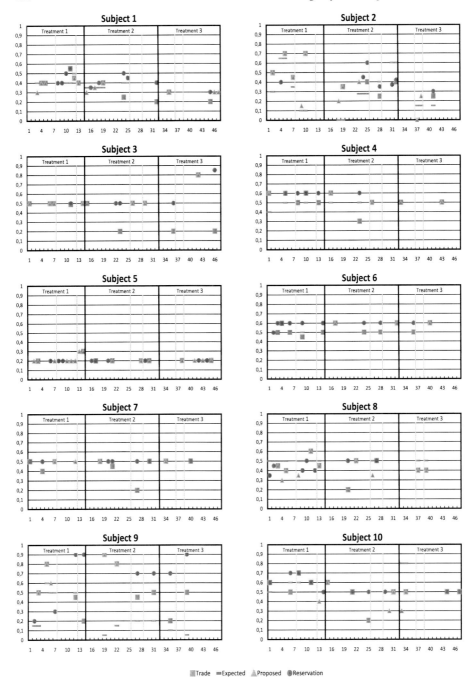

Fig. 7.4 Prices by subject over periods—buyers

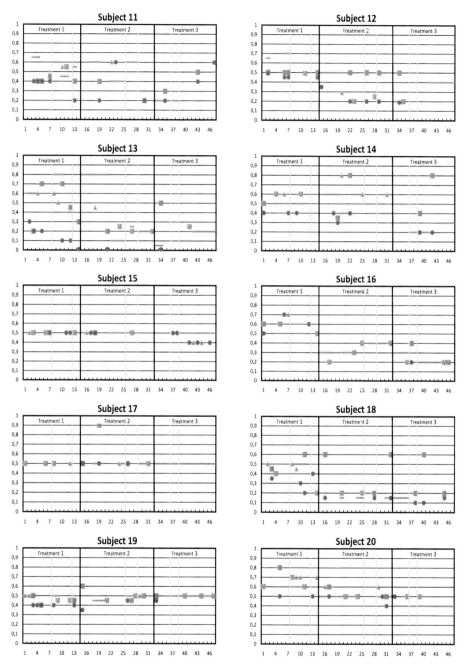

Fig. 7.5 Prices by subject over periods—sellers

Table 7.4 Actions and classifications of subjects

Subject	Ultimatum offer pre-experiment	Classification based on pre-experiment	Average market actions treatments 1, 2, and 3	Classification based on market actions
1	40 %		0.422, 0.394, 0.300	Adaptive
2	49 %	Fair	0.483, 0.393, 0.275	Adaptive
3	50 %	Fair	0.500, 0.500, 0.717	Adaptive
4	50 %	Fair	0.600, 0.567, 0.500	Fair
5	10 %		0.218, 0.200, 0.200	Adaptive
6	50 %	Fair	0.583, 0.600, 0.600	Fair
7	50 %	Fair	0.500, 0.500, 0.500	Fair
8	45 %	Fair	0.423, 0.463, 0.400	Fair
9	50 %	Fair	0.600, 0.775, 0.800	Adaptive
10	50 %	Fair	0.583, 0.483, 0.450	Fair
11	50 %	Fair	0.414, 0.400, 0.400	Fair
12	50 %	Fair	0.466, 0.241, 0.195	Adaptive
13	50 %	Fair	0.290, 0.222, 0.130	Adaptive
14	50 %	Fair	0.500, 0.517, 0.200	Adaptive
15	50 %	Fair	0.500, 0.500, 0.429	Fair
16	30 %		0.600, 0.325, 0.200	Adaptive
17	50 %	Fair	0.500, 0.500, na	Fair
18	50 %	Fair	0.367, 0.170, 0.117	Adaptive
19	50 %	Fair	0.433, 0.457, 0.488	Fair
20	50 %	Fair	0.625, 0.514, 0.500	Fair

Another way to classify the subjects is to split the subject pool into "fair" and "adaptive" players by evaluating their market actions. The result is also given in table 7.4, which shows the average price either offered or entered as reservation value by treatment by subject. Standard theory would predict that this value is 0.5 for the first treatment and decreases to approx. 0.25 for the last treatment. In case subjects responded less to the treatment variables and reduced their values by less than half of the standard prediction,[15] we classify them as "fair." All remaining subjects are classified as "adaptive;"[16] compare the last column of table 7.4. This results in half of the subject pool being classified as fair, which roughly matches the patterns that can be identified by investigating the details of figures 7.4 and 7.5.[17]

We take the fact that the share of fair subjects was only 50% in the market game (compared to 85% in the ultimatum pre-experiment) as an indication that less subjects are fair-minded under market conditions than in pure one-on-one ultimatum bargaining. However, still a substantial share (50% in our case) of subjects preserved

---

[15] So that all averages are in the range of 0.375 to 0.625.

[16] On purpose we refrained from classifying subjects as *unfair*, *selfish*, or *self-interested*. Just the fact that subjects did not act in a strongly fair-minded way does not imply that they acted unfairly. They merely were not driven mostly by fairness, but more by other concerns. As we cannot distinguish fairness and other concerns, we decided to classify subjects by what could be observed, i.e., adaptive behavior regarding the treatment variables and the history of play.

[17] Analysis of the average expected market price shows basically the same picture, but we focussed on the actual actions, as the expected price the subjects entered was not payoff relevant.

their fairness considerations in the market we investigated. In contrast, those 15% of our subjects who made low offers in the ultimatum pre-experiment all acted "adaptive" in the market. Subjects that acted fairly in the market were a strict subset of those subjects that acted fairly as ultimatum proposers.

The subject classification based on the results of the pre-experimental ultimatum game enables us to cut the data in an interesting way: we can look at those market prices generated when both trading partners were fair-minded *ultimatum proposers*, and those when one of them was not. First we examine the results when one of the trading partners was not classified as fair based on the ultimatum game results. Compare table 7.5 to see how these market prices on average compare to the standard prediction without fairness. If we again ignored the issue of dependence, we could calculate the confidence intervals for the average trade price to the confidence level of $1 - \alpha = 0.95$.[18] Then we would find that the prediction based on material payoff maximization is well within this interval. To us, this is an indicator that the theoretical model does apply to the experiment we designed, and that subjects without fairness concern do act approximately as predicted by the model when we assume material payoff maximization.

Table 7.5 Market prices by *not* fair-minded subjects relative to standard prediction

Treatment no.	Number of observations	Standard prediction	Average observed price	Standard deviation	Confidence interval for $1 - \alpha = 0.95$
1	10	0.500	0.440	0.129	[0.348;0.532]
2	10	0.327	0.275	0.092	[0.209;0.341]
3	7	0.245	0.243	0.979	[0.170;0.316]

Furthermore we can investigate the remaining trades, which are all between subjects classified as fair based on their ultimatum behavior. In our pre-experimental ultimatum game we also asked all subjects about the minimum share they would accept. We can use this information to calculate subjects' fairness parameters β in the spirit of the model that is discussed in chapter 5. Under the premise that an even split is the reference in the ultimatum game for all subjects, the average β for subjects that we classified as fair based on their ultimatum bargaining behavior turns out to be $\beta_B = 9$ for the buyers and $\beta_S = 2.9$ for the sellers. Figure 7.6 shows the prices that were generated by fair subjects plotted against the behavioral prediction, and the remaining prices plotted against the standard prediction.[19] Average market prices by treatment generated by fair subjects are marked with *circles*, while the averages of the remaining prices are marked with *small squares*. The model prediction for fair

---

[18] The confidence intervals are given by $\left[\bar{p} - t(1 - \frac{\alpha}{2}, n - 1) \frac{s}{\sqrt{n}}; \bar{p} + t(1 - \frac{\alpha}{2}, n - 1) \frac{s}{\sqrt{n}} \right]$, with $\bar{p}$ being the average observed price, n the number of observations, s the standard deviation, and $t(\cdot)$ the quantile of the Student distribution.

[19] The behavioral prediction was generated using $\delta = 0.9, \beta_B = 9, \beta_S = 2.9$ and $\alpha_B = \alpha_S = 0$. Higher α-values would not change the result qualitatively. The corresponding standard prediction is based on $\delta = 0.9, \beta_B = \beta_S = \alpha_B = \alpha_S = 0$.

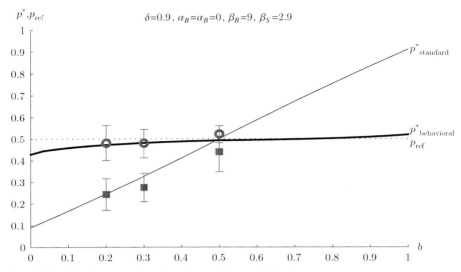

Fig. 7.6 Predicted vs. actual market prices—fair vs. unfair subjects

subjects is close to the experimental data. Table 7.6 shows these results and the confidence intervals for the average trade price to the confidence level of $1 - \alpha = 0.95$
that would result if we ignored the issue of dependence. These confidence intervals
are also marked in figure 7.6. We would find that the behavioral prediction is well
within the bounds of this confidence interval and that the confidence intervals for
treatments 2 and 3 would not overlap with those for adaptive subjects. The interpretation would be that the experimental results for fair subjects do not contradict
the model's behavioral prediction, while they could not be explained with standard
theory.

Table 7.6 Market prices by fair subjects relative to behavioral prediction

Treatment no.	Number of observations	Behavioral prediction	Average observed price	Standard deviation	Confidence interval for $1 - \alpha = 0.95$
1	31	0.493	0.521	0.111	[0.480;0.561]
2	27	0.481	0.478	0.167	[0.412;0.544]
3	14	0.472	0.482	0.141	[0.401;0.563]

7.5 Concluding Remarks

We want to demonstrate empirically that subjects' behavior in an experimental matching market involving bargaining is better predicted and explained by a behavioral theory involving fairness preferences than by "standard" theory based on simple *material* payoff maximization: prices are closer to a fair split of gains than standard theory would predict. Since matching markets form the basis of search theory, this may have interesting implications for labor and monetary economics. In contrast to the experimental findings obtained for double auctions, fairness effects are predicted to persist over time for this practically relevant set of market institutions.

We are not aware of any former empirical research that clarifies actual bargaining behavior and outcomes of agents interacting in such a matching market. We conjecture that agents exhibit a preference for fairness in such markets. In contrast to double-auction markets in which the market design prevents behavioral preferences from shifting the market equilibrium away from the competitive equilibrium, these behavioral preferences do affect the bargaining agreements in matching markets.

To date only the trial study has been conducted, but the results of this trial study are encouraging enough to follow up on this topic with the described full study. Because all observed market prices of the trial study are dependent on each other, this study only represents one single independent observation, and we do not have sufficient data for sound statistic conclusions yet. Nevertheless we want to give an "as if" interpretation in the following that we could defend in case the full study would confirm our trial findings.

We started off with the conjecture that if we implemented the matching market in the way described above in a laboratory setting, we would observe behavior that deviates from the standard prediction. Indeed we could now reject the hypothesis that observed behavior can be described with the standard approach, in which solely the absolute monetary gains are of interest to the market participants. The model that is discussed in chapter 5 proposes an alternative behavioral prediction, one that takes the relation of the absolute gains to a reference or fair price into account. And we would have found a surprisingly good fit between the prediction based on this model and actual behavior. This is especially true if we differentiate between subjects that care about fairness and those that seem to be without pronounced regard for any fairness norms. With this differentiation we would find that if fair subjects bargain with each other, then prices are well predicted with the behavioral approach. Otherwise prices are better explained by simple material payoff maximization.

One interesting area of further research would therefore be to develop a method to accurately predict a subject's type for the market setting. On one hand, we found that purely selfish behavior in an ultimatum bargaining setting is an indicator of "adaptive" behavior in such a matching and bargaining market. On the other hand, some subjects act fair during the ultimatum game, but this does not translate into fair behavior in such a market. Therefore a more accurate up-front classification method would be helpful in case one wants to use the given behavioral model for real-life predictions of specific agents' behavior. Nevertheless, even without such a classification method a prediction of average market outcomes should still be possible, given some basic knowledge about the distribution of types in the population.

Therefore we deem our proposed study important for investigations involving matching markets: the study could demonstrate that actual agreements in such markets are shifted towards the even split of gains. Furthermore, we conjecture that reference points different from the even split would induce a similar effect on prices in such markets.[20] If we were successful to show that market prices are biased towards these distinct reference points, then we would have found a mechanism to explain price stickiness: Agents may form a reference price based on, for example, past prices.[21] This reference price in conjunction with fairness preferences makes market prices stick close to this reference price, even when market fundamentals shift.

As mentioned in the introduction, models using calibrated matching markets to explain real-life phenomena, for example, in the labor market, typically employ an assumed fixed share of the match surplus the worker receives. This assumed fixed share is commonly 0.5 for applications of the Mortensen-Pissarides framework; compare, for example, Den Haan et al. (2000, p. 491) or Walsh (2005, p. 838). We conjecture that this assumption needs to be revised or at least treated with caution. Agents might well agree on a varying share depending on their reference point, and this may be a reference point different from the commonly assumed 0.5. Take the following example from a labor market: Imagine the value of a specific type of worker to a company is €3000, and the workers bring a reservation wage of €1000 to the bargaining table. Given this scenario, they agree on the 0.5 split, which is a wage of €2000. Now let there be a shock to the economy, and the reservation values change to €2500 and €500, respectively. If the split of gains from trade is a fixed parameter, new agreements would be settled for a wage of €1500. However, if the former wage agreements of €2000 are a reference wage and relevant for the bargaining considerations as proposed in chapter 5, the new wage agreements would still be around this reference wage of €2000, although the reservation values and market fundamentals might have changed drastically. The bargainers would adjust the *shares* of surplus each party receives, and this share adjustment results in sticky absolute wages. Overall, this amounts to a novel approach to explaining price or wage stickiness with a behavioral foundation.

Besides the price response to changes in the buyer–seller ratio, also price responses to changes in the discount factor (or in terms used in the proposed experimental implementation, the termination probability) are investigated in chapter 5. The prediction is that a higher discount factor (less discounting) leads to even "stick-

---

[20] To prove this conjecture, we would also run treatments in which we induce distinct reference prices in the beginning. Compare also the classroom experiment described in chapter 4. In chapter 4 the instructions of an ultimatum bargaining experiment were used to guide subjects towards distinct reference points. Although this was only cheap talk and not payoff relevant, it did significantly affect the bargaining outcomes.

[21] See, for example, Bolton et al (2003) for some thoughts on the formation of such beliefs. The belief an agent forms about such a reference may depend on various factors, and history of play is very likely to be an important factor.

ier" prices, intensifying the effects of fairness considerations. In the laboratory we would also be able to investigate this effect by introducing treatments with a different termination probability in a second step and comparing the results to the original ones.

Matching markets are not yet well explored in laboratory settings, but do play an important role in investigations of various kinds of real-life markets that employ, for example, the Mortensen-Pissarides framework. The experiment described here would constitute a good starting point for further research in this domain.

Appendix: Instructions

The appendix contains the English translation of the original German instructions for the experiment.

General Instruction (for all Participants)

You are now taking part in an economic experiment. Please read the following instructions carefully. Everything that you need to know in order to participate in this experiment is explained below. Should you have any difficulties in understanding these instructions please notify us. We will answer your questions at your cubicle.

For showing up today, you receive €5.00. During the course of the experiment, you can earn more money. The currency in this experiment is *points*.[22] The amount of points that you gain during the experiment depends on your decisions and the decisions of other participants. All points that you gain during the course of the experiment will be exchanged into euros at the end of the experiment. The exchange rate will be:

$$1\ point\ =\ €0.01$$
$$100\ points\ =\ €1.00$$

At the end of the experiment you will receive the money that you earned during the experiment in addition to your show-up fee of €5.00 in cash.

Please note that communication between participants is strictly prohibited during the experiment. In addition we would like to point out that you may only use the computer functions which are required for the experiment. Communication between participants and unnecessary interference with computers will lead to exclusion from the experiment. The procedure will be as follows:

1. Every one is assigned to a computer. For these assignments we use cards that we distribute randomly to you.

---

[22] In the German original, we used the word "Taler."

2. You will then go to your computer, and you will find instructions on the screen for a short pre-phase. Please follow these instructions.
3. As soon as all participants conclude the pre-phase, we will distribute instructions for the main experiment. Please read these instructions carefully and answer the few, short control questions at the end. When you are done with the control questions, please hold up the sheet so that we can collect it.
4. When all participants have understood the control questions, the main experiment will begin. This experiment will take place on the computer.
5. As soon as the main experiment is finished, we will call you one by one to see us, so that we can pay out your earnings. After receiving these, you may leave the laboratory.

In case you have any questions, please don't hesitate to contact us.

An Overview of the Experimental Procedures (Instructions for Buyers)

Prior to the experiment the 20 participants were divided into 2 groups: buyers and sellers. In this experiment there are 10 buyers and 10 sellers. *You are a buyer throughout the whole experiment.* The buyers and sellers will interact in markets.

The experiment consists of multiple sequential markets (one market after the other). The time is divided into periods. In some periods you have to make decisions, which you will enter on the computer screen.

The experiment will be divided into *three parts*, and each part consists of multiple markets that last several periods each.

In each part, the markets will be the same over time. The markets of the three different parts differ only with regard to the number of buyers and sellers in each market. So in the first part the markets might, for example, always have five buyers and five sellers, while the markets in the second part might have, for example, three buyers and seven sellers.

The setup will always be such that of the 20 participants of the experiment, only 10 will be in a market at any time. Each market runs for multiple periods, and for those periods that you are not in a market, you have to do nothing but wait for the next period.

Participants are randomly selected to enter the market. Once you enter a market you stay in this market until either you make a deal, or the market terminates.

In each period the computer randomly matches each buyer with one seller into trading couples. If there are more sellers than buyers in the market as in the example of three buyers and seven sellers, some sellers in the market will remain unmatched. If you are matched with another participant as trading partner, you will engage in a simple bargaining session with her/him. You *or* your trading partner will propose a price. If the other party *accepts this price*, the trade is carried out and both trading partners *leave the market. If the offer is rejected*, both you and your trading partner will *remain in the market*.

A market ends after a number of periods that we determined beforehand. You and the other participants do not know how many periods it will run before it ends. You only know that it will end for sure after a while. So the market may last just a few periods or quite long. The knowledge of how many periods one market lasted will not help you to determine how long the next or any other market will last. The number of periods of any given market has been fixed so that however many periods it already lasted, you can estimate that *it will always continue for another period with a 90% chance*. This makes it more likely for a market to last, for example, 11 periods than 3 periods. However, from your perspective, *the market continues in 9 of 10 cases, and ends in 1 of 10 cases after any period.*[23]

If the market continues, each couple that agreed on a price and therefore left the market will be replaced with a new couple of participants, so that the number of buyers and sellers in a market remains constant. Those couples that did not agree on a price will stay in the market and will be matched with a different partner in the next period. If the *market terminates*, all players in the market at that period leave the market and receive a profit of zero.

You may enter markets several times during each part of the three parts of this experimental session. Each time, you will end up with *one* potential profit in points: either you agree on a price, then you earn a *positive potential profit*; or the market terminates before you made an agreement, then you earn a *potential profit of zero points*. At the end of each of the three parts, the computer selects *by random exactly one* of your potential profits, and you will be paid for exactly this selected profit at the end of the experiment.

The three randomly selected profits from the three parts of the experiment will be *summed up* at the end of the experiment, exchanged into euros, and paid together with your show-up fee and your earnings from the pre-phase in cash.

The Experimental Procedures in Detail (Instructions for Buyers)

During the experiment you will see important information and enter your decisions on the computer screen. The following describes in detail what you will see and how you can make your decisions in each period.

In each period you will only see information on the screen that is relevant for you in that period. The screen is divided into several parts:

At the top you will see the period number, and below, if you are waiting to enter a market, or if you are in a market (see figure 7.7).

At the bottom of the screen you will often see an "OK" button. Once you have finished reading and made your decisions (if needed), *please click on this button to*

---

[23] Binmore et al. (1991) first used this description in their implementation of an infinite game in the lab.

Fig. 7.7 The header tells you if you are in a market

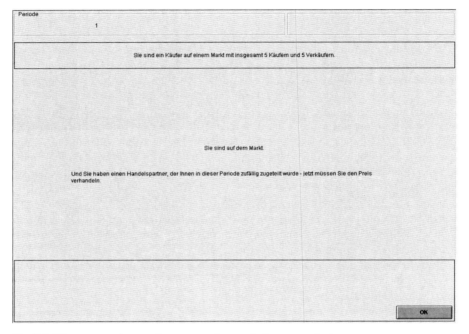

Fig. 7.8 When you are in a market you may be matched or unmatched

continue the experiment. This is important, because often all participants need to wait until everybody has clicked the button (see figure 7.8).

The beginning and the end of all three parts of the experiment and the beginning and the end of each market will be announced on the screen.

Each time you enter a market, but before you know if you propose the price or your trading partner proposes the price, you will be asked about your expectation regarding the price you will get. Please enter your expectation and click on "OK." This expectation will *not* be shown to any other participant.

If you are in a market, you will see how many buyers and how many sellers are in this market. Furthermore, each period that you are in a market, the computer determines randomly whether you are matched with a trading partner. The match is also random and will be a new random choice in each period, so you will, with high probability, not be matched with the same trading partner twice. You will also not receive any information about your trading partner and he will not receive any information about you (see figure 7.8).

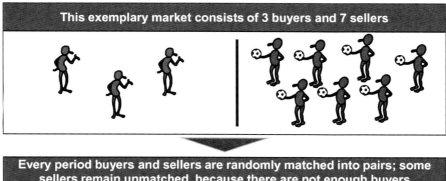

Fig. 7.9 Not all sellers have a trading partner in every period

Whenever there are not the same number of buyers and sellers in the market, some participants remain unmatched. For example, if there are 3 buyers and 7 sellers, only 3 couples will be formed, and 4 sellers remain unmatched in any period (see figure 7.9).

In case you are in a market *and* matched with a trading partner, you engage in a simple bargaining session. There are two possibilities: either you propose the price, or your trading partner proposes the price. This is determined at random with equal probability, so the likelihood that you propose the price is 50% each time.

If you propose the price, you can enter your proposal at the bottom of the screen. *The good you are buying is worth 1000 points to you and nothing (0 points) to the seller.* You may interpret this the following way: By making an agreement with your trading partner, you and your trading partner create a joint surplus of 1000 points. The price then determines how much of this surplus the buyer and the seller each receive. Type in your proposed price between 0 and 1000 points. The remaining time you have to decide is displayed on the screen as a countdown. Click on "OK" to send your offer; see figure 7.10.

If your trading partner proposes a price, then you have to decide which is the highest selling price you would just be willing to accept. Type in the *highest* price between 0 and 1000 points you would be willing to pay (your *reservation price*). Your trading partner will not see this information; it will only be used to determine if you accept or reject the offer your partner makes. Example: You enter 400 points as the highest price you would pay as a buyer (your reservation price). If the seller proposes a price of 500 points, this offer is automatically rejected because it is higher

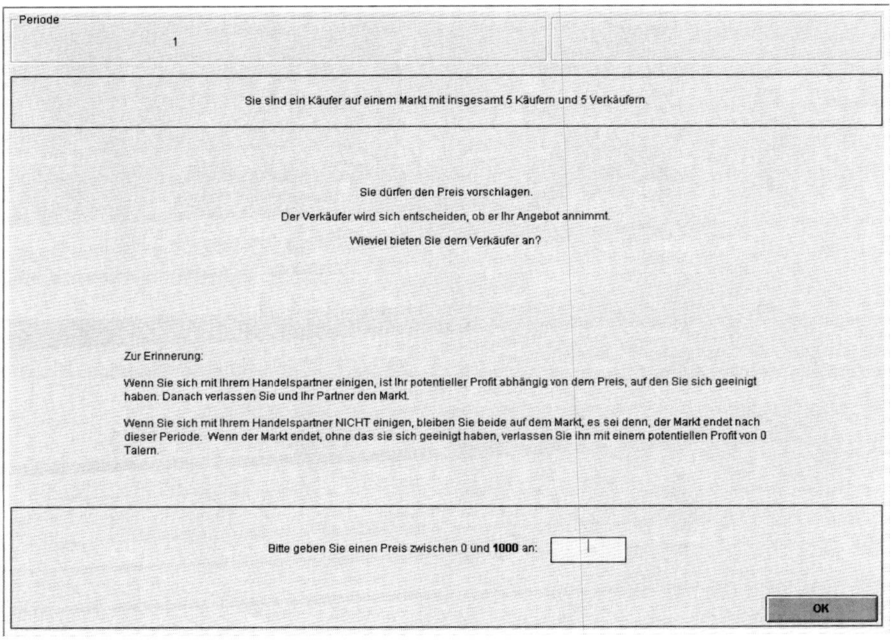

┌─ Periode ──┐
│   │
│   1   │
│   │
│ ┌──┐   │
│ │   │   │
│ │   Sie sind ein Käufer auf einem Markt mit insgesamt 5 Käufern und 5 Verkäufern │ │
│ │   │   │
│ │   │   │
│ │   Sie dürfen den Preis vorschlagen.   │   │
│ │   Der Verkäufer wird sich entscheiden, ob er Ihr Angebot annimmt. │   │
│ │   Wieviel bieten Sie dem Verkäufer an?   │   │
│ │   │   │
│ │   Zur Erinnerung: │   │
│ │   Wenn Sie sich mit Ihrem Handelspartner einigen, ist Ihr potentieller Profit abhängig von dem Preis, auf den Sie sich geeinigt │
│ │   haben. Danach verlassen Sie und Ihr Partner den Markt.   │   │
│ │   Wenn Sie sich mit Ihrem Handelspartner NICHT einigen, bleiben Sie beide auf dem Markt, es sei denn, der Markt endet nach │
│ │   dieser Periode. Wenn der Markt endet, ohne das sie sich geeinigt haben, verlassen Sie ihn mit einem potentiellen Profit von 0 │
│ │   Talern.   │   │
│ └──┘   │
│   │
│   Bitte geben Sie einen Preis zwischen 0 und **1000** an: [|]   │
│   │
│   [OK   ]   │
└──┘

Fig. 7.10 When you are selected to propose a price, enter your proposal in the box

than 400 points. If instead the seller proposes 300 points, the offer is accepted, because it is less than the 400 points you are willing to pay (your reservation price). If the offer is accepted, your potential profit is calculated *based on the actual offer, not on your reservation price*. In this last example the price you pay would be 300 points (figure 7.11).

You only have one round of bargaining in each period, so there is no "haggling", but only a *one-time proposal* that can be accepted or rejected.

Afterwards an information screen is displayed that shows you the outcome of the bargaining (price offered and if it was accepted or not), and the potential profit you and your partner received in case you agreed on the price. In case you agreed on the price, the seller receives the points you pay and you (the buyer) receive 1000 points minus the points you paid for it. Example: You agree on buying the good for 400 points. Then the seller receives a potential profit of 400 points and you (the buyer) receive $1000 - 400 = 600$; i.e., six hundred points. In simple notation: profit of seller = price, and profit of buyer = $1000 -$ price. The total profit (sum for buyer and seller) of both trading partners that agree on a price is always 1000 points, but the price determines how much of these 1000 points are allotted to the buyer and the seller, see figure 7.12 (in which the actual amounts were rendered unrecognizable).

In case you are in a market and you were either not matched with a trading partner, or you were matched but you did not agree on a price, you would normally remain in the market for the next period. It might happen that the market terminates

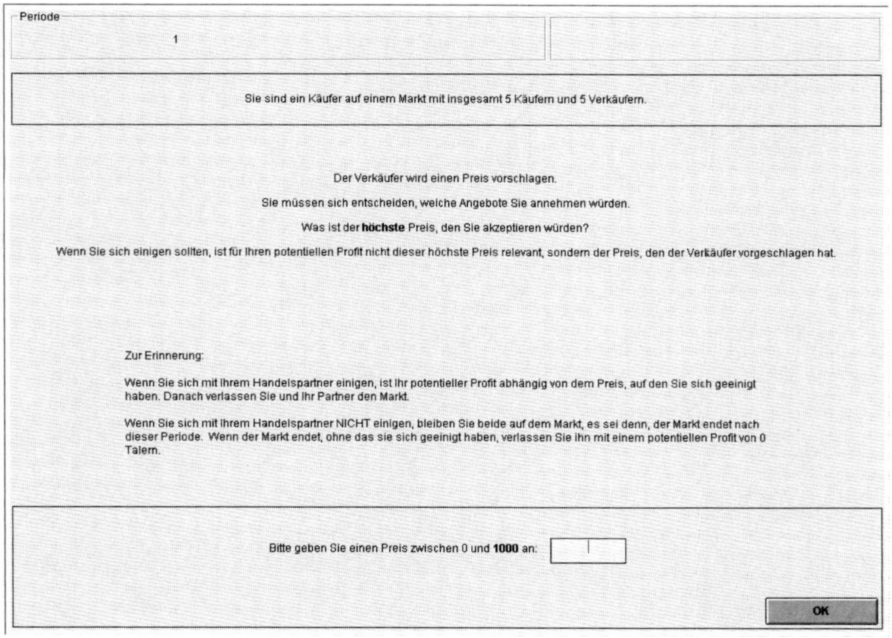

Fig. 7.11 When your partner proposes a price, you enter your reservation price

and you are forced to leave the market. In this event, you receive a potential profit of zero (0 points). As explained above, you do not know when the market will terminate. You can only estimate that *it will continue with a probability of 90% and end with a probability of 10%*. In case a market ends, there will be a message announcing this to all participants.

You may have more than one potential profit during each of the three parts of the experiment. At the end of each part, the computer randomly selects which of your potential profits will be paid in cash to you in the end. Because any of your potential profits might be chosen at random, you need to be careful: If you are in a market and the market terminates before you make an agreement, you receive a potential profit of zero. In addition, this profit of zero might be chosen to be paid. See figure 7.13 for an example, with three potential profits, two of which were created by agreements, and one by the termination of the market before agreement was reached. Of these three potential profits, the first was randomly selected to be paid out at the end of the experiment. (The actual numbers were rendered unrecognizable in this example.)

The sum of all three randomly chosen profits (one for each part) will be paid to you together with your show-up fee and your earnings from the pre-phase at the end of the experiment.

All participants (buyers and sellers) receive the same information and know how to calculate the profits for both—buyers and sellers.

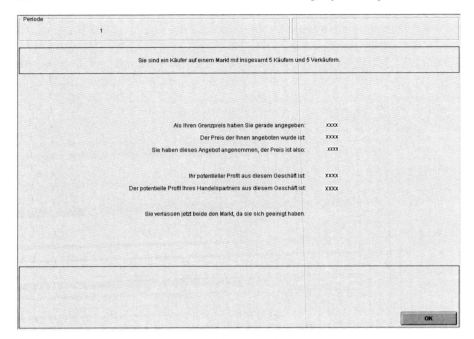

Fig. 7.12 After the bargaining a screen explains the results

The experiment will not start until all participants are completely familiar with all procedures. In order to secure that this is the case, we kindly ask you to solve the exercises below. Afterwards the experiment will begin.

Control Questionnaire—You Are a Buyer

Please solve the following exercises completely. If you have questions ask the experimenter.

Exercise 1   You remained idle because you were not selected to be in the market in a period.

- Will you receive a potential profit in this period? (To remind you: a potential profit may be selected for payout at the end of a part of the experiment.)
- If yes, what would be your potential profit?

Exercise 2   You are in a market, but you were not matched with a trading partner. The market does not terminate, but continues.

- Will you receive a potential profit in this period?

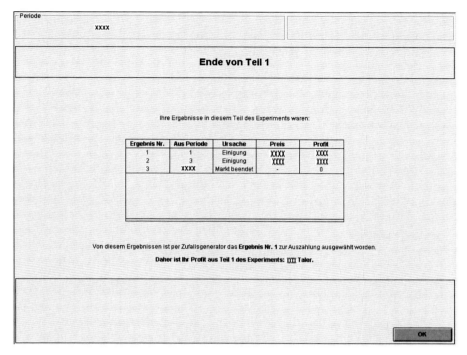

Fig. 7.13 When a part ends, one potential profit is selected randomly

- If yes, what would be your potential profit?

Exercise 3   You are in a market, but you were not matched with a trading partner. The market terminates after this period.

- Will you receive a potential profit in this period?
- If yes, what would be your potential profit?

Exercise 4   You are in a market, and you were matched with a trading partner. You proposed a price of 300 points, and this offer was rejected. The market does not terminate, but continues.

- Will you receive a potential profit in this period?
- If yes, what would be your potential profit?
- Will the seller that was matched with you receive a potential profit?
- If yes, what would be his potential profit?

Exercise 5   You are in a market, and you were matched with a trading partner. You proposed a price of 400 points, and this offer was accepted by the seller. The market does not terminate, but continues.

- Will you receive a potential profit in this period?
- If yes, what would be your potential profit?
- Will the seller that was matched with you receive a potential profit?
- If yes, what would be his potential profit?

Exercise 6   You are in a market, and you were matched with a trading partner. You had to enter your reservation price, for which you entered a price of 600 points. You partner (the seller) proposed a price of 500 points. The market terminates after this period.

- Will this offer be accepted?
- Will you receive a potential profit in this period?
- If yes, what would be your potential profit?
- Will the seller that was matched with you receive a potential profit?
- If yes, what would be his potential profit?

Exercise 7   You are in a market, and you were matched with a trading partner. You had to enter your reservation price, for which you entered a price of 600 points. You partner (the seller) proposed a price of 700 points. The market terminates after this period.

- Will this offer be accepted?
- Will you receive a potential profit in this period?
- If yes, what would be your potential profit?
- Will the seller that was matched with you receive a potential profit?
- If yes, what would be his potential profit?

When you have finished the exercises please hold up this sheet, and we will collect and check it. While you wait please think about the decisions you will make during the experiment.

References

Albrecht J, Anderson A, Smith E, Vroman S (2007) Opportunistic matching in the housing market. Int Econ Rev 48(2):641–664

Arai M (2003) Wages, profits, and capital intensity: Evidence from matched worker-firm data. J Labor Econ 21(3):593–618

Binmore KG, Morgan P, Shaked A, Sutton J (1991) Do people exploit their bargaining power? An experimental study. Games Econom Behav 3(3):295–322

Binmore KG, Swierzbinski J, Hsu S, Proulx C (1993) Focal points and bargaining. Int J Game Theor 22(4):381–409

Bolton LE, Warlop L, Alba JW (2003) Consumer perceptions of price (un)fairness. J Consum Res 29(4):474–491

Brown M, Falk A, Fehr E (2004) Relational contracts and the nature of market interactions. Econometrica 72(3):747–780

Camerer CF (2003) Behavioral Game Theory: Experiments in Strategic Interaction. Princeton University Press, Princeton, NJ

Cason TN, Friedman D, Milam GH (2003) Bargaining versus posted price competition in customer markets. Int J Ind Organ 21(2):223–251

Den Haan WJ, Ramey G, Watson J (2000) Job destruction and propagation of shocks. Am Econ Rev 90(3):482–498

Diamond PA, Maskin E (1979) An equilibrium analysis of search and breach of contract, I: Steady states. Bell J Econ 10(1):282–316

Fehr E, Schmidt KM (1999) A theory of fairness, competition and cooperation. Q J Econ 114(3):817–868

Fehr E, Kirchler E, Weichbold A, Gächter S (1998) When social norms overpower competition: Gift exchange in experimental labor markets. J Labor Econ 16(2):324–351

Fischbacher U (2007) z-tree: Zurich toolbox for ready-made economic experiments. Exp Econ 10(2):171–178

Kachelmeier SJ, Shehata M (1992) Culture and competition: A laboratory market comparison between China and the West. J Econ Behav Organ 19(2):145–168

Kachelmeier SJ, Limberg ST, Schadewald MS (1991) A laboratory market examination of the consumer price response to information about producers' cost and profits. Account Rev 66(4):694–717

Krainer J, LeRoy SF (2002) Equilibrium valuation of illiquid assets. Econ Theor 19(2):223–242

Kujal P, Smith VL (2008) Fairness and short run price adjustment in posted offer markets. In: Plott CR, Smith VL (eds) Handbook of Experimental Economics Results, vol 1, North-Holland, Amsterdam, Netherlands, chap 6, pp 55–61

Mortensen DT (1982) The matching process as a noncooperative bargaining game. In: McCall JJ (ed) The Economics of Information and Uncertainty, The University of Chicago Press, Chicago, IL, pp 233–254

Mortensen DT, Pissarides CA (1999) New developments in models of search in the labor market. In: Ashenfelter O, Card D (eds) Handbook of Labor Economics, vol 3, Elsevier, Amsterdam, Netherlands, chap 39, pp 2567–2627

Plott CR, Smith VL (1978) An experimental examination of two exchange institutions. Rev Econ Stud 45(1):133–153

Rocheteau G, Wright R (2005) Money in search equilibrium, in competitive equilibrium, and in competitive search equilibrium. Econometrica 73(1):175–202

Rogerson R, Shimer R, Wright R (2005) Search-theoretic models of the labor market: A survey. J Econ Lit 43(4):959–988

Roth AE (1995) Bargaining experiments. In: Kagel JH, Roth AE (eds) The Handbook of Experimental Economics, Princeton University Press, Princeton, NJ, chap 4, pp 254–348

Rubinstein A, Wolinsky A (1985) Equilibrium in a market with sequential bargaining. Econometrica 53(5):1133–1150

Shi S (2001) Liquidity, bargaining, and multiple equilibria in a search monetary model. Ann Econ Finance 2(2):325–251

Smith VL, Williams AW (1982) The effects of rent asymmetries in experimental auction markets. J Econ Behav Organ 3(1):99–116

Walsh CE (2005) Labor market search, sticky prices, and interest rate policies. Rev Econ Dynam 8(4):829–849

Young HP, Burke MA (2001) Competition and custom in economic contracts: A case study of Illinois agriculture. Am Econ Rev 91(3):559–573

List of Figures

List of Tables

Index